CW01594057

The Kingdom of God Is Within You

By

graf Leo Tolstoy

PREFACE.

In the year 1884 I wrote a book under the title "What I Believe," in which I did in fact make a sincere statement of my beliefs.

In affirming my belief in Christ's teaching, I could not help explaining why I do not believe, and consider as mistaken, the Church's doctrine, which is usually called Christianity.

Among the many points in which this doctrine falls short of the doctrine of Christ I pointed out as the principal one the absence of any commandment of non-resistance to evil by force. The perversion of Christ's teaching by the teaching of the Church is more clearly apparent in this than in any other point of difference.

I know--as we all do--very little of the practice and the spoken and written doctrine of former times on the subject of non-resistance to evil. I knew what had been said on the subject by the fathers of the Church--Origen, Tertullian, and others--I knew too of the existence of some so-called sects of Mennonites, Herrnhuters, and Quakers, who do not allow a Christian the use of weapons, and do not enter military service; but I knew little of what had been done by these so-called sects toward expounding the question.

My book was, as I had anticipated, suppressed by the Russian censorship; but partly owing to my literary reputation, partly because the book had excited people's curiosity, it circulated in manuscript and in lithographed copies in Russia and through translations abroad, and it evolved, on one side, from those who shared my convictions, a series of essays with a great deal of information on the subject, on the other side a series of criticisms on the principles laid down in my book.

A great deal was made clear to me by both hostile and sympathetic criticism, and also by the historical events of late years; and I was led to fresh results and conclusions, which I wish now to expound.

First I will speak of the information I received on the history of the question of non-resistance to evil; then of the views of this question maintained by spiritual critics, that is, by professed believers in the Christian religion, and also by temporal ones, that is, those who do not profess the Christian religion; and lastly I will speak of the conclusions to which I have been brought by all this in the light of the historical events of late years.

L. TOLSTOI.
YASNAÏA POLIANA,
May 14/26, 1893.

CONTENTS.

I. THE DOCTRINE OF NON-RESISTANCE TO EVIL BY FORCE HAS BEEN PROFESSED BY A MINORITY OF MEN FROM THE VERY FOUNDATION OF CHRISTIANITY

II. CRITICISMS OF THE DOCTRINE OF NON-RESISTANCE TO EVIL BY FORCE ON THE PART OF BELIEVERS AND OF UNBELIEVERS

III. CHRISTIANITY MISUNDERSTOOD BY BELIEVERS

IV. CHRISTIANITY MISUNDERSTOOD BY MEN OF SCIENCE

V. CONTRADICTION BETWEEN OUR LIFE AND OUR CHRISTIAN CONSCIENCE

VI. ATTITUDE OF MEN OF THE PRESENT DAY TO WAR

VII. SIGNIFICANCE OF COMPULSORY SERVICE

VIII. DOCTRINE OF NON-RESISTANCE TO EVIL BY FORCE MUST INEVITABLY BE ACCEPTED BY MEN OF THE PRESENT DAY

IX. THE ACCEPTANCE OF THE CHRISTIAN CONCEPTION OF LIFE WILL EMANCIPATE MEN FROM THE MISERIES OF OUR PAGAN LIFE

X. EVIL CANNOT BE SUPRESSED BY THE PHYSICAL FORCE OF THE GOVERNMENT--THE MORAL PROGRESS OF HUMANITY IS BROUGHT ABOUT NOT ONLY BY INDIVIDUAL RECOGNITION OF THE TRUTH BUT ALSO THROUGH THE ESTABLISHMENT OF A PUBLIC OPINION

XI. THE CHRISTIAN CONCEPTION OF LIFE HAS ALREADY ARISEN IN OUR SOCIETY, AND WILL INFALLIBLY PUT AN END TO THE PRESENT ORGANIZATION OF OUR LIFE BASED ON FORCE--WHEN THAT WILL BE

XII. CONCLUSION--REPENT YE, FOR THE KINGDOM OF HEAVEN IS AT HAND

"Ye shall know the truth, and the truth shall make you free. "--John viii. 32.

"Fear not them which kill the body, but are not able to kill the soul; but rather fear him which is able to destroy both soul and body in hell."--MATT. x. 28.

"Ye have been bought with a price; be not ye the servants of men."--I COR. vii. 23.

"THE KINGDOM OF GOD IS WITHIN YOU."

CHAPTER I.

THE DOCTRINE OF NON-RESISTANCE TO EVIL BY FORCE HAS BEEN PROFESSED BY A MINORITY OF MEN FROM THE VERY FOUNDATION OF CHRISTIANITY.

Of the Book "What I Believe"--The Correspondence Evoked by it--Letters from Quakers--Garrison's Declaration--Adin Ballou, his Works, his Catechism--Helchitsky's "Net of Faith"--The Attitude of the World to Works Elucidating Christ's Teaching--Dymond's Book "On War"--Musser's "Non-resistance Asserted"--Attitude of the Government in 1818 to Men who Refused to Serve in the Army--Hostile Attitude of Governments Generally and of Liberals to Those who Refuse to Assist in Acts of State Violence, and their Conscious Efforts to Silence and Suppress these Manifestations of Christian Non-resistance.

Among the first responses called forth by my book were some letters from American Quakers. In these letters, expressing their sympathy with my views on the unlawfulness for a Christian of war and the use of force of any kind, the Quakers gave me details of their own so-called sect, which for more than two hundred years has actually professed the teaching of Christ on non-resistance to evil by force, and does not make use of weapons in self-defense. The Quakers sent me books, from which I learnt how they had, years ago, established beyond doubt the duty for a Christian of fulfilling the command of non-resistance to evil by force, and had exposed the error of the Church's teaching in allowing war and capital punishment.

In a whole series of arguments and texts showing that war--that is, the wounding and killing of men--is inconsistent with a religion founded on peace and good will toward men, the Quakers maintain and prove that nothing has contributed so much to the obscuring of Christian truth in the eyes of the heathen, and has hindered so much the diffusion of Christianity through the world, as the disregard of this command by men calling themselves Christians, and the permission of war and violence to Christians.

"Christ's teaching, which came to be known to men, not by means of violence and the sword," they say, "but by means of non-resistance to evil, gentleness, meekness, and peaceableness, can only be diffused through the world by the example of peace, harmony, and love among its followers."

"A Christian, according to the teaching of God himself, can act only peaceably toward all men, and therefore there can be no authority able to force the Christian to act in opposition to the teaching of God and to the principal virtue of the Christian in his relation with his neighbors."

"The law of state necessity," they say, "can force only those to change the law of God who, for the sake of earthly gains, try to reconcile the irreconcilable; but for a Christian who sincerely believes that following Christ's teaching will give him salvation, such considerations of state can have no force."

Further acquaintance with the labors of the Quakers and their works--with Fox, Penn, and especially the work of Dymond (published in 1827)--showed me not only that the impossibility of reconciling Christianity with force and war had been recognized long, long ago, but that this irreconcilability had been long ago proved so clearly and so indubitably that one could only wonder how this impossible reconciliation of Christian teaching with the use of force, which has been, and is still, preached in the churches, could have been maintained in spite of it.

In addition to what I learned from the Quakers I received about the same time, also from America, some information on the subject from a source perfectly distinct and previously unknown to me.

The son of William Lloyd Garrison, the famous champion of the emancipation of the negroes, wrote to me that he had read my book, in which he found ideas similar to those expressed by his father in the year 1838, and that, thinking it would be interesting to me to know this, he sent me a declaration or proclamation of "non-resistance" drawn up by his father nearly fifty years ago.

This declaration came about under the following circumstances: William Lloyd Garrison took part in a discussion on the means of suppressing war in the Society for the Establishment of Peace among Men, which existed in 1838 in America. He came to the conclusion that the establishment of universal peace can only be founded on the open profession of the doctrine of non-resistance to evil by violence (Matt. v. 39), in its full significance, as understood by the Quakers, with whom Garrison happened to be on friendly relations. Having come to this conclusion, Garrison thereupon composed and laid before the society a declaration, which was signed at the time--in 1838--by many members.

"DECLARATION OF SENTIMENTS ADOPTED BY PEACE CONVENTION.

"Boston, 1838.

"We the undersigned, regard it as due to ourselves, to the cause which we love, to the country in which we live, to publish a declaration expressive of the purposes we aim to accomplish and the measures we shall adopt to carry forward the work of peaceful universal reformation.

"We do not acknowledge allegiance to any human government. We recognize but one King and Lawgiver, one Judge and Ruler of mankind. Our country is the world, our countrymen are all mankind. We love the land of our nativity only as we love all other lands. The interests and rights of American citizens are not dearer to us than those of the whole human race. Hence we can allow no appeal to patriotism to revenge any national insult or injury...

"We conceive that a nation has no right to defend itself against foreign enemies or to punish its invaders, and no individual possesses that right in his own case, and the unit cannot be of greater importance than the aggregate. If soldiers thronging from abroad with intent to commit rapine and destroy life may not be resisted by the people or the magistracy, then ought no resistance to be offered to domestic troublers of the public peace or of private security.

"The dogma that all the governments of the world are approvingly ordained of God, and that the powers that be in the United States, in Russia, in Turkey, are in accordance with his will, is no less absurd than impious. It makes the impartial Author of our existence unequal and tyrannical. It cannot be affirmed that the powers that be in any nation are actuated by the spirit or guided by the example of Christ in the treatment of enemies; therefore they cannot be agreeable to the will of God, and therefore their overthrow by a spiritual regeneration of their subjects is inevitable.

"We regard as unchristian and unlawful not only all wars,

whether offensive or defensive, but all preparations for war; every naval ship, every arsenal, every fortification, we regard as unchristian and unlawful; the existence of any kind of standing army, all military chieftains, all monuments commemorative of victory over a fallen foe, all trophies won in battle, all celebrations in honor of military exploits, all appropriations for defense by arms; we regard as unchristian and unlawful every edict of government requiring of its subjects military service.

"Hence we deem it unlawful to bear arms, and we cannot hold any office which imposes on its incumbent the obligation to compel men to do right on pain of imprisonment or death. We therefore voluntarily exclude ourselves from every legislative and judicial body, and repudiate all human politics, worldly honors, and stations of authority. If we cannot occupy a seat in the legislature or on the bench, neither can we elect others to act as our substitutes in any such capacity. It follows that we cannot sue any man at law to force him to return anything he may have wrongly taken from us; if he has seized our coat, we shall surrender him our cloak also rather than subject him to punishment.

"We believe that the penal code of the old covenant--an eye for an eye, and a tooth for a tooth--has been abrogated by Jesus Christ, and that under the new covenant the forgiveness instead of the punishment of enemies has been enjoined on all his disciples in all cases whatsoever. To extort money from enemies, cast them into prison, exile or execute them, is obviously not to forgive but to take retribution.

"The history of mankind is crowded with evidences proving that physical coercion is not adapted to moral regeneration, and that the sinful dispositions of men can be subdued only by love; that evil can be exterminated only by good; that it is not safe to rely upon the strength of an arm to preserve us from harm; that there is great security in being gentle, long-suffering, and abundant in mercy; that it is only the meek who shall inherit the earth; for those who take up the sword shall perish by the sword.

"Hence as a measure of sound policy--of safety to property, life, and liberty--of public quietude and private enjoyment--as well as on the ground of allegiance to Him who is King of kings and Lord of lords, we cordially adopt the non-resistance principle, being confident that it provides for all possible consequences, is armed with omnipotent power, and must ultimately triumph over every assailing force.

"We advocate no Jacobinical doctrines. The spirit of Jacobinism is the spirit of retaliation, violence, and murder. It neither fears God nor regards man. We would be filled with the spirit of Christ. If we abide evil by our fundamental principle of not opposing evil by evil we cannot participate in sedition, treason, or violence. We shall submit to every ordinance and every requirement of government, except such as are contrary to the commands of the Gospel, and in no case resist the operation of law, except by meekly submitting to the penalty of disobedience.

"But while we shall adhere to the doctrine of non-resistance and passive submission to enemies, we purpose, in a moral and spiritual sense, to assail iniquity in high places and in low places, to apply our principles to all existing evil, political, legal, and ecclesiastical institutions, and to hasten the time when the kingdoms of this world will have become the kingdom of our Lord Jesus Christ. It appears to us a self-evident truth that whatever the Gospel is designed to destroy at any period of the world, being contrary to it, ought now to be abandoned. If, then, the time is predicted when swords shall be beaten into plowshares and spears into pruning hooks, and men shall not learn the art of war any more, it follows that all who manufacture, sell, or wield these deadly weapons do thus array themselves against the peaceful dominion of the Son of God on earth.

"Having thus stated our principles, we proceed to specify the measures we propose to adopt in carrying our object into effect.

"We expect to prevail through the Foolishness of Preaching. We shall endeavor to promulgate our views among all persons, to whatever nation, sect, or grade of society they may belong. Hence we shall organize public lectures, circulate tracts and publications, form societies, and petition every governing body. It will be our leading object to devise ways and means for effecting a radical change in the views, feelings, and practices of society respecting the sinfulness of war and the treatment of enemies.

"In entering upon the great work before us, we are not unmindful that in its prosecution we may be called to test our sincerity even as in a fiery ordeal. It may subject us to insult, outrage, suffering, yea, even death itself. We anticipate no small amount of misconception, misrepresentation, and calumny. Tumults may arise against us. The proud and pharisaical, the ambitious and tyrannical, principalities and powers, may combine to crush us. So they treated the Messiah whose example we are humbly striving to imitate. We shall not be afraid of their terror. Our confidence is in the Lord Almighty and not in man. Having withdrawn from human protection, what can sustain us but that faith which overcomes the world? We shall not think it strange concerning the fiery trial which is to try us, but rejoice inasmuch as we are partakers of Christ's sufferings.

"Wherefore we commit the keeping of our souls to God. For every one that forsakes houses, or brethren, or sisters, or father, or mother, or wife, or children, or lands for Christ's sake, shall receive a hundredfold, and shall inherit everlasting life.

"Firmly relying upon the certain and universal triumph of the sentiments contained in this declaration, however formidable may be the opposition arrayed against them, we hereby affix our signatures to it; commending it to the reason and conscience of mankind, and resolving, in the strength of the Lord God, to calmly and meekly abide the issue."

Immediately after this declaration a Society for Non-resistance was founded by Garrison, and a journal called the NON-RESISTANT, in which the doctrine of non-resistance was advocated in its full significance and in all its consequences, as it had been expounded in the declaration. Further information as to the ultimate destiny of the society and the journal I gained from the excellent biography of W. L. Garrison, the work of his son.

The society and the journal did not exist for long. The greater number of Garrison's fellow-workers in the movement for the liberation of the slaves, fearing that the too radical programme of the journal, the NON-RESISTANT, might keep people away from the practical work of negro-emancipation, gave up the profession of the principle of non-resistance as it had been expressed in the declaration, and both society and journal ceased to exist.

This declaration of Garrison's gave so powerful and eloquent an expression of a confession of faith of such importance to men, that one would have thought it must have produced a strong impression on people, and have become known throughout the world and the subject of discussion on every side. But nothing of the kind occurred. Not only was it unknown in Europe, even the Americans, who have such a high opinion of Garrison, hardly knew of the declaration.

Another champion of non-resistance has been overlooked in the same way--the American Adin Ballou, who lately died, after spending fifty years in preaching this doctrine. Lord God, to calmly and meekly abide the doctrine. How great the ignorance is of everything relating to the question of non-resistance may be seen from the fact that Garrison the son, who has written an excellent biography of his father in four great volumes, in answer to my inquiry whether there are existing now societies for non-resistance, and adherents of the doctrine, told me that as far as he knew that society had broken up, and that there were no adherents of that doctrine, while at the very time when he was writing to me there was living, at Hopedale in Massachusetts, Adin

Ballou, who had taken part in the labors of Garrison the father, and had devoted fifty years of his life to advocating, both orally and in print, the doctrine of non-resistance. Later on I received a letter from Wilson, a pupil and colleague of Ballou's, and entered into correspondence with Ballou himself. I wrote to Ballou, and he answered me and sent me his works. Here is the summary of some extracts from them:

> "Jesus Christ is my Lord and teacher," says Ballou in one of his essays exposing the inconsistency of Christians who allowed a right of self-defense and of warfare. "I have promised leaving all else, to follow good and through evil, to death itself. But I am a citizen of the democratic republic of the United States; and in allegiance to it I have sworn to defend the Constitution of my country, if need be, with my life. Christ requires of me to do unto others as I would they should do unto me. The Constitution of the United States requires of me to do unto two millions of slaves [at that time there were slaves; now one might venture to substitute the word 'laborers'] the very opposite of what I would they should do unto me--that is to help to keep them in their present condition of slavery. And, in spite of this, I continue to elect or be elected, I propose to vote, I am even ready to be appointed to any office under government. That will not hinder me from being a Christian. I shall still profess Christianity, and shall find no difficulty in carrying out my covenant with Christ and with the government.

"Jesus Christ forbids me to resist evil doers, and to take from them an eye for an eye, a tooth for a tooth, bloodshed for bloodshed, and life for life.

"My government demands from me quite the opposite, and bases a system of self-defense on gallows, musket, and sword, to be used against its foreign and domestic foes. And the land is filled accordingly with gibbets, prisons, arsenals, ships of war, and soldiers.

"In the maintenance and use of these expensive appliances for murder, we can very suitably exercise to the full the virtues of forgiveness to those who injure us, love toward our enemies, blessings to those who curse us, and doing good to those who hate us.

"For this we have a succession of Christian priests to pray for us and beseech the blessing of Heaven on the holy work of slaughter.

"I see all this (i. e., the contradiction between profession and practice), and I continue to profess religion and take part in government, and pride myself on being at the same time a devout Christian and a devoted servant of the government. I do not want to agree with these senseless notions of non-resistance.

> I cannot renounce my authority and leave only immoral men in control of the government. The Constitution says the government has the right to declare war, and I assent to this and support it, and swear that I will support it. And I do not for that cease to be a Christian. War, too, is a Christian duty. Is it not a Christian duty to kill hundreds of thousands of one's fellow-men, to outrage women, to raze and burn towns, and to practice every possible cruelty? It is time to dismiss all these false sentimentalities. It is the truest means of forgiving injuries and loving enemies. If we only do it in the spirit of love, nothing can be more Christian than such murder."

In another pamphlet, entitled "How many Men are Necessary to Change a Crime into a Virtue?" he says: "One man may not kill. If he kills a fellow-creature, he is a murderer. If two, ten, a hundred men do so, they, too, are murderers. But a government or a nation may kill as many men as it chooses, and that will not be murder, but a great and noble action. Only gather the people together on a large scale, and a battle of ten thousand men becomes an innocent action. But precisely how many people must there be to make it so?--that is the question. One man cannot plunder and pillage, but a whole nation can. But precisely how many are needed to make it permissible? Why is it that one man, ten, a hundred, may not break the law of God, but a great number may?"

And here is a version of Ballou's catechism composed for his flock:

CATECHISM OF NON-RESISTANCE.

Q. Whence is the word "non-resistance" derived?

A. From the command, "Resist not evil." (M. v. 39.)

Q. What does this word express?

A. It expresses a lofty Christian virtue enjoined on us by Christ.

Q. Ought the word "non-resistance" to be taken in its widest sense--that is to say, as intending that we should not offer any resistance of any kind to evil?

A. No; it ought to be taken in the exact sense of our Saviour's teaching--that is, not repaying evil for evil. We ought to oppose evil by every righteous means in our power, but not by evil.

Q. What is there to show that Christ enjoined non-resistance in that sense?

A. It is shown by the words he uttered at the same time. He said: "Ye have heard, it was said of old, An eye for an eye, and a tooth for a tooth. But I say unto you Resist not evil. But if one smites thee on the right cheek, turn him the other also; and if one will go to law with thee to take thy coat from thee, give him thy cloak also."

Q. Of whom was he speaking in the words, "Ye have heard it was said of old"?

A. Of the patriarchs and the prophets, contained in the Old Testament, which the Hebrews ordinarily call the Law and the Prophets.

Q. What utterances did Christ refer to in the words, "It was said of old"?

A. The utterances of Noah, Moses, and the other prophets, in which they admit the right of doing bodily harm to those who inflict harm, so as to punish and prevent evil deeds.

Q. Quote such utterances.

A. "Whoso sheddeth man's blood, by man shall his blood be shed."--GEN. ix. 6.

"He that smiteth a man, so that he die, shall be surely put to death... And if any mischief follow, then thou shalt give life for life, eye for eye, tooth for tooth, hand for hand, foot for foot, burning for burning, wound for wound, stripe for stripe." --Ex. xxi. 12 and 23-25.

"He that killeth any man shall surely be put to death. And if a man cause a blemish in his neighbor, as he hath done, so shall it be done unto him: breach for breach, eye for eye, tooth for tooth."--LEV. xxiv. 17, 19, 20.

"Then the judges shall make diligent inquisition; and behold, if the witness be a false witness, and hath testified falsely against his brother, then shall ye do unto him as he had thought to have done unto his brother... And thine eye shall not pity; but life shall go for life, eye for eye, tooth for tooth, hand for hand, foot for foot."--DEUT. xix. 18, 21.

Noah, Moses, and the Prophets taught that he who kills, maims, or injures his neighbors does evil. To resist such evil, and to prevent it, the evil doer must be punished with death, or maiming, or some physical injury. Wrong must be opposed by wrong, murder by murder, injury by injury, evil by evil. Thus taught Noah, Moses, and the Prophets. But Christ rejects all this. "I say unto you," is written in the Gospel, "resist not evil," do not oppose injury with injury, but rather bear repeated injury from the evil doer. What was permitted is forbidden. When we understand what kind of resistance they taught, we know exactly what resistance Christ forbade.

Q. Then the ancients allowed the resistance of injury by injury?

A. Yes. But Jesus forbids it. The Christian has in no case the right to put to death his neighbor who has done him evil, or to do him injury in return.

Q. May he kill or maim him in self-defense?

A. No.

Q. May he go with a complaint to the judge that he who has wronged him may be punished?

A. No. What he does through others, he is in reality doing himself.

Q. Can he fight in conflict with foreign enemies or disturbers of the peace?

A. Certainly not. He cannot take any part in war or in

preparations for war. He cannot make use of a deadly weapon. He cannot oppose injury to injury, whether he is alone or with others, either in person or through other people.

Q. Can he voluntarily vote or furnish soldiers for the government?

A. He can do nothing of that kind if he wishes to be faithful to Christ's law.

Q. Can he voluntarily give money to aid a government resting on military force, capital punishment, and violence in general?

A. No, unless the money is destined for some special object, right in itself, and good both in aim and means.

Q. Can he pay taxes to such a government?

A. No; he ought not voluntarily to pay taxes, but he ought not to resist the collecting of taxes. A tax is levied by the government, and is exacted independently of the will of the subject. It is impossible to resist it without having recourse to violence of some kind. Since the Christian cannot employ violence, he is obliged to offer his property at once to the loss by violence inflicted on it by the authorities.

Q. Can a Christian give a vote at elections, or take part in government or law business?

A. No; participation in election, government, or law business is participation in government by force.

Q. Wherein lies the chief significance of the doctrine of non-resistance?

A. In the fact that it alone allows of the possibility of eradicating evil from one's own heart, and also from one's neighbor's. This doctrine forbids doing that whereby evil has endured for ages and multiplied in the world. He who attacks another and injures him, kindles in the other a feeling of hatred, the root of every evil. To injure another because he has injured us, even with the aim of overcoming evil, is doubling the harm for him and for oneself; it is begetting, or at least setting free and inciting, that evil spirit which we should wish to drive out. Satan can never be driven out by Satan. Error can never be corrected by error, and evil cannot be vanquished by evil.

True non-resistance is the only real resistance to evil. It is crushing the serpent's head. It destroys and in the end extirpates the evil feeling.

Q. But if that is the true meaning of the rule of non-resistance, can it always put into practice?

A. It can be put into practice like every virtue enjoined by the law of God. A virtue cannot be practiced in all circumstances without self-sacrifice, privation, suffering, and in extreme cases loss of life itself. But he who esteems life more than fulfilling the will of God is already dead to the only true life. Trying to save his life he loses it. Besides, generally speaking, where non-resistance costs the sacrifice of a single life or of some material welfare, resistance costs a thousand such sacrifices.

Non-resistance is Salvation; Resistance is Ruin.

It is incomparably less dangerous to act justly than unjustly, to submit to injuries than to resist them with violence, less dangerous even in one's relations to the present life. If all men refused to resist evil by evil our world would be happy.

Q. But so long as only a few act thus, what will happen to them?

A. If only one man acted thus, and all the rest agreed to crucify him, would it not be nobler for him to die in the glory of non-resisting love, praying for his enemies, than to live to wear the crown of Caesar stained with the blood of the slain? However, one man, or a thousand men, firmly resolved not to oppose evil by evil are far more free from danger by violence than those who resort to violence, whether among civilized or savage neighbors. The robber, the murderer, and the cheat will leave them in peace, sooner than those who oppose them with arms, and those who take up the sword shall perish by the sword, but those who seek after peace, and behave kindly and harmlessly, forgiving and forgetting injuries, for the most part enjoy peace, or, if they die, they die blessed. In this way, if all kept the ordinance of non-resistance, there would obviously be no evil nor crime. If the majority acted thus they would establish the rule of love and good will even over evil doers, never opposing evil with evil, and never resorting to force. If there were a moderately large minority of such men, they would exercise such a salutary moral influence on society that every cruel punishment would be abolished, and violence and feud would be replaced by peace and love. Even if there were only a small minority of them, they would rarely experience anything worse than the world's contempt, and meantime the world, though unconscious of it, and not grateful for it, would be continually becoming wiser and better for their unseen action on it. And if in the worst case some members of the minority were persecuted to death, in dying for the truth they would have left behind them their doctrine, sanctified by the blood of their martyrdom. Peace, then, to all who seek peace, and may overruling love be the imperishable heritage of every soul who obeys willingly Christ's word, "Resist not evil."

ADIN BALLOU.

For fifty years Ballou wrote and published books dealing principally with the question of non-resistance to evil by force. In these works, which are distinguished by the clearness of their thought and eloquence of exposition, the question is looked at from every possible side, and the binding nature of this command on every Christian who acknowledges the Bible as the revelation of God is firmly established. All the ordinary objections to the doctrine of non-resistance from the Old and New Testaments are brought forward, such as the expulsion of the moneychangers from the Temple, and so on, and arguments follow in disproof of them all. The practical reasonableness of this rule of conduct is shown independently of Scripture, and all the objections ordinarily made against its practicability are stated and refuted. Thus one chapter in a book of his treats of non-resistance in exceptional cases, and he owns in this connection that if there were cases in which the rule of non-resistance were impossible of application, it would prove that the law was not universally authoritative. Quoting these cases, he shows that it is precisely in them that the application of the rule is both necessary and reasonable. There is no aspect of the question, either on his side or on his opponents', which he has not followed up in his writings. I mention all this to show the unmistakable interest which such works ought to have for men who make a profession of Christianity, and because one would have thought Ballou's work would have been well known, and the ideas expressed by him would lave been either accepted or refuted; but such has not been the case.

The work of Garrison, the father, in his foundation of the Society of Non-resistants and his Declaration, even more than my correspondence with the Quakers, convinced me of the fact that the departure of the ruling form of Christianity from the law of Christ on non-resistance by force is an error that has long been observed and pointed out, and that men have labored, and are still laboring, to correct. Ballou's work confirmed me still more in this view. But the fate of Garrison, still more that of Ballou, in being completely unrecognized in spite of fifty years of obstinate and persistent work in the same direction, confirmed me in the idea that there exists a kind of tacit but steadfast conspiracy of silence about all such efforts.

Ballou died in August, 1890, and there was as obituary notice of him in an American journal of Christian views (RELIGIO-PHILOSOPHICAL JOURNAL, August 23). In this laudatory notice it is recorded that Ballou was the spiritual director of a parish, that he delivered from eight to nine thousand sermons, married one thousand couples, and wrote about five hundred articles; but there is not a single word said of the object to which he devoted his life; even the word "non-resistance" is not mentioned. Precisely as it was with all the preaching of the Quakers for two hundred years and, too, with the efforts of Garrison the father, the foundation of his society and journal, and his Declaration, so it is with the life-work of Ballou. It seems just as though it did not exist and never had existed.

We have an astounding example of the obscurity of works which aim at expounding the doctrine of non-resistance to evil by force, and at confuting those who do not recognize this commandment, in the book of the Tsech Helchitsky, which has only lately been noticed and has not hitherto been printed.

Soon after the appearance of my book in German, I received a letter from Prague, from a professor of the university there, informing me of the existence of a work, never yet printed, by Helchitsky, a Tsech of the fifteenth century, entitled "The Net of Faith." In this work, the professor told me, Helchitsky expressed precisely the same view as to true and false Christianity as I had expressed in my book "What I Believe." The professor wrote to me that Helchitsky's work was to be published for the first time in the Tsech language in the JOURNAL OF THE PETERSBURG ACADEMY OF SILENCE. Since I could not obtain the book itself, I tried to make myself acquainted with what was known of Helchitsky, and I gained the following information from a German book sent me by the

Prague professor and from Pypin's history of Tsech literature. This was Pypin's account:

"'The Net of Faith' is Christ's teaching, which ought to draw man up out of the dark depths of the sea of worldliness and his own iniquity. True faith consists in believing God's Word; but now a time has come when men mistake the true faith for heresy, and therefore it is for the reason to point out what the true faith consists in, if anyone does not know this. It is hidden in darkness from men, and they do not recognize the true law of Christ.

"To make this law plain, Helchitsky points to the primitive organization of Christian society--the organization which, he says, is now regarded in the Roman Church as an abominable heresy. This Primitive Church was his special ideal of social organization, founded on equality, liberty, and fraternity. Christianity, in Helchitsky's view, still preserves these elements, and it is only necessary for society to return to its pure doctrine to render unnecessary every other form of social order in which kings and popes are essential; the law of love would alone be sufficient in every case.

"Historically, Helchitsky attributes the degeneration of Christianity to the times of Constantine the Great, whom he Pope Sylvester admitted into the Christian Church with all his heathen morals and life. Constantine, in his turn, endowed the Pope with worldly riches and power. From that time forward these two ruling powers were constantly aiding one another to strive for nothing but outward glory. Divines and ecclesiastical dignitaries began to concern themselves only about subduing the whole world to their authority, incited men against one another to murder and plunder, and in creed and life reduced Christianity to a nullity. Helchitsky denies completely the right to make war and to inflict the punishment of death; every soldier, even the 'knight,' is only a violent evil doer--a murderer."

The same account is given by the German book, with the addition of a few biographical details and some extracts from Helchitsky's writings.

Having learnt the drift of Helchitsky's teaching in this way, I awaited all the more impatiently the appearance of "The Net of Faith" in the journal of the Academy. But one year passed, then two and three, and still the book did not appear. It was only in 1888 that I learned that the printing of the book, which had been begun, was stopped. I obtained the proofs of what had been printed and read them through. It is a marvelous book from every point of view.

Its general tenor is given with perfect accuracy by Pypin.

Helchitsky's fundamental idea is that Christianity, by allying itself with temporal power in the days of Constantine, and by continuing to develop in such conditions, has become completely distorted, and has ceased to be Christian altogether. Helchitsky gave the title "The Net of Faith" to his book, taking as his motto the verse of the Gospel about the calling of the disciples to be fishers of men; and, developing this metaphor, he says:

> "Christ, by means of his disciples, would have caught all the world in his net of faith, but the greater fishes broke the net and escaped out of it, and all the rest have slipped through the holes made by the greater fishes, so that the net has remained quite empty. The greater fishes who broke the net are the rulers, emperors, popes, kings, who have not renounced power, and instead of true Christianity have put on what is simply a mask of it."

Helchitsky teaches precisely what has been and is taught in these days by the non-resistant Mennonites and Quakers, and in former tunes by the Bogomilites, Paulicians, and many others. He teaches that Christianity, expecting from its adherents gentleness, meekness, peaceableness, forgiveness of injuries, turning the other cheek when one is struck, and love for enemies, is inconsistent with the use of force, which is an indispensable condition of authority.

The Christian, according to Helchitsky's reasoning, not only cannot be a ruler or a soldier; he cannot take any part in government nor in trade, or even be a landowner; he can only be an artisan or a husbandman.

This book is one of the few works attacking official Christianity which has escaped being burned. All such so-called heretical works were burned at the stake, together with their authors, so that there are few ancient works exposing the errors of official Christianity. The book has a special interest for this reason alone. But apart from its interest from every point of view, it is one of the most remarkable products of thought for its depth of aim, for the astounding strength and beauty of the national language in which it is written, and for its antiquity. And yet for more than four centuries it has remained unprinted, and is still unknown, except to a few learned specialists.

One would have thought that all such works, whether of the Quakers, of Garrison, of Ballou, or of Helchitsky, asserting and proving as they do, on the principles of the Gospel, that our modern world takes a false view of Christ's teaching, would have awakened interest, excitement, talk, and discussion among spiritual teachers and their flocks alike.

Works of this kind, dealing with the very essence of Christian doctrine, ought, one would have thought, to have been examined and accepted as true, or refuted and rejected. But nothing of the kind has occurred, and the same fate has been repeated with all those works. Men of the most diverse views, believers, and, what is surprising, unbelieving liberals also, as though by agreement, all preserve the same persistent silence about them, and all that has been done by people to explain the true meaning of Christ's doctrine remains either ignored or forgotten.

But it is still more astonishing that two other books, of which I heard on the appearance of my book, should be so little known, I mean Dymond's book "On War," published for the first time in London in 1824, and Daniel Musser's book on "Non-resistance," written in 1864. It is particularly astonishing that these books should be unknown, because, apart from their intrinsic merits, both books treat not so much of the theory as of the practical application of the theory to life, of the attitude of Christianity to military service, which is especially important and interesting now in these clays of universal conscription.

People will ask, perhaps: How ought a subject to behave who believes that war is inconsistent with his religion while the government demands from him that he should enter military service?

This question is, I think, a most vital one, and the answer to it is specially important in these days of universal conscription. All--or at least the great majority of the people--are Christians, and all men are called upon for military service. How ought a man, as a Christian, to meet this demand? This is the gist of Dymond's answer:

"His duty is humbly but steadfastly to refuse to serve."

There are some people, who, without any definite reasoning about it, conclude straightway that the responsibility of government measures rests entirely on those who resolve on them, or that the governments and sovereigns decide the question of what is good or bad for their subjects, and the duty of the subjects is merely to obey. I think that arguments of this kind only obscure men's conscience. I cannot take part in the councils of government, and therefore I am not responsible for its misdeeds.. Indeed, but we are responsible for our own misdeeds. And the misdeeds of our rulers become our own, if we, knowing that they are misdeeds, assist in carrying, them out. Those who suppose that they are bound to obey the government, and that the responsibility for the misdeeds they commit is transferred from them to their rulers, deceive themselves. They say: "We give our acts up to the will of others, and our acts cannot be good or bad; there is no merit in what is good nor responsibility for what is evil in our actions, since they are not done of our own will."

It is remarkable that the very same thing is said in the instructions to soldiers which they make them learn--that is, that the officer is alone responsible for the consequences of his command. But this is not right. A man cannot get rid of the responsibility, for his own actions. And that is clear from the following example. If your officer commands you to kill your neighbor's child, to kill your father or your mother, would you obey? If you would not obey, the whole argument falls to the ground, for if you can disobey the governors in one case, where do you draw the line up to which you can obey them? There is no line other than that laid down by Christianity, and that line is both reasonable and practicable.

And therefore we consider it the duty of every man who thinks war inconsistent with Christianity, meekly but firmly to refuse to serve in the army. And let those whose lot it is to act thus, remember that the fulfillment of a great duty rests with them. The destiny of humanity in the world depends, so far as it depends on men at all, on their fidelity to their religion. Let them confess their conviction, and stand up for it, and not in words alone, but in sufferings too, if need be. If you believe that Christ forbade murder, pay no heed to the arguments nor to the commands of those who call on you to bear a hand in it. By such a steadfast refusal to make use of force, you call down on yourselves the blessing promised to those "who hear these sayings and do them," and the time will come when the world will recognize you as having aided in the reformation of mankind.

Musser's book is called "Non-resistance Asserted," or "Kingdom of Christ and Kingdoms of this World Separated." This book is devoted to the same question, and was written when the American Government was exacting military service from its citizens at the time of the Civil War. And it has, too, a value for all time, dealing with the question how, in such circumstances, people should and can refuse to enter military service. Here is the tenor of the author's introductory remarks:

> "It is well known that there are many persons in the United States who refuse to fight on grounds of conscience. They are called the 'defenseless,' or 'non-resistant' Christians. These Christians refuse to defend their country, to bear arms, or at the call of government to make war on its enemies. Till lately this religious scruple seemed a valid excuse to the government, and those who urged it were let off service. But at the beginning of our Civil War public opinion was agitated on this subject. It was natural that persons who considered it their duty to bear all the hardships and dangers of war in defense of their country should feel resentment against those persons who had for long shared with them the advantages of the protection of government, and who now in time of need and danger would not share in bearing the labors and dangers of its defense. It was even natural that they should declare the attitude of such men monstrous, irrational, and suspicious."

A host of orators and writers, our author tells us, arose to oppose this attitude, and tried to prove the sinfulness of non-resistance, both from Scripture and on common-sense grounds. And this was perfectly natural, and in many cases the authors were right--right, that is, in regard to persons who did not renounce the benefits they received from the government and tried to avoid the hardships of military service, but not right in regard to the principle of non-resistance itself. Above all, our author proves the binding nature of the rule of non-resistance for a Christian, pointing out that this command is perfectly clear, and is enjoined upon every Christian by Christ without possibility of misinterpretation. "Bethink yourselves whether it is righteous to obey man more than God," said Peter and John. And this is precisely what ought to be the attitude to every man who wishes to be Christian to the claim on him for military service, when Christ has said, "Resist not evil by force." As for the question of the principle itself, the author regards that as decided. As to the second question, whether people have the right to refuse to serve in the army who have not refused the benefits conferred by a government resting on force, the author considers it in detail, and arrives at the conclusion that a Christian following the law of Christ, since he does not go to war, ought not either to take advantage of any institutions of government, courts of law, or elections, and that in his private concerns he must not have recourse to the authorities, the police, or the law. Further on in the book he treats of the relation of the Old Testament to the New, the value of government for those who are Christians, and makes some observations on the doctrine of non-resistance and the attacks made on it. The author concludes his book by saying: "Christians do not need government, and therefore they cannot either obey it in what is contrary to Christ's teaching nor, still less, take part in it." Christ took his disciples out of the world, he says. They do not expect worldly blessings and worldly happiness, but they expect eternal life. The Spirit in whom they live makes them contented and happy in every position. If the world tolerates them, they are always happy. If the world will not leave them in peace, they will go elsewhere, since they are pilgrims on the earth and they have no fixed place of habitation. They believe that "the dead may bury their dead." One thing only is needful for them, "to follow their Master."

Even putting aside the question as to the principle laid down in these two books as to the Christian's duty in his attitude to war, one cannot help perceiving the practical importance and the urgent need of deciding the question.

There are people, hundreds of thousands of Quakers, Mennonites, all our Douhobortsi, Molokani, and others who do not belong to any definite sect, who consider that the use of force--and, consequently, military service--is inconsistent with Christianity. Consequently there are every year among us in Russia some men called upon for military service who refuse to serve on the ground of their religious convictions. Does the government let them off then? No. Does it compel them to go, and in case of disobedience punish them? No. This was how the government treated them in

1818. Here is an extract from the diary of Nicholas Myravyov of Kars, which was not passed by the censor, and is not known in Russia:

"Tiflis, October 2, 1818.

"In the morning the commandant told me that five peasants belonging to a landowner in the Tamboff government had lately been sent to Georgia. These men had been sent for soldiers, but they would not serve; they had been several times flogged and made to run the gauntlet, but they would submit readily to the cruelest tortures, and even to death, rather than serve. 'Let us go,' they said, 'and leave us alone; we will not hurt anyone; all men are equal, and the Tzar is a man like us; why should we pay him tribute; why should I expose my life to danger to kill in battle some man who has done me no harm? You can cut us to pieces and we will not be soldiers. He who has compassion on us will give us charity, but as for the government rations, we have not had them and we do not want to have them.' These were the words of those peasants, who declare that there are numbers like them Russia. They brought them four times before the Committee of Ministers, and at last decided to lay the matter before the Tzar who gave orders that they should be taken to Georgia for correction, and commanded the commander-in-chief to send him a report every month of their gradual success in bringing these peasants to a better mind."

How the correction ended is not known, as the whole episode indeed was unknown, having been kept in profound secrecy.

This was how the government behaved seventy-five years ago--this is how it has behaved in a great cumber of cases, studiously concealed from the people. And this is how the government behaves now, except in the case of the German Mennonites, living in the province of Kherson, whose plea against military service is considered well grounded. They are made to work off their term of service in labor in the forests.

But in the recent cases of refusal on the part of Mennonites to serve in the army on religious grounds, the government authorities have acted in the following manner:

To begin with, they have recourse to every means of coercion used in our times to "correct" the culprit and bring him to "a better mind," and these measures are carried out with the greatest secrecy. I know that in the case of one man who declined to serve in 1884 in Moscow, the official correspondence on the subject had two months after his refusal accumulated into a big folio, and was kept absolutely secret among the Ministry.

They usually begin by sending the culprit to the priests, and the latter, to their shame be it said, always exhort him to obedience. But since the exhortation in Christ's name to forswear Christ is for the most part unsuccessful, after he has received the admonitions of the spiritual authorities, they send him to the gendarmes, and the latter, finding, as a rule, no political cause for offense in him, dispatch him back again, and then he is sent to the learned men, to the doctors, and to the madhouse. During all these vicissitudes he is deprived of liberty and has to endure every kind of humiliation and suffering as a convicted criminal. (All this has been repeated in four cases.) The doctors let him out of the madhouse, and then every kind of secret shift is employed to prevent him from going free--whereby others would be encouraged to refuse to serve as he has done--and at the same time to avoid leaving him among the soldiers, for fear they too should learn from him that military service is not at all their duty by the law of God, as they are assured, but quite contrary to it.

The most convenient thing for the government would be to kill the non-resistant by flogging him to death or some other means, as was done in former days. But to put a man openly to death because he believes in the creed we all confess is impossible. To let a man alone who has refused obedience is also impossible. And so the government tries either to compel the man by ill-treatment to renounce Christ, or in some way or other to get rid of him unobserved, without openly putting him to death, and to hide somehow both the action and the man himself from other people.

And so all kinds of shifts and wiles and cruelties are set on foot against him. They either send him to the frontier or provoke him to insubordination, and then try him for breach of discipline and shut him up in the prison of the disciplinary battalion, where they can ill treat him freely unseen by anyone, or they declare him mad, and lock him up in a lunatic asylum. They sent one man in this way to Tashkend--that is, they pretended to transfer to the Tashkend army; another to Omsk; a third him they convicted of insubordination and shut up in prison; a fourth they sent to a lunatic asylum.

Everywhere the same story is repeated. Not only the government, but the great majority of liberal, advanced people, as they are called, studiously turn away from everything that has been said, written, or done, or is being done by men to prove the incompatibility of force in its most awful, gross, and glaring form--in the form, that is, of an army of soldiers prepared to murder anyone, whoever it may be--with the teachings of Christianity, or even of the humanity which society professes as its creed.

So that the information I have gained of the attitude of the higher ruling classes, not only in Russia but in Europe and America, toward the elucidation of this question has convinced me that there exists in these ruling classes a consciously hostile attitude to true Christianity, which is shown pre-eminently in their reticence in regard to all manifestations of it.

CHAPTER II.

CRITICISMS OF THE DOCTRINE OF NON-RESISTANCE TO EVIL BY FORCE ON THE PART OF BELIEVERS AND OF UNBELIEVERS.

Fate of the Book "What I Believe"--Evasive Character of Religious Criticisms of Principles of my Book--1st Reply: Use of Force not Opposed to Christianity--2d Reply: Use of Force Necessary to Restrain Evil Doers--3d Reply: Duty of Using Force in Defense of One's Neighbor--4th Reply: The Breach of the Command of Non-resistance to be Regarded Simply as a Weakness--5th Reply: Reply Evaded by Making Believe that the Question has long been Decided--To Devise such Subterfuges and to take Refuge Behind the Authority of the Church, of Antiquity, and of Religion is all that Ecclesiastical Critics can do to get out of the Contradiction between Use of Force and Christianity in Theory and in Practice--General Attitude of the Ecclesiastical World and of the Authorities to Profession of True Christianity--General Character of Russian Freethinking Critics--Foreign Freethinking Critics--Mistaken Arguments of these Critics the Result of Misunderstanding the True Meaning of Christ's Teaching.

The impression I gained of a desire to conceal, to hush up, what I had tried to express in my book, led me to judge the book itself afresh.

On its appearance it had, as I had anticipated, been forbidden, and ought therefore by law to have been burnt. But, at the same time, it was discussed among officials, and circulated in a great number of manuscript and lithograph copies, and in translations printed abroad.

And very quickly after the book, criticisms, both religious and secular in character, made their appearance, and these the government tolerated, and even encouraged. So that the refutation of a book which no one was supposed to know anything about was even chosen as the subject for theological dissertations in the academies.

The criticisms of my book, Russian and foreign alike, fall under two general divisions--the religious criticisms of men who regard themselves as believers, and secular criticisms, that is, those of freethinkers.

I will begin with the first class. In my book I made it an accusation against the teachers of the Church that their teaching is opposed to Christ's commands clearly and definitely expressed in the Sermon on the Mount, and opposed in especial to his command in regard to resistance to evil, and that in this way they deprive Christ's teaching of all value. The Church authorities accept the teaching of the Sermon on the Mount on non-resistance to evil by force as divine revelation; and therefore one would have thought that if they felt called upon to write about my book at all, they would have found it inevitable before everything else to reply to the principal point of my charge against them, and to say plainly, do they or do they not admit the teaching of the Sermon on the Mount and the commandment of non-resistance to evil as binding on a Christian. And they were bound to answer this question, not after the usual fashion (i. e., "that although on the one side one cannot absolutely deny, yet on the other side one cannot main fully assent, all the more seeing that," etc., etc.). No; they should have answered the question as plainly as it was put in my book--Did Christ really demand from his disciples that they should carry out what he taught them in the Sermon on the Mount? And can a Christian, then, or can he not, always remaining a Christian, go to law or make any use of the law, or seek his own protection in the law? And can the Christian, or can he not, remaining a Christian, take part in the administration of government, using compulsion against his neighbors? And--the most important question hanging over the heads of all of us in these days of universal military service--can the Christian, or can he not, remaining a Christian, against Christ's direct prohibition, promise obedience in future actions directly opposed to his teaching? And can he, by taking his share of service in the army, prepare himself to murder men, and even actually murder them?

These questions were put plainly and directly, and seemed to require a plain and direct answer; but in all the criticisms of my book there was no such plain and direct answer. No; my book received precisely the same treatment as all the attacks upon the teachers of the Church for their defection from the Law of Christ of which history from the days of Constantine is full.

A very great deal was said in connection with my book of my having incorrectly interpreted this and other passages of the Gospel, of my being in error in not recognizing the Trinity, the redemption, and the immortality of the soul. A very great deal was said, but not a word about the one thing which for every Christian is the most essential question in life--how to reconcile the duty of forgiveness, meekness, patience, and love for all, neighbors and enemies alike, which is so clearly expressed in the words of our teacher, and in the heart of each of us--how to reconcile this duty with the obligation of using force in war upon men of our own or a foreign people.

All that are worth calling answers to this question can be brought under the following five heads. I have tried to bring together in this connection all I could, not only from the criticisms on my book, but from what has been written in past times on this theme.

The first and crudest form of reply consists in the bold assertion that the use of force is not opposed by the teaching of Christ;

that it is permitted, and even enjoined, on the Christian by the Old and New Testaments.

Assertions of this kind proceed, for the most part, from men who have attained the highest ranks in the governing or ecclesiastical hierarchy, and who are consequently perfectly assured that no one will dare to contradict their assertion, and that if anyone does contradict it they will hear nothing of the contradiction. These men have, for the most part, through the intoxication of power, so lost the right idea of what that Christianity is in the name of which they hold their position that what is Christian in Christianity presents itself to them as heresy, while everything in the Old and New Testaments which can be distorted into an antichristian and heathen meaning they regard as the foundation of Christianity. In support of their assertion that Christianity is not opposed to the use of force, these men usually, with the greatest audacity, bring together all the most obscure passages from the Old and New Testaments, interpreting them in the most unchristian way--the punishment of Ananias and Sapphira, of Simon the Sorcerer, etc. They quote all those sayings of Christ's which can possibly be interpreted as justification of cruelty: the expulsion from the Temple; "It shall be more tolerable for the land of Sodom than for this city," etc., etc. According to these people's notions, a Christian government is not in the least bound to be guided by the spirit of peace, forgiveness of injuries, and love for enemies.

To refute such an assertion is useless, because the very people who make this assertion refute themselves, or, rather, renounce Christ, inventing a Christianity and a Christ of their own in the place of him in whose name the Church itself exists, as well as their office in it. If all men were to learn that the Church professes to believe in a Christ of punishment and warfare, not of forgiveness, no one would believe in the Church and it could not prove to anyone what it is trying to prove.

The second, somewhat less gross, form of argument consists in declaring that, though Christ did indeed preach that we should turn the left cheek, and give the cloak also, and this is the highest moral duty, yet that there are wicked men in the world, and if these wicked men mere not restrained by force, the whole world and all good men would come to ruin through them. This argument I found for the first time in John Chrysostom, and I show how he is mistaken in my book "What I believe."

This argument is ill grounded, because if we allow ourselves to regard any men as intrinsically wicked men, then in the first place we annul, by so doing, the whole idea of the Christian teaching, according to which we are all equals and brothers, as sons of one father in heaven. Secondly, it is ill founded, because even if to use force against wicked men had been permitted by God, since it is impossible to find a perfect and unfailing distinction by which one could positively know the wicked from the good, so it would come to all individual men and societies of men mutually regarding each other as wicked men, as is the case now. Thirdly, even if it were possible to distinguish the wicked from the good unfailingly, even then it would be impossible to kill or injure or shut up in prison these wicked men, because there would be no one in a Christian society to carry out such punishment, since every Christian, as a Christian, has been commanded to use no force against the wicked.

The third kind of answer, still more subtle than the preceding, consists in asserting that though the command of non-resistance to evil by force is binding on the Christian when the evil is directed against himself personally, it ceases to be binding when the evil is directed against his neighbors, and that then the Christian is not only not bound to fulfill the commandment, but is even bound to act in opposition to it in defense of his neighbors, and to use force against transgressors by force. This assertion is an absolute assumption, and one cannot find in all Christ's teaching any confirmation of such an argument. Such an argument is not only a limitation, but a direct contradiction and negation of the commandment. If every man has the right to have recourse to force in face of a danger threatening an other, the question of the use of force is reduced to a question of the definition of danger for another. If my private judgment is to decide the question of what is danger for another, there is no occasion for the use of force which could not be justified on the ground of danger threatening some other man. They killed and burnt witches, they killed aristocrats and girondists, they killed their enemies because those who were in authority regarded them as dangerous for the people.

If this important limitation, which fundamentally undermines the whole value of the commandment, had entered into Christ's meaning, there must have been mention of it somewhere. This restriction is made nowhere in our Saviour's life or preaching. On the contrary, warning is given precisely against this treacherous and scandalous restriction which nullifies the commandment. The error and impossibility of such a limitation is shown in the Gospel with special clearness in the account of the judgment of Caiaphas, who makes precisely this distinction. He acknowledged that it was wrong to punish the innocent Jesus, but he saw in him a source of danger not for himself, but for the whole people, and therefore he said: It is better for one man to die, that the whole people perish not. And the erroneousness of such a limitation is still more clearly expressed in the words spoken to Peter when he tried to resist by force evil directed against Jesus (Matt. xxvi. 52). Peter was not defending himself, but his beloved and heavenly Master. And Christ at once reproved him for this, saying, that he who takes up the sword shall perish by the sword.

Besides, apologies for violence used against one's neighbor in defense of another neighbor from greater violence are always untrustworthy, because when force is used against one who has not yet carried out his evil intent, I can never know which would be greater--the evil of my act of violence or of the act I want to prevent. We kill the criminal that society may be rid of him, and we never know whether the criminal of to-day would not have been a changed man tomorrow, and whether our punishment of him is not useless cruelty. We shut up the dangerous--as we think--member of society, but the next day this man might cease to be dangerous and his imprisonment might be for nothing. I see that a man I know to be a ruffian is pursuing a young girl. I have a gun in my hand--I kill the ruffian and save the girl. But the death or the wounding of the ruffian has positively taken place, while what would have happened if this had not been I cannot know. And what an immense mass of evil must result, and indeed does result, from allowing men to assume the right of anticipating what may happen. Ninety-nine per cent of the evil of the world is founded on this reasoning--from the Inquisition to dynamite bombs, and the executions or punishments of tens of thousands of political criminals.

A fourth, still more refined, reply to the question, What ought to be the Christian's attitude to Christ's command of non-resistance to evil by force? consists in declaring that they do not deny the command of non-resisting evil, but recognize it; but they only do not ascribe to this command the special exclusive value attached to it by sectarians. To regard this command as the indispensable condition of Christian life, as Garrison, Ballou, Dymond, the

Quakers, the Mennonites and the Shakers do now, and as the Moravian brothers, the Waldenses, the Albigenses, the Bogomilites, and the Paulicians did in the past, is a one-sided heresy. This command has neither more nor less value than all the other commands, and the man who through weakness transgresses any command whatever, the command of non-resistance included, does not cease to be a Christian if he hold the true faith. This is a very skillful device, and many people who wish to be deceived are easily deceived by it. The device consists in reducing a direct conscious denial of a command to a casual breach of it. But one need only compare the attitude of the teachers of the Church to this and to other commands which they really do recognize, to be convinced that their attitude to this is completely different from their attitude to other duties.

The command against fornication they do really recognize, and consequently they do not admit that in any case fornication can cease to be wrong. The Church preachers never point out cases in which the command against fornication can be broken, and always teach that we must avoid seductions which lead to temptation to fornication. But not so with the command of non-resistance. All church preachers recognize cases in which that command can be broken, and teach the people accordingly. And they not only do not teach teat we should avoid temptations to break it, chief of which is the military oath, but they themselves administer it.
The preachers of the Church never in any other case advocate the

breaking of any other commandment. But in connection with the commandment of non-resistance they openly teach that we must not understand it too literally, but that there are conditions and circumstances in which we must do the direct opposite, that is, go to law, fight, punish. So that occasions for fulfilling the commandment of non-resistance to evil by force are taught for the most part as occasions for not fulfilling it. The fulfillment of this command, they say, is very difficult and pertains only to perfection. And how can it not be difficult, when the breach of it is not only not forbidden, but law courts, prisons, cannons, guns, armies, and wars are under the immediate sanction of the Church? It cannot be true, then, that this command is recognized by the preachers of the Church as on a level with other commands.

The preachers of the Church clearly, do not recognize it; only not daring to acknowledge this, they try to conceal their not recognizing it.

So much for the fourth reply.

The fifth kind of answer, which is the subtlest, the most often used, and the most effective, consists in avoiding answering, in making believe that this question is one which has long ago been decided perfectly clearly and satisfactorily, and that it is not worth while to talk about it. This method of reply is employed by all the more or less cultivated religious writers, that is to say, those who feel the laws of Christ binding for themselves. Knowing that the contradiction existing between the teaching of Christ which we profess with our lips and the whole order of our lives cannot be removed by words, and that touching upon it can only make it more obvious, they, with more or less ingenuity, evade it, pretending that the question of reconciling Christianity with the use of force has been decided already, or does not exist at all.

[Footnote: I only know one work which differs somewhat from this general definition, and that is not a criticism in the precise meaning of the word, but an article treating of the same subject and having my book in view. I mean the pamphlet of Mr. Troizky (published at Kazan), "A Sermon for the People." The author obviously accepts Christ's teaching in its true meaning. He says that the prohibition of resistance to evil by force means exactly what it does mean; and the same with the prohibition of swearing. He does not, as others do, deny the meaning of Christ's teaching, but unfortunately he does not draw from this admission the inevitable deductions which present themselves spontaneously in our life when we understand Christ's teaching in that way. If we must not oppose evil by force, nor swear, everyone naturally asks, "How, then, about military service? and the oath of obedience?" To this question the author gives no reply; but it must be answered. And if he cannot answer, then he would do better no to speak on the subject at all, as such silence leads to error.]

The majority of religious critics of my book use this fifth method of replying to it. I could quote dozens of such critics, in all of whom, without exception, we find the same thing repeated: everything is discussed except what constitutes the principal subject of the book. As a characteristic example of such criticisms, I will quote the article of a well-known and ingenious English writer and preacher--Farrar--who, like many learned theologians, is a great master of the art of circuitously evading a question. The article was published in an American journal, the FORUM, in October, 1888.

After conscientiously explaining in brief the contents of my book, Farrar says:

> "Tolstoy came to the conclusion that a coarse deceit had been palmed upon the world when these words 'Resist not evil,' were held by civil society to be compatible with war, courts of justice, capital punishment, divorce, oaths, national prejudice, and, indeed, with most of the institutions of civil and social life. He now believes that the kingdom of God would come if all men kept these five commandments of Christ, viz.: 1. Live in peace with all men. 2. Be pure. 3. Take no oaths. 4. Resist not evil. 5. Renounce national distinctions.

> "Tolstoy," he says, "rejects the inspiration of the Old Testament; hence he rejects the chief doctrines of the Church--that of the Atonement by blood, the Trinity, the descent of the Holy Ghost on the Apostles, and his transmission through the priesthood." And he recognizes only the words and commands of Christ. "But is this interpretation of Christ a true one?" he says. "Are all men bound to act as Tolstoy teaches--i. e., to carry out these five commandments of Christ?"

You expect, then, that in answer to this essential question, which is the only one that could induce a man to write an article about the book, he will say either that this interpretation of Christ's teaching is true and we ought to follow it, or he will say that such an interpretation is untrue, will show why, and will give some other correct interpretation of those words which I interpret incorrectly. But nothing of this kind is done. Farrar only expresses his "belief" that,

> "although actuated by the noblest sincerity, Count Tolstoy has been misled by partial and one-sided interpretations of the meaning of the Gospel and the mind and will of Christ." What this error consists in is not made clear; it is only said:
> "To enter into the proof of this is impossible in this article, for I have already exceeded the space at my command."

And he concludes in a tranquil spirit:

> "Meanwhile, the reader who feels troubled lest it should be his duty also to forsake all the conditions of his life and to take up the position and work of a common laborer, may rest for the present on the principle, SECURUS JUDICAT ORBIS TERRARUM. With few and rare exceptions," he continues, "the whole of Christendom, from the days of the Apostles down to our own, has come to the firm conclusion that it was the object of Christ to lay down great eternal principles, but not to disturb the bases and revolutionize the institutions of all human society, which themselves rest on divine sanctions as well as on inevitable conditions. Were it my object to prove how untenable is the doctrine of communism, based by Count Tolstoy upon the divine paradoxes [sic], which can be interpreted only on historical principles in accordance with the whole method of the teaching of Jesus, it would require an ampler canvas than I have here at my disposal."

What a pity he has not an "ampler canvas at his disposal"! And what a strange thing it is that for all these last fifteen centuries no one has had a "canvas ample enough" to prove that Christ, whom we profess to believe in, says something utterly unlike what he does say! Still, they could prove it if they wanted to. But it is not worth while to prove what everyone knows; it is enough to say "SECURUS JUDICAT ORBIS TERRARUM."

And of this kind, without exception, are all the criticisms of educated believers, who must, as such, understand the danger of their position. The sole escape from it for them lies in their hope that they may be able, by using the authority of the Church, of antiquity, and of their sacred office, to overawe the reader and draw him away from the idea of reading the Gospel for himself and thinking out the question in his own mind for himself. And in this they are successful; for, indeed, how could the notion occur to any one that all that has been repeated from century to century with such earnestness and solemnity by all those archdeacons, bishops, archbishops, holy synods, and popes, is all of it a base lie and a calumny foisted upon Christ by them for the sake of keeping safe the money they must have to live luxuriously on the necks of other men? And it is a lie and a calumny so transparent that the only way of keeping it up consists in overawing people by their earnestness, their conscientiousness. It is just what has taken place of late years at recruiting sessions; at a table before the zertzal--the symbol of the Tzars authority--in the seat of honor under the life-size portrait of the Tzar, sit dignified old officials, wearing decorations, conversing freely and easily, writing notes, summoning men before them, and giving orders. Here, wearing a cross on his breast, near them, is prosperous-looking old Priest in a silken cassock, with long gray hair flowing on to his cope; before a lectern who wears the golden cross and has a Gospel bound in gold.

They summon Iran Petroff. A young man comes in, wretchedly, shabbily dressed, and in terror, the muscles of his face working, his eyes bright and restless; and in a broken voice, hardly above a whisper, he says: "I--by Christ's law--as a Christian--I cannot." "What is he muttering?" asks the president, frowning impatiently and raising his eyes from his book to listen. "Speak louder," the colonel with shining epaulets shouts to him. "I--I as a Christian--" And at last it appears that the young man refuses to serve in the army because he is a Christian. "Don't talk nonsense. Stand to be measured. Doctor, may I trouble you to measure him. He is all right?" "Yes." "Reverend father, administer the oath to him."

No one is the least disturbed by what the poor scared young man is muttering. They do not even pay attention to it. "They all mutter something, but we've no time to listen to it, we have to enroll so many."

The recruit tries to say something still. "It's opposed to the law of Christ." "Go along, go along; we know without your help what is opposed to the law and what's not; and you soothe his mind, reverend father, soothe him. Next: Vassily Nikitin." And they lead the trembling youth away. And it does not strike anyone --the guards, or Vassily Nikitin, whom they are bringing in, or any of the spectators of this scene--that these inarticulate words of the young man, at once suppressed by the authorities, contain the truth, and that the loud, solemnly uttered sentences of the calm, self-confident official and the priest are a lie and a deception.

Such is the impression produced not only by Farrar's article, but by all those solemn sermons, articles, and books which make their appearance from all sides directly there is anywhere a glimpse of truth exposing a predominant falsehood. At once begins the series of long, clever, ingenious, and solemn speeches and writings, which deal with questions nearly related to the subject, but skillfully avoid touching the subject itself.

That is the essence of the fifth and most effective means of getting out of the contradictions in which Church Christianity has placed itself, by professing its faith in Christ's teaching in words, while it denies it in its life, and teaches people to do the same.

Those who justify themselves by the first method, directly, crudely asserting that Christ sanctioned violence, wars, and murder, repudiate Christ's doctrine directly; those who find their defense in the second, the third, or the fourth method are confused and can easily be convicted of error; but this last class, who do not argue, who do not condescend to argue about it, but take shelter behind their own grandeur, and make a show of all this having been decided by them or at least by someone long ago, and no longer offering a possibility of doubt to anyone--they seem safe from attack, and will be beyond attack till men come to realize that they are under the narcotic influence exerted on them by governments and churches, and are no longer affected by it.

Such was the attitude of the spiritual critics--i. e., those professing faith in Christ--to my book. And their attitude could not have been different. They are bound to take up this attitude by the contradictory position in which they find themselves between belief in the divinity of their Master and disbelief in his clearest utterances, and they want to escape from this contradiction. So that one cannot expect from them free discussion of the very essence of the question--that is, of the change in men's life which must result from applying Christ's teaching to the existing order of the world. Such free discussion I only expected from worldly, freethinking critics who are not bound to Christ's teaching in any way, and can therefore take an independent view of it. I had anticipated that freethinking writers would look at Christ, not merely, like the Churchmen, as the founder of a religion of personal salvation, but, to express it in their language, as a reformer who laid down new principles of life and destroyed the old, and whose reforms are not yet complete, but are still in progress even now.

Such a view of Christ and his teaching follows from my book. But to my astonishment, out of the great number of critics of my book there was not one, either Russian or foreign, who treated the subject from the side from which it was approached in the book--that is, who criticised

Christ's doctrines as philosophical, moral, and social principles, to use their scientific expressions. This was not done in a single criticism. The freethinking Russian critics taking my book as though its whole contents could be reduced to non-resistance to evil, and understanding the doctrine of non-resistance to evil itself (no doubt for greater convenience in refuting it) as though it would prohibit every kind of conflict with evil, fell vehemently upon this doctrine, and for some years past have been very successfully proving that Christ's teaching is mistaken in so far as it forbids resistance to evil. Their refutations of this hypothetical doctrine of Christ were all the more successful since they knew beforehand that their arguments could not be contested or corrected, for the censorship, not having passed the book, did not pass articles in its defense.

It is a remarkable thing that among us, where one cannot say a word about the Holy Scriptures without the prohibition of the censorship, for some years past there have been in all the journals constant attacks and criticisms on the command of Christ simply and directly stated in Matt. v. 39. The Russian advanced critics, obviously unaware of all that has been done to elucidate the question of non-resistance, and sometimes even imagining apparently that the rule of non-resistance to evil had been invented by me personally, fell foul of the very idea of it. They opposed it and attacked it, and advancing with great heat arguments which had long ago been analyzed and refuted from every point of view, they demonstrated that a man ought invariably to defend (with violence) all the injured and oppressed, and that thus the doctrine of non-resistance to evil is an immoral doctrine.

To all Russian critics the whole import of Christ's command seemed reducible to the fact that it would hinder them from the active opposition to evil to which they are accustomed. So that the principle of non-resistance to evil by force has been attacked by two opposing camps: the conservatives, because this principle would hinder their activity in resistance to evil as applied to the revolutionists, in persecution and punishment of them; the revolutionists, too, because this principle would hinder their resistance to evil as applied to the conservatives and the overthrowing of them. The conservatives were indignant at the doctrine of non-resistance to evil by force hindering the energetic destruction of the revolutionary elements, which may ruin the national prosperity; the revolutionists were indignant at the doctrine of non-resistance to evil by force hindering the overthrow of the conservatives, who are ruining the national prosperity. It is worthy of remark in this connection that the revolutionists have attacked the principle of non-resistance to evil by force, in spite of the fact that it is the greatest terror and danger for every despotism. For ever since the beginning of the world, the use of violence of every kind, from the Inquisition to the Schlüsselburg fortress, has rested and still rests on the opposite principle of the necessity of resisting evil by force.

Besides this, the Russian critics have pointed out the fact that the application of the command of non-resistance to practical life would turn mankind aside out of the path of civilization along which it is moving. The path of civilization on which mankind in Europe is moving is in their opinion the one along which all mankind ought always to move.

So much for the general character of the Russian critics.

Foreign critics started from the same premises, but their discussions of my book were somewhat different from those of Russian critics, not only in being less bitter, and in showing more culture, but even in the subject-matter.

In discussing my book and the Gospel teaching generally, as it is expressed in the Sermon on the Mount, the foreign critics maintained that such doctrine is not peculiarly Christian (Christian doctrine is either Catholicism or Protestantism according to their views)--the teaching of the Sermon on the Mount is only a string of very pretty impracticable dreams DU CHARMANT DOCTEUR, as Reran says, fit for the simple and half-savage inhabitants of Galilee who lived eighteen hundred years ago, and for the half-savage Russian peasants--Sutaev and Bondarev--and the Russian mystic Tolstoy, but not at all consistent with a high degree of European culture.

The foreign freethinking critics have tried in a delicate manner, without being offensive to me, to give the impression that my conviction that mankind could be guided by such a naïve doctrine as that of the Sermon on the Mount proceeds from two causes: that such a conviction is partly due to my want of knowledge, my ignorance of history, my ignorance of all the vain attempts to apply the principles of the Sermon on the Mount to life, which have been made in history and have led to nothing; and partly it is due to my failing to appreciate the full value of the lofty civilization to which mankind has attained at present, with its Krupp cannons, smokeless powder, colonization of Africa, Irish Coercion Bill, parliamentary government, journalism, strikes, and the Eiffel Tower.

So wrote de Vogüé and Leroy Beaulieu and Matthew Arnold; so wrote the American author Savage, and Ingersoll, the popular freethinking American preacher, and many others.

"Christ's teaching is no use, because it is inconsistent with our industrial age," says Ingersoll naïvely, expressing in this utterance, with perfect directness and simplicity, the exact notion of Christ's teaching held by persons of refinement and culture of our times. The teaching is no use for our industrial age, precisely as though the existence of this industrial age were a sacred fact which ought not to and could not be changed. It is just as though drunkards when advised how they could be brought to habits of sobriety should answer that the advice is incompatible with their habit of taking alcohol.

The arguments of all the freethinking critics, Russian and foreign alike, different as they may be in tone and manner of presentation, all amount essentially to the same strange misapprehension--namely, that Christ's teaching, one of the consequences of which is non-resistance to evil, is of no use to us because it requires a change of our life.

Christ's teaching is useless because, if it were carried into practice, life could not go on as at present; we must add: if we have begun by living sinfully, as we do live and are accustomed to live. Not only is the question of non-resistance to evil not discussed; the very mention of the fact that the duty of non-resistance enters into Christ's teaching is regarded as satisfactory proof of the impracticability of the whole teaching.

Meanwhile one would have thought it was necessary to point out at least some kind of solution of the following question, since it is at the root of almost everything that interests us.

The question amounts to this: In what way are we to decide men's disputes, when some men consider evil what others consider good, and VICE VERSA? And to reply that that is evil which I think evil, in spite of the fact that my opponent thinks it good, is not a solution of the difficulty. There can only be two solutions: either to find a real unquestionable criterion of what is evil or not to resist evil by force.

The first course has been tried ever since the beginning of historical times, and, as we all know, it has not hitherto led to any successful results.

The second solution--not forcibly to resist what we consider evil until we have found a universal criterion--that is the solution given by Christ.

We may consider the answer given by Christ unsatisfactory; we may replace it by another and better, by finding a criterion by which evil could be defined for all men unanimously and simultaneously; we may simply, like savage nations, not recognize the existence of the question. But we cannot treat the question as the learned critics of Christianity do. They pretend either that no such question exists at all or that the question is solved by granting to certain persons or assemblies of persons the right to define evil and to resist it by force. But we know all the while that granting such a right to certain persons does not decide the question (still less so when we are ourselves the certain persons), since there are always people who do not recognize this right in the authorized persons or assemblies.

But this assumption, that what seems evil to us is really evil, shows a complete misunderstanding of the question, and lies at the root of the argument of freethinking critics about the Christian religion. In this way, then, the discussions of my book on the part of Churchmen and freethinking critics alike showed me that the majority of men simply do not understand either Christ's teaching or the questions which Christ's teaching solves.

CHAPTER III.

CHRISTIANITY MISUNDERSTOOD BY BELIEVERS.

Meaning of Christian Doctrine, Understood by a Minority, has Become Completely Incomprehensible for the Majority of Men--Reason of this to be Found in Misinterpretation of Christianity and Mistaken Conviction of Believers and Unbelievers Alike that they Understand it--The Meaning of Christianity Obscured for Believers by the Church--The First Appearance of Christ's Teaching--Its Essence and Difference from Heathen Religions--Christianity not Fully Comprehended at the Beginning, Became More and More Clear to those who Accepted it from its Correspondence with Truth--Simultaneously with this Arose the Claim to Possession of the Authentic Meaning of the Doctrine Based on the Miraculous Nature of its Transmission--Assembly of Disciples as Described in the Acts--The Authoritative Claim to the Sole Possession of the True Meaning of Christ's Teaching Supported by Miraculous Evidence has Led by Logical Development to the Creeds of the Churches--A Church Could Not be Founded by Christ--Definitions of a Church According to the Catechisms--The Churches have Always been Several in Number and Hostile to One Another--What is Heresy--The Work of G. Arnold on Heresies--Heresies the Manifestations of Progress in the Churches--Churches Cause Dissension among Men, and are Always Hostile to Christianity--Account of the Work Done by the Russian Church--Matt. xxiii. 23--The Sermon on the Mount or the Creed--The Orthodox Church Conceals from the People the True Meaning of Christianity--The Same Thing is Done by the Other Churches--All the

External Conditions of Modern Life are such as to Destroy the Doctrine of the Church, and therefore the Churches use Every Effort to Support their Doctrines.

Thus the information I received, after my book came out, went to show that the Christian doctrine, in its direct and simple sense, was understood, and had always been understood, by a minority of men, while the critics, ecclesiastical and freethinking alike, denied the possibility of taking Christ's teaching in its direct sense. All this convinced me that while on one hand the true understanding of this doctrine had never been lost to a minority, but had been established more and more clearly, on the other hand the meaning of it had been more and more obscured for the majority. So that at last such a depth of obscurity has been reached that men do not take in their direct sense even the simplest precepts, expressed in the simplest words, in the Gospel.

Christ's teaching is not generally understood in its true, simple, and direct sense even in these days, when the light of the Gospel has penetrated even to the darkest recesses of human consciousness; when, in the words of Christ, that which was spoken in the ear is proclaimed from the housetops; and when the Gospel is influencing every side of human life--domestic, economic, civic, legislative, and international. This lack of true understanding of Christ's words at such a time would be inexplicable, if there were not causes to account for it.

One of these causes is the fact that believers and unbelievers alike are firmly persuaded that they have understood Christ's teaching a long time, and that they understand it so fully, indubitably, and conclusively that it can have no other significance than the one they attribute to it. And the reason of this conviction is that the false interpretation and consequent misapprehension of the Gospel is an error of such long standing. Even the strongest current of water cannot add a drop to a cup which is already full.

The most difficult subjects can be explained to the most slow-witted man if he has not formed any idea of them already; but the simplest thing cannot be made clear to the most intelligent man if he is firmly persuaded that he knows already, without a shadow of doubt, what is laid before him.

The Christian doctrine is presented to the men of our world to-day as a doctrine which everyone has known so long and accepted so unhesitatingly in all its minutest details that it cannot be understood in any other way than it is understood now.

Christianity is understood now by all who profess the doctrines of the Church as a supernatural miraculous revelation of everything which is repeated in the Creed. By unbelievers it is regarded as an illustration of man's craving for a belief in the supernatural, which mankind has now outgrown, as an historical phenomenon which has received full expression in Catholicism, Greek Orthodoxy, and Protestantism, and has no longer any living significance for us. The significance of the Gospel is hidden from believers by the Church, from unbelievers by Science.

I will speak first of the former. Eighteen hundred years ago there appeared in the midst of the heathen Roman world a strange new doctrine, unlike any of the old religions, and attributed to a man, Christ.

This new doctrine was in both form and content absolutely new to the Jewish world in which it originated, and still more to the Roman world in which it was preached and diffused.

In the midst of the elaborate religious observances of Judaism, in which, in the words of Isaiah, law was laid upon law, and in the midst of the Roman legal system worked out to the highest point of perfection, a new doctrine appeared, which denied not only every deity, and all fear and worship of them, but even all human institutions and all necessity for them. In place of all the rules of the old religions, this doctrine sets up only a type of inward perfection, truth, and love in the person of Christ, and--as a result of this inward perfection being attained by men--also the outward perfection foretold by the Prophets--the kingdom of God, when all men will cease to learn to make war, when all shall be taught of God and united in love, and the lion will lie down with the lamb. Instead of the threats of punishment which all the old laws of religions and governments alike laid down for non-fulfillment of their rules, instead of promises of rewards for fulfillment of them, this doctrine called men to it only because it was the truth. John vii. 17: "If any man will do His will, he shall know of the doctrine whether it be of God." John viii. 46: "If I say the truth, why do ye not believe me? But ye seek to kill me, a man that hath told you the truth. Ye shall know the truth, and the truth shall make you free. God is a spirit, and they that worship him must worship him in spirit and in truth. Keep my sayings, and ye shall know of my sayings whether they be true." No proofs of this doctrine were offered except its truth, the correspondence of the doctrine with the truth. The whole teaching consisted in the recognition of truth and following it, in a greater and greater attainment of truth, and a closer and closer following of it in the acts of life. There are no acts in this doctrine which could justify a man and make him saved. There is only the image of truth to guide-him, for inward perfection in the person of Christ, and for outward perfection in the establishment of the kingdom of God. The fulfillment of this teaching consists only in walking in the chosen way, in getting nearer to inward perfection in the imitation of Christ, and outward perfection in the establishment of the kingdom of God. The greater or less blessedness of a man depends, according to this doctrine, not on the degree of perfection to which he has attained, but on the greater or less swiftness with which he is pursuing it.

The progress toward perfection of the publican Zaccheus, of the woman that was a sinner, of the robber on the cross, is a greater state of blessedness, according to this doctrine, than the stationary righteousness of the Pharisee. The lost sheep is dearer than ninety-nine that were not lost. The prodigal son, the piece of money that was lost and found again, are dearer, more precious to God than those which have not been lost.

Every condition, according to this doctrine, is only a particular step in the attainment of inward and outward perfection, and therefore has no significance of itself. Blessedness consists in progress toward perfection; to stand still in any condition whatever means the cessation of this blessedness.

"Let not thy left hand know what they right hand doeth." "No man having put his hand to the plow and looking back is fit for the Kingdom of God." "Rejoice not that the spirits are subject to you, but seek rather that your names be written in heaven." "Be ye perfect even as your Father in heaven is perfect." "Seek ye first the kingdom of heaven and its righteousness."

The fulfillment of this precept is only to be found in uninterrupted progress toward the attainment of ever higher truth, toward establishing more and more firmly an ever greater love within oneself, and establishing more and more widely the kingdom of God outside oneself.

It is obvious that, appearing as it did in the midst of the Jewish and heathen world, such teaching could not be accepted by the majority of men, who were living a life absolutely different from what was required by it. It is obvious, too, that even for those by whom it was accepted, it was so absolutely opposed to all their old views that it could not be comprehensible in its full significance.

It has been only by a succession of misunderstandings, errors, partial explanations, and the corrections and additions of generations that the meaning of the Christian doctrine has grown continually more and more clear to men. The Christian view of life has exerted an influence on the Jewish and heathen, and the heathen and Jewish view of life has, too, exerted an influence on the Christian. And Christianity, as the living force, has gained more and more upon the extinct Judaism and heathenism, and has grown continually clearer and clearer, as it freed itself from the admixture of falsehood which had overlaid it. Men went further and further in the attainment of the meaning of Christianity, and realized it more and more in life.

The longer mankind lived, the clearer and clearer became the meaning of Christianity, as must always be the case with every theory of life.

Succeeding generations corrected the errors of their predecessors, and grew ever nearer and nearer to a comprehension of the true meaning. It was thus from the very earliest times of Christianity. And so, too, from the earliest times of Christianity there were men who began to assert on their own authority that the meaning they attribute to the doctrine is the only true one, and as proof bring forward supernatural occurrences in support of the correctness of their interpretation.

This was the principal cause at first of the misunderstanding of the doctrine, and afterward of the complete distortion of it.

It was supposed that Christ's teaching was transmitted to men not like every other truth, but in a special miraculous way. Thus the truth of the teaching was not proved by its correspondence with the needs of the mind and the whole nature of man, but by the miraculous manner of its transmission, which was advanced as an irrefutable proof of the truth of the interpretation put on it.
This hypothesis originated from misunderstanding of the teaching, and its result was to make it impossible to understand it rightly.

And this happened first in the earliest times, when the doctrine was still not so fully understood and often interpreted wrongly, as we see by the Gospels and the Acts. The less the doctrine was understood, the more obscure it appeared and the more necessary were external proofs of its truth. The proposition that we ought not to do unto others as we would not they should do unto us, did not need to be proved by miracles and needed no exercise of faith, because this proposition is in itself convincing and in harmony with man's mind and nature; but the proposition that Christ was God had to be proved by miracles completely beyond our comprehension.

The more the understanding of Christ's teaching was obscured, the more the miraculous was introduced into it; and the more the miraculous was introduced into it, the more the doctrine was strained from its meaning and the more obscure it became; and the more it was strained from its meaning and the more obscure it became, the more strongly its infallibility had to be asserted, and the less comprehensible the doctrine became.

One can see by the Gospels, the Acts, and the Epistles how from the earliest times the non-comprehension of the doctrine called forth the need for proofs through the miraculous and incomprehensible.

The first example in the book of Acts is the assembly which gathered together in Jerusalem to decide the question which had arisen, whether to baptize or not the uncircumcised and those who had eaten of food sacrificed to idols.

The very fact of this question being raised showed that

those who discussed it did not understand the teaching of Christ, who rejected all outward observances--ablutions, purifications, fasts, and sabbaths. It was plainly said, "Not that which goeth into a man's mouth, but that which cometh out of a man's mouth, defileth him," and therefore the question of baptizing the uncircumcised could only have arisen among men who, though they loved their Master and dimly felt the grandeur of his teaching, still did not understand the teaching itself very clearly. And this was the fact.

Just in proportion to the failure of the members of the assembly to understand the doctrine was their need of external confirmation of their incomplete interpretation of it. And then to settle this question, the very asking of which proved their misunderstanding of the doctrine, there was uttered in this assembly, as is described in the Acts, that strange phrase, which was for the first time found necessary to give external confirmation to certain assertions, and which has been productive of so much evil.

That is, it was asserted that the correctness of what they had decided was guaranteed by the miraculous participation of the Holy Ghost, that is, of God, in their decision. But the assertion that the Holy Ghost, that is, God, spoke through the Apostles, in its turn wanted proof. And thus it was necessary, to confirm this, that the Holy Ghost should descend at Pentecost in tongues of fire upon those who made this assertion. (In the account of it, the descent of the Holy Ghost precedes the assembly, but the book of Acts was written much later than both events.) But the descent of the Holy Ghost too had to be proved for those who had not seen the tongues of fire (though it is not easy to understand why a tongue of fire burning above a man's head should prove that what that man is going to say will be infallibly the truth). And so arose the necessity for still more miracles and changes, raisings of the dead to life, and strikings of the living dead, and all those marvels which have been a stumbling-block to men, of which the Acts is full, and which, far from ever convincing one of the truth of the Christian doctrine, can only repel men from it. The result of such a means of confirming the truth was that the more these confirmations of truth by tales of miracles were heaped up one after another, the more the doctrine was distorted from its original meaning, aid the more incomprehensible it became.

Thus it was from the earliest times, and so it went on, constantly increasing, till it reached in our day the logical climax of the dogmas of transubstantiation and the infallibility of the Pope, or of the bishops, or of Scripture, and of requiring a blind faith rendered incomprehensible and utterly meaningless, not in God, but in Christ, not in a doctrine, but in a person, as in Catholicism, or in persons, as in Greek Orthodoxy, or in a book, as in Protestantism. The more widely Christianity was diffused, and the greater the number of people unprepared for it who were brought under its sway, the less it was understood, the more absolutely was its infallibility insisted on, and the less possible it became to understand the true meaning of the doctrine. In the times of Constantine the whole interpretation of the doctrine had been already reduced to a RÉSUMÉ--supported by the temporal authority--of the disputes that had taken place in the Council--to a creed which reckoned off--I believe in so and so, and so and so, and so and so to the end--to one holy, Apostolic Church, which means the infallibility of those persons who call themselves the Church. So that it all amounts to a man no longer believing in God nor Christ, as they are revealed to him, but believing in what the Church orders him to believe in.

But the Church is holy; the Church was founded by Christ. God could not leave men to interpret his teaching at random--therefore he founded the Church. All those statements are so utterly untrue and unfounded that one is ashamed to refute them. Nowhere nor in anything, except in the assertion of the Church, can we find that God or Christ founded anything like what Churchmen understand by the Church. In the Gospels there is a warning against the Church, as it is an external authority, a warning most clear and obvious in the passage where it is said that Christ's followers should "call no man master." But nowhere is anything said of the foundation of what Churchmen call the Church.

The word church is used twice in the Gospels--once in the sense of an assembly of men to decide a dispute, the other time in connection with the obscure utterance about a stone--Peter, and the gates of hell. From these two passages in which the word church is used, in the signification merely of an assembly, has been deduced all that we now understand by the Church.

But Christ could not have founded the Church, that is, what we now understand by that word. For nothing like the idea of the Church as we know it now, with its sacraments, miracles, and above all its claim to infallibility, is to be found either in Christ's words or in the ideas of the men of that time.

The fact that men called what was formed afterward by the same word as Christ used for something totally different, does not give them the right to assert that Christ founded the one, true Church.

Besides, if Christ had really founded such an institution as the Church for the foundation of all his teaching and the whole faith, he would certainly have described this institution clearly and definitely, and would have given the only true Church, besides tales of miracles, which are used to support every kind of superstition, some tokens so unmistakable that no doubt of its genuineness could ever have arisen. But nothing of the sort was done by him. And there have been and still are different institutions, each calling itself the true Church.

The Catholic catechism says: "L'Église est la société des fidéles établie par notre Seigneur Jésus Christ, répandue sur toute la terre et soumise à l'authorité des pasteurs légitimes, principalement notre Saint Père le Pape," [see Footnote] understanding by the words "pasteurs légitimes" an association of men having the Pope at its head, and consisting of certain individuals bound together by a certain organization.

[Footnote: "The Church is the society of the faithful, established by our Lord Jesus Christ, spread over the whole earth, and subject to the authority of its lawful pastors, and chief of them our Holy Father the Pope."]

The Greek Orthodox catechism says: "The Church is a society founded upon earth by Jesus Christ, which is united into one whole, by one divine doctrine and by sacraments, under the rule and guidance of a priesthood appointed by God," meaning by the "priesthood appointed by God" the Greek Orthodox priesthood, consisting of certain individuals who happen to be in such or such positions.

The Lutheran catechism says: "The Church is holy Christianity, or the collection of all believers under Christ, their head, to whom the Holy Ghost through the Gospels and sacraments promises, communicates, and administers heavenly salvation," meaning that the Catholic Church is lost in error, and that the true means of salvation is in Lutheranism.

For Catholics the Church of God coincides with the Roman priesthood and the Pope. For the Greek Orthodox believer the Church of God coincides with the establishment and priesthood of Russia. [See Footnote]

[Footnote: Homyakov's definition of the Church, which was received with some favor among Russians, does not improve matters, if we are to agree with Homyakov in considering the Greek Orthodox Church as the one true Church. Homyakov asserts that a church is a collection of men (all without distinction of clergy and laymen) united together by love, and that only to men united by love is the truth revealed (let us love each other, that in the unity of thought, etc.), and that such a church is the church which, in the first place, recognizes the Nicene Creed, and in the second place does not, after the division of the churches, recognize the popes and new dogmas. But with such a definition of the church, there is still more difficulty in reconciling, as Homyakov tries to do, the church united by love with the church that recognizes the Nicene Creed and the doctrine of Photius. So that Homyakov's assertion that this church, united by love, and consequently holy, is the same church as the Greek Orthodox priesthood profess faith in, is even more arbitrary than the assertions of the Catholics or the Orthodox. If we admit the idea of a church in the sense Homyakov gives to it--that is, a body of men bound together by love and truth--then all that any man can predicate in regard to this body, if such an one exists, is its love and truth, but there can be no outer signs by which one could reckon oneself or another as a member of this holy body, nor by which one could put anyone outside it; so that no institution having an external existence can correspond to this idea.]

For Lutherans the Church of God coincides with a body of men who recognize the authority of the Bible and Luther's catechism.

Ordinarily, when speaking of the rise of Christianity, men belonging to one of the existing churches use the word church in the singular, as though there were and had been only one church. But this is absolutely incorrect. The Church, as an institution which asserted that it possessed infallible truth, did not make its appearance singly; there were at least two churches directly this claim was made.

While believers were agreed among themselves and the body was one, it had no need to declare itself as a church. It was only when believers were split up into opposing parties, renouncing one another, that it seemed necessary to each party to confirm their own truth by ascribing to themselves infallibility. The conception of one church only arose when there were two sides divided and disputing, who each called the other side heresy, and recognized their own side only as the infallible church.

If we knew that there was a church which decided in the year 51 to receive the uncircumcised, it is only so because there was another church--of the Judaists--who decided to keep the uncircumcised out.

If there is a Catholic Church now which asserts its own infallibility, that is only because there are churches--Greco-Russian, Old Orthodox, and Lutheran--each asserting its own infallibility and denying that of all other churches. So that the one Church is only a fantastic imagination which has not the least trace of reality about it.

As a real historical fact there has existed, and still exist, several bodies of men, each asserting that it is the one Church, founded by Christ, and that all the others who call themselves churches are only sects and heresies.

The catechisms of the churches of the most world-wide influence--the Catholic, the Old Orthodox, and the Lutheran--openly assert this.

In the Catholic catechism it is said: "Quels sont ceux qui sont hors de l'église? Les infidèles, les hérétiques, les schismatiques." [Footnote: "Who are those who are outside the

Church? Infidels, heretics, and schismatics."] The so-called Greek Orthodox are regarded as schismatics, the Lutherans as heretics; so that according to the Catholic catechism the only people in the Church are Catholics.

In the so-called Orthodox catechism it is said: By the one Christian Church is understood the Orthodox, which remains fully in accord with the Universal Church. As for the Roman Church and other sects (the Lutherans and the rest they do not even dignify by the name of church), they cannot be included in the one true Church, since they have themselves separated from it.

According to this definition the Catholics and Lutherans are outside the Church, and there are only Orthodox in the Church.

The Lutheran catechism says: "Die wahre kirche wird darein erkannt, dass in ihr das Wort Gottes lauter und rein ohne Menschenzusätze gelehrt and die Sacramente treu nach Christi Einsetzung gewahret werden." [Footnote: "The true Church will be known by the Word of God being studied clear and unmixed with man's additions and the sacraments being maintained faithful to Christ's teaching."]

According to this definition all those who have added anything to the teaching of Christ and the apostles, as the Catholic and Greek churches have done, are outside the Church. And in the Church there are only Protestants.

The Catholics assert that the Holy Ghost has been transmitted without a break in their priesthood. The Orthodox assert that the same Holy Ghost has been transmitted without a break in their priesthood. The Arians asserted that the Holy Ghost was transmitted in their priesthood (they asserted this with just as much right as the churches in authority now). The Protestants of every kind--Lutherans, Reformed Church, Presbyterians, Methodists, Swedenborgians, Mormons--assert that the Holy Ghost is only present in their communities. If the Catholics assert that the Holy Ghost, at the time of the division of the Church into Arian and Greek, left the Church that fell away and remained in the one true Church, with precisely the same right the Protestants of every denomination can assert that at the time of the separation of their Church from the Catholic the Holy Ghost left the Catholic and passed into the Church they professed. And this is just what they do.

Every church traces its creed through an uninterrupted transmission from Christ and the Apostles. And truly every Christian creed that has been derived from Christ must have come down to the present generation through a certain transmission. But that does not prove that it alone of all that has been transmuted, excluding all the rest, can be the sole truth, admitting of no doubt.

Every branch in a tree comes from the root in unbroken connection; but the fact that each branch comes from the one root, does not prove at all that each branch was the only one. It is precisely the same with the Church. Every church presents exactly the same proofs of the succession, and even the same miracles, in support of its authenticity, as every other. So that there is but one strict and exact definition of what is a church (not of something fantastic which we would wish it to be, but of what it is and has been in reality)--a church is a body of men who claim for themselves that they are in complete and sole possession of the truth. And these bodies, having in course of time, aided by the support of the temporal authorities, developed into powerful institutions, have been the principal obstacles to the diffusion of a true comprehension of the teaching of Christ.

It could not be otherwise. The chief peculiarity which distinguished Christ's teaching from previous religions consisted in the fact that those who accepted it strove ever more and more to comprehend and realize its teaching. But the Church doctrine asserted its own complete and final comprehension and realization of it.

Strange though it may seem to us who have been brought up in the erroneous view of the Church as a Christian institution, and in contempt for heresy, yet the fact is that only in what was called heresy was there any true movement, that is, true Christianity, and that it only ceased to be so when those heresies stopped short in their movement and also petrified into the fixed forms of a church.

And, indeed what is a heresy? Read all the theological works one after another. In all of them heresy is the subject which first presents itself for definition; since every theological work deals with the true doctrine of Christ as distinguished from the erroneous doctrines which surround it, that is, heresies. Yet you will not find anywhere anything like a definition of heresy.

The treatment of this subject by the learned historian of Christianity, E. de Pressensé, in his "Histoire du Dogme" (Paris, 1869), under the heading "Ubi Christus, ibi Ecclesia," may serve as an illustration of the complete absence of anything like a definition of what is understood by the word heresy. Here is what he says in his introduction (p. 3):

> "Je sais que l'on nous conteste le droit de qualifier ainsi [that is, to call heresies] les tendances qui furent si vivement combattues par les premiers Pères. La désignation même d'hérésie semble une atteinte portée à la liberté de conscience et de pensée. Nous ne pouvons partager ce scrupule, car il n'irait à rien moins qu'à enlever au Christianisme tout caractère distinctif." [see Footnote]

[Footnote: "I know that our right to qualify thus the tendencies which were so actively opposed by the early Fathers is contested. The very use of the word heresy seems an attack upon liberty of conscience and thought. We cannot share this scruple; for it would amount to nothing less than depriving Christianity of all distinctive character."]

And though he tells us that after Constantine's time the Church did actually abuse its power by designating those who dissented from it as heretics and persecuting them, yet he says, when speaking of early times:

"L'église est une libre association; il y a tout profit a se séparer d'elle. La polémique contre l'erreur n'a d'autres ressources que la pensée et le sentiment. Un type doctrinal uniforme n'a pas encore été élaboré; les divergences secondaires se produisent en Orient et en Occident avec une entière liberté; la théologie n'est point liée a d'invariables formules. Si au sein de cette diversité apparait un fonds commun de croyances, n'est-on pas en droit d'y voir non pas un système formulé et composé par les représentants d'une autorité d'école, mais la foi elle-même dons son instinct le plus sûr et sa manifestation la plus spontanée? Si cette même unanimité qui se révèle dans les croyances essentielles, se retrouve pour repousser telles ou telles tendances ne serons nous pas en droit de conclure que ces tendances étaient en désacord flagrant avec les principes fondamentaux du christianisme? Cette présomption ne se transformerait-elle pas en certitude si nous reconnaissons dans la doctrine

universellement repoussée par l'Église les traits caractéristiques de l'une des religions du passé? Pour dire que le gnosticisme ou l'ébionitisme sont les formes légitimes de la pensée chrétienne il faut dire hardiment qu'il n'y a pas de pensée chrétienne, ni de caractère spécifique qui la fasse reconnaître. Sous prétexte de l'élargir, on la dissout. Personne au temps de Platon n'eût osé couvrir de son nom une doctrine qui n'eut pas fait place à la théorie des idées; et l'on eût excité les justes moqueries de la Grèce, en voulant faire d'Epicure ou de Zénon un disciple de l'Académie. Reconnaissons donc que s'il existe une religion ou une doctrine qui s'appelle christianisme, elle peut avoir ses hérésies." [see Footnote]

[Footnote: "The Church is a free association; there is much to be gained by separation from it. Conflict with error has no weapons other than thought and feeling. One uniform type of doctrine has not yet been elaborated; divergencies in secondary matters arise freely in East and West; theology is not wedded to invariable formulas. If in the midst of this diversity a mass of beliefs common to all is apparent, is one not justified in seeing in it, not a formulated system, framed by the representatives of pedantic authority, but faith itself in its surest instinct and its most spontaneous manifestation? If the same unanimity which is revealed in essential points of belief is found also in rejecting certain tendencies, are we not justified in concluding that these tendencies were in flagrant opposition to the fundamental principles of Christianity? And will not this presumption be transformed into certainty if we recognize in the doctrine universally rejected by the Church the characteristic features of one of the religions of the past? To say that gnosticism or ebionitism are legitimate forms of Christian thought, one must boldly deny the existence of Christian thought at all, or any specific character by which it could be recognized. While ostensibly widening its realm, one undermines it. No one in the time of Plato would have ventured to give his name to a doctrine in which the theory of ideas had no place, and one would deservedly have excited the ridicule of Greece by trying to pass off Epicurus or Zeno as a disciple of the Academy. Let us recognize, then, that if a religion or a doctrine exists which is called Christianity, it may have its heresies."]

The author's whole argument amounts to this: that every opinion which differs from the code of dogmas we believe in at a given time, is heresy. But of course at any given time and place men always believe in something or other; and this belief in something, indefinite at any place, at some time, cannot be a criterion of truth.

It all amounts to this: since ubi Christus ibi Ecclesia, then Christus is where we are.

Every so-called heresy, regarding, as it does, its own creed as the truth, can just as easily find in Church history a series of illustrations of its own creed, can use all Pressensé's arguments on its own behalf, and can call its own creed the one truly Christian creed. And that is just what all heresies do and have always done.

The only definition of heresy (the word [GREEK WORD], means a part) is this: the name given by a body of men to any opinion which rejects a part of the Creed professed by that body. The more frequent meaning, more often ascribed to the word heresy, is --that of an opinion which rejects the Church doctrine founded and supported by the temporal authorities.

[TRANSCRIBIST'S NOTE: The GREEK WORD above used Greek letters, spelled: alpha(followed by an apostrophe)-iota(with accent)-rho-epsilon-sigma-iota-zeta]

There is a remarkable and voluminous work, very little known, "Unpartheyische Kirchen- und Ketzer-Historie," 1729, by Gottfried Arnold, which deals with precisely this subject, and points out all the unlawfulness, the arbitrariness, the senselessness, and the cruelty of using the word heretic in the sense of reprobate. This book is an attempt to write the history of Christianity in the form of a history of heresy.

In the introduction the author propounds a series of questions: (1) Of those who make heretics; (2) Of those whom they made heretics; (3) Of heretical subjects themselves; (4) Of the method of making heretics; and (5) Of the object and result of making heretics.

On each of these points he propounds ten more questions, the answers to which he gives later on from the works of well-known theologians. But he leaves the reader to draw for himself the principal conclusion from the expositions in the whole book. As examples of these questions, in which the answers are to some extent included also, I will quote the following. Under the 4th head, of the manner in which heretics are made, he says, in one of the questions (in the 7th):

> "Does not all history show that the greatest makers of heretics and masters of that craft were just these wise men, from whom the Father hid his secrets, that is, the hypocrites,

the Pharisees, and lawyers, men utterly godless and perverted (Question 20-21)? And in the corrupt times of Christianity were not these very men cast out, denounced by the hypocrites and envious, who were endowed by God with great gifts and who would in the days of pure Christianity have been held in high honor? And, on the other hand, would not the men who, in the decline of Christianity raised themselves above all, and regarded themselves as the teachers of the purest Christianity, would not these very men, in the times of the apostles and disciples of Christ, have been regarded as the most shameless heretics and anti-Christians?"

He expounds, among other things in these questions, the theory that any verbal expression of faith, such as was demanded by the Church, and the departure from which was reckoned as heresy, could never fully cover the exact religious ideas of a believer, and that therefore the demand for an expression of faith in certain words was ever productive of heresy, and he says, in Question 21:

"And if heavenly things and thoughts present themselves to a man's mind as so great and so profound that he does not find corresponding words to express them, ought one to call him a heretic, because he cannot express his idea with perfect exactness?"

And in Question 33:

"And is not the fact that there was no heresy in the earliest days due to the fact that the Christians did not judge one another by verbal expressions, but by deed and by heart, since they had perfect liberty to express their ideas without the dread of being called heretics; was it not the easiest and most ordinary ecclesiastical proceeding, if the clergy wanted to get rid of or to ruin anyone, for them to cast suspicion on the person's belief, and to throw a cloak of heresy upon him, and by this means to procure his condemnation and removal?

"True though it may be that there were sins and errors among the so-called heretics, it is no less true and evident," he says farther on, "from the innumerable examples quoted here (i. e., in the history of the Church and of heresy), that there was not a single sincere and conscientious man of any importance whom the Churchmen would not from envy or other causes have ruined."

Thus, almost two hundred years ago, the real meaning of heresy was understood. And notwithstanding that, the same conception of it has gone on existing up to now. And it cannot fail to exist so long as the conception of a church exists. Heresy is the obverse side of the Church. Wherever there is a church, there must be the conception of heresy. A church is a body of men who assert that they are in possession of infallible truth. Heresy is the opinion of the men who do not admit the infallibility of the Church's truth.

Heresy makes its appearance in the Church. It is the effort to break through the petrified authority of the Church. All effort after a living comprehension of the doctrine has been made by heretics. Tertullian, Origen, Augustine, Luther, Huss, Savonarola, Helchitsky, and the rest were heretics. It could not be otherwise.

The follower of Christ, whose service means an ever-growing understanding of his teaching, and an ever-closer fulfillment of it, in progress toward perfection, cannot, just because he is a follower, of Christ, claim for himself or any other that he understands Christ's teaching fully and fulfills it. Still less can he claim this for any body of men.

To whatever degree of understanding and perfection the follower of Christ may have attained, he always feels the insufficiency of his understanding and fulfillment of it, and is always striving toward a fuller understanding and fulfillment. And therefore, to assert of one's self or of any body of men, that one is or they are in possession of perfect understanding and fulfillment of Christ's word, is to renounce the very spirit of Christ's teaching.

Strange as it may seem, the churches as churches have always been, and cannot but be, institutions not only alien in spirit to Christ's teaching, but even directly antagonistic to it. With good reason Voltaire calls the Church l'infâme; with good reason have all or almost all so-called sects of Christians recognized the Church as the scarlet woman foretold in the Apocalypse; with good reason is the history of the Church the history of the greatest cruelties and horrors.

The churches as churches are not, as many people suppose, institutions which have Christian principles for their basis, even though they may have strayed a little away from the straight path. The churches as churches, as bodies which assert their own infallibility, are institutions opposed to Christianity. There is not only nothing in common between the churches as such and Christianity, except the name, but they represent two principles fundamentally opposed and antagonistic to one another. One represents pride, violence, self-assertion, stagnation, and death; the other, meekness, penitence, humility, progress, and life.

We cannot serve these two masters; we have to choose between them.

The servants of the churches of all denominations, especially of later times, try to show themselves champions of progress in Christianity. They make concessions, wish to correct the abuses that have slipped into the Church, and maintain that one cannot, on account of these abuses, deny the principle itself of a Christian church, which alone can bind all men together in unity and be a mediator between men and God. But this is all a mistake. Not only have churches never bound men together in unity; they have always been one of the principal causes of division between men, of their hatred of one another, of wars, battles, inquisitions, massacres of St. Bartholomew, and so on. And the churches have never served as mediators between men and God. Such mediation is not wanted, and was directly forbidden by Christ, who has revealed his teaching directly and immediately to each man. But the churches set up dead forms in the place of God, and far from revealing God, they obscure him from men's sight. The churches, which originated from misunderstanding of Christ's teaching and have maintained this misunderstanding by their immovability, cannot but persecute and refuse to recognize all true understanding of Christ's words. They try to conceal this, but in vain; for every step forward along the path pointed out for us by Christ is a step toward their destruction.

To hear and to read the sermons and articles in which Church writers of later times of all denominations speak of Christian truths and virtues; to hear or read these skillful arguments that have been elaborated during centuries, and exhortations and professions, which sometimes seem like sincere professions, one is ready to doubt whether the churches can be antagonistic to Christianity. "It cannot be," one says, "that these people who can point to such men as Chrysostom, Fénelon, Butler, and others professing the Christian faith, were antagonistic to Christianity." One is tempted to say, "The churches may have strayed away from Christianity, they may be in error, but they cannot be hostile to it." But we must look to the fruit to judge the tree, as Christ taught us. And if we see that their fruits were evil, that the results of their activity were antagonistic to Christianity, we cannot but admit that however good the men were--the work of the Church in which these men took part was not Christian. The goodness and worth of these men who served the churches was the goodness and worth of the men, and not of the institution they served. All the good men, such as Francis of Assisi, and Francis of Sales, our Tihon Zadonsky, Thomas à Kempis, and others, were good men in spite of their serving an institution hostile to Christianity, and they would have been still better if they had not been under the influence of the error which they were serving.

But why should we speak of the past and judge from the past, which may have been misrepresented and misunderstood by us? The churches, with their principles and their practice, are not a thing of the past. The churches are before us to-day, and we can judge of them to some purpose by their practical activity, their influence on men.

What is the practical work of the churches to-day? What is their influence upon men? What is done by the churches among us, among the Catholics and the Protestants of all denominations--what is their practical work? and what are the results of their practical work?

The practice of our Russian so-called Orthodox Church is plain to all. It is an enormous fact which there is no possibility of hiding and about which there can be no disputing.

What constitutes the practical work of this Russian Church, this immense, intensely active institution, which consists of a regiment of half a million men and costs the people tens of millions of rubles?

The practical business of the Church consists in instilling by every conceivable means into the mass of one hundred millions of the Russian people those extinct relics of beliefs for which there is nowadays no kind of justification, "in which scarcely anyone now believes, and often not even those whose duty it is to diffuse these false beliefs." To instill into the people the formulas of Byzantine theology, of the Trinity, of the Mother of God, of Sacraments, of Grace, and so on, extinct conceptions, foreign to us, and having no kind of meaning for men of our times, forms only one part of the work of the Russian Church. Another part of its practice consists in the maintenance of idol-worship in the most literal meaning of the word; in the veneration of holy relics, and of ikons, the offering of sacrifices to them, and the expectation of their answers to prayer. I am not going to speak of what is preached and what is written by clergy of scientific or liberal tendencies in the theological journals. I am going to speak of what is actually done by the clergy through the wide expanse of the Russian land among a people of one hundred millions. What do they, diligently, assiduously, everywhere alike, without intermission, teach the people? What do they demand from the people in virtue of their (so-called) Christian faith?

I will begin from the beginning with the birth of a child. At the birth of a child they teach them that they must recite a prayer over the child and mother to purify them, as though without this prayer the mother of a newborn child were unclean. To do this the priest holds the child in his arms before the images of the saints (called by the people plainly gods) and reads words of exorcizing power, and this purifies the mother. Then it is suggested to the parents, and even exacted of them, under fear of punishment for non-fulfillment, that the child must be baptized; that is, be dipped by the priest three times into the water, while certain words, understood by no one, are read aloud, and certain actions, still less understood, are performed; various parts of the body are rubbed with oil, and the hair is cut, while the sponsors blow and spit at an imaginary devil. All this is necessary to purify the child and to make him a Christian. Then it is instilled into the parents that they ought to administer the sacrament to the child, that is, give him, in the guise of bread and wine, a portion of Christ's body to eat, as a result of which the child receives the grace of God within it, and so on. Then it is suggested that the child as it grows up must be taught to pray. To pray means to place himself directly before the wooden boards on which are painted the faces of Christ, the Mother of God, and the saints, to bow his head and his whole body, and to touch his forehead, his shoulders and his stomach with his right hand, holding his fingers in a certain position, and to utter some words of Slavonic, the most usual of which as taught to all children are: Mother of God, virgin, rejoice thee, etc., etc.

Then it is instilled into the child as it is brought up that at the sight of any church or ikon he must repeat the same action--i. e., cross himself. Then it is instilled into him that on holidays (holidays are the days on which Christ was born, though no one knows when that was, on which he was circumcised, on which the Mother of God died, on which the cross was carried in procession, on which ikons have been set up, on which a lunatic saw a vision, and so on)--on holidays he must dress himself in his best clothes and go to church, and must buy candles and place them there before the images of the saints. Then he must give offerings and prayers for the dead, and little loaves to be cut up into three-cornered pieces, and must pray many times for the health and prosperity of the Tzar and the bishops, and for himself and his own affairs, and then kiss the cross and the hand of the priest.

Besides these observances, it is instilled into him that at least once a year he must confess. To confess means to go to the church and to tell the priest his sins, on the theory that this informing a stranger of his sins completely purifies him from them. And after that he must eat with a little spoon a morsel of bread with wine, which will purify him still more. Next it is instilled into him that if a man and woman want their physical union to be sanctified they must go to church, put on metal crowns, drink certain potions, walk three times round a table to the sound of singing, and that then the physical union of a man and woman becomes sacred and altogether different from all other such unions.

Further it is instilled into him in his life that he must observe the following rules: not to eat butter or milk on certain days, and on certain other days to sing Te Deums and requiems for the dead, on holidays to entertain the priest and give him money, and several times in the year to bring the ikons from the church, and to carry them slung on his shoulders through the fields and houses. It is instilled into him that on his death-bed a man must not fail to eat bread and wine with a spoon, and that it will be still better if he has time to be rubbed with sacred oil. This will guarantee his welfare in the future life. After his death it is instilled into his relatives that it is a good thing for the salvation of the dead man to place a printed paper of prayers in his hands; it is a good thing further to read aloud a certain book over the dead body, and to pronounce the dead man's name in church at a certain time. All this is regarded as faith obligatory on everyone.

But if anyone wants to take particular care of his soul, then according to this faith he is instructed that the greatest security of the salvation of the soul in the world is attained by offering money to the churches and monasteries, and engaging the holy men by this means to pray for him. Entering monasteries too and kissing relics and miraculous ikons, are further means of salvation for the soul.

According to this faith ikons and relics communicate a special sanctity, power, and grace, and even proximity to these objects, touching them, kissing them, putting candles before them, crawling under them while they are being carried along, are all efficacious for salvation, as well as Te Deums repeated before these holy things.

So this, and nothing else, is the faith called Orthodox, that is the actual faith which, under the guise of Christianity, has been with all the forces of the Church, and is now with especial zeal, instilled into the people.

And let no one say that the Orthodox teachers place the essential part of their teaching in something else, and that all these are only ancient forms, which it is not thought necessary to do away with. That is false. This, and nothing but this, is the faith taught through the whole of Russia by the whole of the Russian clergy, and of late years with especial zeal. There is nothing else taught. Something different may be talked of and written of in the capitals; but among the hundred millions of the people this is what is done, this is what is taught, and nothing more. Churchmen may talk of something else, but this is what they teach by every means in their power.

All this, and the worship of relics and of ikons, has been introduced into works of theology and into the catechisms. Thus they teach it to the people in theory and in practice, using every resource of authority, solemnity, pomp, and violence to impress them. They compel the people, by overawing them, to believe in this, and jealously guard this faith from any attempt to free the people from these barbarous superstitions.

As I said when I published my book, Christ's teaching and his very words about non-resistance to evil were for many years a subject for ridicule and low jesting in my eyes, and Churchmen, far from opposing it, even encouraged this scoffing at sacred things. But try the experiment of saying a disrespectful word about a hideous idol which is carried sacrilegiously about Moscow by drunken men under the name of the ikon of the Iversky virgin, and you will raise a groan of indignation from these same Churchmen. All that they preach is an external observance of the rites of idolatry. And let it not be said that the one does not hinder the other, that "These ought ye to have done, and not to leave the other undone." "All, therefore, whatsoever they bid you observe, that observe and do; but do not ye after their works: for they say, and do not" (Matt. xxiii. 23, 3).

This was spoken of the Pharisees, who fulfilled all the external observances prescribed by the law, and therefore the words "whatsoever they bid you observe, that observe and do," refer to works of mercy and goodness, and the words "do not ye after their works, for they say and do not," refer to their observance of ceremonies and their neglect of good works, and have exactly the opposite meaning to that which the Churchmen try to give to the passage, interpreting it as an injunction to observe ceremonies. External observances and the service of truth and goodness are for the most part difficult to combine; the one excludes the other. So it was with the Pharisees, so it is now with Church Christians.

If a man can be saved by the redemption, by sacraments, and by prayer, then he does not need good works.

The Sermon on the Mount, or the Creed. One cannot believe in both. And Churchmen have chosen the latter. The Creed is taught and is read as a prayer in the churches, but the Sermon on the Mount is excluded even from the Gospel passages read in the churches, so that the congregation never hears it in church, except on those days when the whole of the Gospel is read. Indeed, it could not be otherwise. People who believe in a wicked and senseless God--who has cursed the human race and devoted his own Son to sacrifice, and a part of mankind to eternal torment--cannot believe in the God of love. The man who believes in a God, in a Christ coming again in glory to judge and to punish the quick and the dead, cannot believe in the Christ who bade us turn the left cheek, judge not, forgive these that wrong us, and love our enemies. The man who believes in the inspiration of the Old Testament and the sacred character of David, who commanded on his deathbed the murder of an old man who had cursed him, and whom he could not kill himself because he was bound by an oath to him, and the similar atrocities of which the Old Testament is full, cannot believe in the holy love of Christ. The man who believes in the Church's doctrine of the compatibility of warfare and capital punishment with Christianity cannot believe in the brotherhood of all men.

And what is most important of all--the man who believes in salvation through faith in the redemption or the sacraments, cannot devote all his powers to realizing Christ's moral teaching in his life.

The man who has been instructed by the Church in the profane doctrine that a man cannot be saved by his own powers, but that there is another means of salvation, will infallibly rely upon this means and not on his own powers, which, they assure him, it is sinful to trust in.

The teaching of every Church, with its redemption and sacraments, excludes the teaching of Christ; most of all the teaching of the Orthodox Church with its idolatrous observances.

"But the people have always believed of their own accord as they believe now," will be said in answer to this. "The whole history of the Russian people proves it. One cannot deprive the people of their traditions." This statement, too, is misleading. The people did certainly at one time believe in something like what the Church believes in now, though it was far from being the same thing. In spite of their superstitious regard for ikons, housespirits, relics, and festivals with wreaths of birch leaves, there has still always been in the people a profound moral and living understanding of Christianity, which there has never been in the Church as a whole, and which is only met with in its best representatives. But the people, notwithstanding all the prejudices instilled into them by the government and the Church, have in their best representatives long outgrown that crude stage of understanding, a fact which is proved by the springing up everywhere of the rationalist sects with which Russia is swarming to-day, and on which Churchmen are now carrying on an ineffectual warfare. The people are advancing to a consciousness of the moral, living side of Christianity. And then the Church comes forward, not borrowing from the people, but zealously instilling into them the petrified formalities of an extinct paganism, and striving to thrust them back again into the darkness from which they are emerging with such effort.

"We teach the people nothing new, nothing but what they believe, only in a more perfect form," say the Churchmen. This is just what the man did who tied up the full-grown chicken and thrust it back into the shell it had come out of.

I have often been irritated, though it would be comic if the consequences were not so awful, by observing how men shut one another in a delusion and cannot get out of this magic circle.

The first question, the first doubt of a Russian who is beginning to think, is a question about the ikons, and still more the miraculous relics: Is it true that they are genuine, and that miracles are worked through them? Hundreds of thousands of men put this question to themselves, and their principal difficulty in answering it is the fact that bishops, metropolitans, and all men in positions of authority kiss the relics and wonder-working ikons. Ask the bishops and men in positions of authority why they do so, and they will say they do it for the sake of the people, while the people kiss them because the bishops and men in authority do so.

In spite of all the external varnish of modernity, learning, and spirituality which the members of the Church begin nowadays to assume in their works, their articles, their theological journals, and their sermons, the practical work of the Russian Church consists of nothing more than keeping the people in their present condition of coarse and savage idolatry, and worse still, strengthening and diffusing superstition and religious ignorance, and suppressing that living understanding of Christianity which exists in the people side by side with idolatry.

I remember once being present in the monks' bookshop of the Optchy Hermitage while an old peasant was choosing books for his grandson, who could read. A monk pressed on him accounts of relics, holidays, miraculous ikons, a psalter, etc. I asked the old man, "Has he the Gospel?" "No." "Give him the Gospel in Russian," I said to the monk. "That will not do for him," answered the monk. There you have an epitome of the work of our Church.

But this is only in barbarous Russia, the European and American reader will observe. And such an observation is just, but only so far as it refers to the government, which aids the Church in its task of stultification and corruption in Russia.

It is true that there is nowhere in Europe a government so despotic and so closely allied with the ruling Church. And therefore the share of the temporal power in the corruption of the people is greatest in Russia. But it is untrue that the Russian Church in its influence on the people is in any respect different from any other church.

The churches are everywhere the same, and if the Catholic, the Anglican, or the Lutheran Church has not at hand a government as compliant as the Russian, it is not due to any indisposition to profit by such a government.

The Church as a church, whatever it may be--Catholic, Anglican, Lutheran, Presbyterian--every church, in so far as it is a church, cannot but strive for the same object as the Russian Church. That object is to conceal the real meaning of Christ's teaching and to replace it by their own, which lays no obligation on them, excludes the possibility of understanding the true teaching of Christ, and what is the chief consideration, justifies the existence of priests supported at the people's expense.

What else has Catholicism done, what else is it doing in its prohibition of reading the Gospel, and in its demand for unreasoning submission to Church authorities and to an infallible Pope? Is the religion of Catholicism any other than that of the Russian Church? There is the same external ritual, the same relics, miracles, and wonder-working images of Notre Dame, and the same processions; the same loftily vague discussions of Christianity in books and sermons, and when it comes to practice, the same supporting of the present idolatry. And is not the same thing done in Anglicanism, Lutheranism, and every denomination of

Protestantism which has been formed into a church? There is the same duty laid on their congregations to believe in the dogmas expressed in the fourth century, which have lost all meaning for men of our times, and the same duty of idolatrous worship, if not of relics and ikons, then of the Sabbath Day and the letter of the Bible. There is always the same activity directed to concealing the real duties of Christianity, and to putting in their place an external respectability and cant, as it is so well described by the English, who are peculiarly oppressed by it. In Protestantism this tendency is specially remarkable because it has not the excuse of antiquity. And does not exactly the same thing show itself even in contemporary revivalism--the revived Calvinism and Evangelicalism, to which the Salvation Army owes its origin?

Uniform is the attitude of all the churches to the teaching of Christ, whose name they assume for their own advantage.

The inconsistency of all church forms of religion with the teaching of Christ is, of course, the reason why special efforts are necessary to conceal this inconsistency from people. Truly, we need only imagine ourselves in the position of any grown-up man, not necessarily educated, even the simplest man of the present day, who has picked up the ideas that are everywhere in the air nowadays of geology, physics, chemistry, cosmography, or history, when he, for the first time, consciously compares them with the articles of belief instilled into him in childhood, and maintained by the churches--that God created the world in six days, and light before the sun; that Noah shut up all the animals in his ark, and so on; that Jesus is also God the Son, who created all before time was; that this God came down upon earth to atone for Adam's sin; that he rose again, ascended into heaven, and sitteth on the right hand of the Father, and will come in the clouds to judge the world, and so on. All these propositions, elaborated by men of the fourth century, had a certain meaning for men of that time, but for men of to-day they have no meaning whatever. Men of the present day can repeat these words with their lips, but believe them they cannot. For such sentences as that God lives in heaven, that the heavens opened and a voice from somewhere said something, that Christ rose again, and ascended somewhere in heaven, and again will come from somewhere on the clouds, and so on, have no meaning for us.

A man who regarded the heavens as a solid, finite vault could believe or disbelieve that God created the heavens, that the heavens opened, that Christ ascended into heaven, but for us all these phrases have no sense whatever. Men of the present can only believe, as indeed they do, that they ought to believe in this; but believe it they cannot, because it has no meaning for them.

Even if all these phrases ought to be interpreted in a figurative sense and are allegories, we know that in the first place all Churchmen are not agreed about it, but, on the contrary, the majority stick to understanding the Holy Scripture in its literal sense; and secondly, that these allegorical interpretations are very varied and are not supported by any evidence.

But even if a man wants to force himself to believe in the doctrines of the Church just as they are taught to him, the universal diffusion of education and of the Gospel and of communication between people of different forms of religion presents a still more insurmountable obstacle to his doing so.

A man of the present day need only buy a Gospel for three copecks and read through the plain words, admitting of no misinterpretation, that Christ said to the Samaritan woman "that the Father seeketh not worshipers at Jerusalem, nor in this mountain nor in that, but worshipers in spirit and in truth," or the saying that "the Christian must not pray like the heathen, nor for show, but secretly, that is, in his closet," or that Christ's follower must call no man master or father--he need only read these words to be thoroughly convinced that the Church pastors, who call themselves teachers in opposition to Christ's precept, and dispute among themselves, constitute no kind of authority, and that what the Churchmen teach us is not Christianity. Less even than that is necessary. Even if a man nowadays did continue to believe in miracles and did not read the Gospel, mere association with people of different forms of religion and faith, which happens so easily in these days, compels him to doubt of the truth of his own faith. It was all very well when a man did not see men of any other form of religion than his own; he believed that his form of religion was the one true one. But a thinking man has only to come into contact--as constantly happens in these days--with people, equally good and bad, of different denominations, who condemn each other's beliefs, to doubt of the truth of the belief he professes himself. In these days only a man who is absolutely ignorant or absolutely indifferent to the vital questions with which religion deals, can remain in the faith of the Church.

What deceptions and what strenuous efforts the churches must employ to continue, in spite of all these tendencies subversive of the faith, to build churches, to perform masses, to preach, to teach, to convert, and, most of all, to receive for it all immense emoluments, as do all these priests, pastors, incumbents, superintendents, abbots, archdeacons, bishops, and archbishops. They need special supernatural efforts. And the churches do, with ever-increasing intensity and zeal, make such efforts. With us in Russia, besides other means, they employ, simple brute force, as there the temporal power is willing to obey the Church. Men who refuse an external assent to the faith, and say so openly, are either directly punished or deprived of their rights; men who strictly keep the external forms of religion are rewarded and given privileges.

That is how the Orthodox clergy proceed; but indeed all churches without exception avail themselves of every means for the purpose

--one of the most important of which is what is now called hypnotism.

Every art, from architecture to poetry, is brought into requisition to work its effect on men's souls and to reduce them to a state of stupefaction, and this effect is constantly produced. This use of hypnotizing influence on men to bring them to a state of stupefaction is especially apparent in the proceedings of the Salvation Army, who employ new practices to which we are unaccustomed: trumpets, drums, songs, flags, costumes, marching, dancing, tears, and dramatic performances.

But this only displeases us because these are new practices. Were not the old practices in churches essentially the same, with their special lighting, gold, splendor, candles, choirs, organ, bells, vestments, intoning, etc.?

But however powerful this hypnotic influence may be, it is not the chief nor the most pernicious activity of the Church. The chief and most pernicious work of the Church is that which is directed to the deception of children--these very children of whom Christ said: "Woe to him that offendeth one of these little ones." From the very first awakening of the consciousness of the child they begin to deceive him, to instill into him with the utmost solemnity what they do not themselves believe in, and they continue to instill it into him till the deception has by habit grown into the child's nature. They studiously deceive the child on the most important subject in life, and when the deception has so grown into his life that it would be difficult to uproot it, then they reveal to him the whole world of science and reality, which cannot by any means be reconciled with the beliefs that have been instilled into him, leaving it to him to find his way as best he can out of these contradictions.

If one set oneself the task of trying to confuse a man so that he could not think clearly nor free himself from the perplexity of two opposing theories of life which had been instilled into him from childhood, one could not invent any means more effectual than the treatment of every young man educated in our so-called Christian society.

It is terrible to think what the churches do to men. But if one imagines oneself in the position of the men who constitute the Church, we see they could not act differently. The churches are placed in a dilemma: the Sermon on the Mount or the Nicene Creed--the one excludes the other. If a man sincerely believes in the Sermon on the Mount, the Nicene Creed must inevitably lose all meaning and significance for him, and the Church and its representatives together with it. If a man believes in the Nicene Creed, that is, in the Church, that is, in those who call themselves its representatives, the Sermon on the Mount becomes superfluous for him. And therefore the churches cannot but make every possible effort to obscure the meaning of the Sermon on the Mount, and to attract men to themselves. It is only due to the intense zeal of the churches in this direction that the influence of the churches has lasted hitherto.

Let the Church stop its work of hypnotizing the masses, and deceiving children even for the briefest interval of time, and men would begin to understand Christ's teaching. But this understanding will be the end of the churches and all their influence. And therefore the churches will not for an instant relax their zeal in the business of hypnotizing grown-up people and deceiving children. This, then, is the work of the churches: to instill a false interpretation of Christ's teaching into men, and to prevent a true interpretation of it for the majority of so-called believers.

CHAPTER IV.

CHRISTIANITY MISUNDERSTOOD BY MEN OF SCIENCE.

Attitude of Men of Science to Religions in General--What Religion is, and What is its Significance for the Life of Humanity--Three Conceptions of Life--Christian Religion the Expression of the Divine Conception of Life--Misinterpretation of Christianity by Men of Science, who Study it in its External Manifestations Due to their Criticising it from Standpoint of Social Conception of Life--Opinion, Resulting from this Misinterpretation, that Christ's Moral Teaching is Exaggerated and Cannot be put into Practice--Expression of Divine Conception of Life in the Gospel--False Ideas of Men of Science on Christianity Proceed from their Conviction that they have an Infallible Method of Criticism--From which come Two Misconceptions in Regard to Christian Doctrine--First Misconception, that the Teaching Cannot be put into Practice, Due to the Christian Religion Directing Life in a Way Different from that of the Social Theory of Life--Christianity holds up Ideal, does not lay down Rules--To the Animal Force of Man Christ Adds the Consciousness of a Divine Force--Christianity Seems to Destroy Possibility of Life only when the Ideal held up is Mistaken for Rule--Ideal Must Not be Lowered--Life, According to Christ's Teaching, is Movement--The Ideal and the Precepts--Second Misconception Shown in Replacing Love and Service of God by Love and Service of Humanity--Men of Science Imagine their Doctrine of Service of Humanity and Christianity are Identical--Doctrine of Service of Humanity Based on Social Conception of

Life--Love for Humanity, Logically Deduced from Love of Self, has No Meaning because Humanity is a Fiction--Christian Love Deduced from Love of God, Finds its Object in the whole World, not in Humanity Alone--Christianity Teaches Man to Live in Accordance with his Divine Nature--It Shows that the Essence of the Soul of Man is Love, and that his Happiness Ensues from Love of God, whom he Recognizes as Love within himself.

Now I will speak of the other view of Christianity which hinders the true understanding of it--the scientific view.

Churchmen substitute for Christianity the version they have framed of it for themselves, and this view of Christianity they regard as the one infallibly true one.

Men of science regard as Christianity only the tenets held by the different churches in the past and present; and finding that these tenets have lost all the significance of Christianity, they accept it as a religion which has outlived its age.

To see clearly how impossible it is to understand the Christian teaching from such a point of view, one must form for oneself an idea of the place actually held by religions in general, by the Christian religion in particular, in the life of mankind, and of the significance attributed to them by science.

Just as the individual man cannot live without having some theory of the meaning of his life, and is always, though often unconsciously, framing his conduct in accordance with the meaning he attributes to his life, so too associations of men living in similar conditions--nations--cannot but have theories of the meaning of their associated life and conduct ensuing from those theories. And as the individual man, when he attains a fresh stage of growth, inevitably changes his philosophy of life, and the grown-up man sees a different meaning in it from the child, so too associations of men--nations--are bound to change their philosophy of life and the conduct ensuing from their philosophy, to correspond with their development.

The difference, as regards this, between the individual man and humanity as a whole, lies in the fact that the individual, in forming the view of life proper to the new period of life on which he is entering and the conduct resulting from it, benefits by the experience of men who have lived before him, who have already passed through the stage of growth upon which he is entering. But humanity cannot have this aid, because it is always moving along a hitherto untrodden track, and has no one to ask how to understand life, and to act in the conditions on which it is entering and through which no one has ever passed before.

Nevertheless, just as a man with wife and children cannot continue to look at life as he looked at it when he was a child, so too in the face of the various changes that are taking place, the greater density of population, the establishment of communication between different peoples, the improvements of the methods of the struggle with nature, and the accumulation of knowledge, humanity cannot continue to look at life as of old, and it must frame a new theory of life, from which conduct may follow adapted to the new conditions on which it has entered and is entering.

To meet this need humanity has the special power of producing men who give a new meaning to the whole of human life--a theory of life from which follow new forms of activity quite different from all preceding them. The formation of this philosophy of life appropriate to humanity in the new conditions on which it is entering, and of the practice resulting from it, is what is called religion.

And therefore, in the first place, religion is not, as science imagines, a manifestation which at one time corresponded with the development of humanity, but is afterward outgrown by it. It is a manifestation always inherent in the life of humanity, and is as indispensable, as inherent in humanity at the present time as at any other. Secondly, religion is always the theory of the practice of the future and not of the past, and therefore it is clear that investigation of past manifestations cannot in any case grasp the essence of religion.

The essence of every religious teaching lies not in the desire for a symbolic expression of the forces of nature, nor in the dread of these forces, nor in the craving for the marvelous, nor in the external forms in which it is manifested, as men of science imagine; the essence of religion lies in the faculty of men of foreseeing and pointing out the path of life along which humanity must move in the discovery of a new theory of life, as a result of which the whole future conduct of humanity is changed and different from all that has been before.

This faculty of foreseeing the path along which humanity must move, is common in a greater or less degree to all men. But in all times there have been men in whom this faculty was especially strong, and these men have given clear and definite expression to what all men felt vaguely, and formed a new philosophy of life from which new lines of action followed for hundreds and thousands of years.

Of such philosophies of life we know three; two have already been passed through by humanity, and the third is that we are passing through now in Christianity. These philosophies of life are three in number, and only three, not because we have arbitrarily brought the various theories of life together under these three heads, but because all men's actions are always based on one of these three views of life--because we cannot view life otherwise than in these three ways.

These three views of life are as follows: First, embracing the individual, or the animal view of life; second, embracing the society, or the pagan view of life; third, embracing the whole world, or the divine view of life.

In the first theory of life a man's life is limited to his one individuality; the aim of life is the satisfaction of the will of this individuality. In the second theory of life a man's life is limited not to his own individuality, but to certain societies and classes of individuals: to the tribe, the family, the clan, the nation; the aim of life is limited to the satisfaction of the will of those associations of individuals. In the third theory of life a man's life is limited not to societies and classes of individuals, but extends to the principle and source of life--to God.

These three conceptions of life form the foundation of all the religious that exist or have existed.

The savage recognizes life only in himself and his personal desires. His interest in life is concentrated on himself alone. The highest happiness for him is the fullest satisfaction of his desires. The motive power of his life is personal enjoyment. His religion consists in propitiating his deity and in worshiping his gods, whom he imagines as persons living only for their personal aims.

The civilized pagan recognizes life not in himself alone, but in societies of men--in the tribe, the clan, the family, the kingdom --and sacrifices his personal good for these societies. The motive power of his life is glory. His religion consists in the exaltation of the glory of those who are allied to him--the founders of his family, his ancestors, his rulers--and in worshiping gods who are exclusively protectors of his clan, his family, his nation, his government [see Footnote].

[Footnote: The fact that so many varied forms of existence, as the life of the family, of the tribe, of the clan, of the state, and even the life of humanity theoretically conceived by the Positivists, are founded on this social or pagan theory of life, does not destroy the unity of this theory of life. All these varied forms of life are founded on the same conception, that the life of the individual is not a sufficient aim of life--that the meaning of life can be found only in societies of individuals.]

The man who holds the divine theory of life recognizes life not in his own individuality, and not in societies of individualities (in the family, the clan, the nation, the tribe, or the government), but in the eternal undying source of life--in God; and to fulfill the will of God he is ready to sacrifice his individual and family and social welfare. The motor power of his life is love. And his religion is the worship in deed and in truth of the principle of the whole--God.

The whole historic existence of mankind is nothing else than the gradual transition from the personal, animal conception of life to the social conception of life, and from the social conception of life to the divine conception of life. The whole history of the ancient peoples, lasting through thousands of years and ending with the history of Rome, is the history of the transition from the animal, personal view of life to the social view of life. The whole of history from the time of the Roman Empire and the appearance of Christianity is the history of the transition, through which we are still passing now, from the social view of life to the divine view of life.

This view of life is the last, and founded upon it is the Christian teaching, which is a guide for the whole of our life and lies at the root of all our activity, practical and theoretic.
Yet men of what is falsely called science, pseudo-scientific men, looking at it only in its externals, regard it as something outgrown and having no value for us.

Reducing it to its dogmatic side only--to the doctrines of the

Trinity, the redemption, the miracles, the Church, the sacraments, and so on--men of science regard it as only one of an immense number of religions which have arisen among mankind, and now, they say, having played out its part in history, it is outliving its own age and fading away before the light of science and of true enlightenment.

We come here upon what, in a large proportion of cases, forms the source of the grossest errors of mankind. Men on a lower level of understanding, when brought into contact with phenomena of a higher order, instead of making efforts to understand them, to raise themselves up to the point of view from which they must look at the subject, judge it from their lower standpoint, and the less they understand what they are talking about, the more confidently and unhesitatingly they pass judgment on it.

To the majority of learned then, looking at the living, moral teaching of Christ from the lower standpoint of the conception of life, this doctrine appears as nothing but very indefinite and incongruous combination of Indian asceticism, Stoic and Neoplatonic philosophy, and insubstantial anti-social visions, which have no serious significance for our times. Its whole meaning is concentrated for them in its external manifestations--in Catholicism, Protestantism, in certain dogmas, or in the conflict with the temporal power. Estimating the value of Christianity by these phenomena is like a deaf man's judging of the character and quality of music by seeing the movements of the musicians.

The result of this is that all these scientific men, from Kant, Strauss, Spencer, and Renan down, do not understand the meaning of Christ's sayings, do not understand the significance, the object, or the reason of their utterance, do not understand even the question to which they form the answer. Yet, without even taking the pains to enter into their meaning, they refuse, if unfavorably disposed, to recognize any reasonableness in his doctrines; or if they want to treat them indulgently, they condescend, from the height of their superiority, to correct them, on the supposition that Christ meant to express precisely their own ideas, but did not succeed in doing so. They behave to his teaching much as self-assertive people talk to those whom they consider beneath them, often supplying their companions' words: "Yes, you mean to say this and that." This correction is always with the aim of reducing the teaching of the higher, divine conception of life to the level of the lower, state conception of life.

They usually say that the moral teaching of Christianity is very fine, but overexaggerated; that to make it quite right we must reject all in it that is superfluous and unnecessary to our manner of life. "And the doctrine that asks too much, and requires what cannot be performed, is worse than that which requires of men what is possible and consistent with their powers," these learned interpreters of Christianity maintain, repeating what was long ago asserted, and could not but be asserted, by those who crucified the Teacher because they did not understand him--the Jews.

It seems that in the judgment of the learned men of our time the Hebrew law--a tooth for a tooth, and an eye for an eye--is a law of just retaliation, known to mankind five thousand years before the law of holiness which Christ taught in its place.

It seems that all that has been done by those men who understood Christ's teaching literally and lived in accordance with such an understanding of it, all that has been said and done by all true Christians, by all the Christian saints, all that is now reforming the world in the shape of socialism and communism--is simply exaggeration, not worth talking about.

After eighteen hundred years of education in Christianity the civilized world, as represented by its most advanced thinkers, holds the conviction that the Christian religion is a religion of dogmas; that its teaching in relation to life is unreasonable, and is an exaggeration, subversive of the real lawful obligations of morality consistent with the nature of man; and that very doctrine of retribution which Christ rejected, and in place of which he put his teaching, is more practically useful for us.

To learned men the doctrine of non-resistance to evil by force is exaggerated and even irrational. Christianity is much better without it, they think, not observing closely what Christianity, as represented by them, amounts to.

They do not see that to say that the doctrine of non-resistance to evil is an exaggeration in Christ's teaching is just like saying that the statement of the equality of the radii of a circle is an exaggeration in the definition of a circle. And those who speak thus are acting precisely like a man who, having no idea of what a circle is, should declare that this requirement, that every point of the circumference should be an equal distance from the center, is exaggerated. To advocate the rejection of Christ's command of non-resistance to evil, or its adaptation to the needs of life, implies a misunderstanding of the teaching of Christ.

And those who do so certainly do not understand it. They do not understand that this teaching is the institution of a new theory of life, corresponding to the new conditions on which men have entered now for eighteen hundred years, and also the definition of the new conduct of life which results from it. They do not believe that Christ meant to say what he said; or he seems to them to have said what he said in the Sermon on the Mount and in other places accidentally, or through his lack of intelligence or of cultivation.

[Footnote: Here, for example, is a characteristic view of that kind from the American journal the ARENA

(October, 1890): "New Basis of Church Life." Treating of the significance of the Sermon on the Mount and non-resistance to evil in particular, the author, being under no necessity, like the Churchmen, to hide its significance, says:

> "Christ in fact preached complete communism and anarchy; but one must learn to regard Christ always in his historical and psychological significance. Like every advocate of the love of humanity, Christ went to the furthest extreme in his teaching. Every step forward toward the moral perfection of humanity is always guided by men who see nothing but their vocation. Christ, in no disparaging sense be it said, had the typical temperament of such a reformer. And therefore we must remember that his precepts cannot be understood literally as a complete philosophy of life. We ought to analyze his words with respect for them, but in the spirit of criticism, accepting what is true," etc.

Christ would have been happy to say what he ought, but he was not able to express himself as exactly and clearly as we can in the spirit of criticism, and therefore let us correct him. All that he said about meekness, sacrifice, lowliness, not caring for the morrow, was said by accident, through lack of knowing how to express himself scientifically.]

Matt. vi. 25-34: "Therefore I say unto you, Take no thought for your life, what ye shall eat, or what ye shall drink; nor yet for your body, what ye shall put on. Is not the life more than meat, and the body than rainment? Behold the fouls of the air; for they sow not, neither do they reap, nor gather into barns; yet your heavenly Father feedeth them. Are ye not much better than they? Which of you by taking thought can add one cubit onto his stature? And why take ye thought for rainment? Consider the lilies of the field how they grow; they toil not, neither do they spin; and yet I say unto you, That even Solomon in all his glory was not arrayed like one of these. Wherefore, if God so clothe the grass of the field, which to-day is, and to-morrow is cast into the oven, shall he not much more clothe you, O ye of little faith? Therefore take no thought, saying, What shall we eat? or, What shall we drink? or, Wherewithal shall we be clothed? (For after all these things do the Gentiles seek), for your heavenly Father knoweth that ye have need of all these things. But seek ye first the kingdom of God, and his righteousness, and all these things shall be added unto you. Take therefore no thought for the morrow; for the morrow shall take thought for the things of itself. Sufficient unto the day is the evil thereof." Luke xii. 33-34: "Sell that ye have, and give alms; provide yourselves bags which wax not old, a treasure in the heavens that faileth not, where no thief approacheth, neither moth corrupteth. For where your treasure is, there will your heart be also." Sell all thou hast and follow me; and he who will not leave father, or mother, or children, or brothers, or fields, or house, he cannot be my disciple. Deny thyself, take up thy cross each day and follow me. My meat is to do the will of him that sent me, and to perform his works. Not my will, but thine be done; not what I will, but as thou wilt. Life is to do not one's will, but the will of God.

All these principles appear to men who regard them from the standpoint of a lower conception of life as the expression of an impulsive enthusiasm, having no direct application to life. These principles, however, follow from the Christian theory of life, just as logically as the principles of paying a part of one's private gains to the commonwealth and of sacrificing one's life in defense of one's country follow from the state theory of life.

As the man of the stale conception of life said to the savage: Reflect, bethink yourself! The life of your individuality cannot be true life, because that life is pitiful and passing. But the life of a society and succession of individuals, family, clan, tribe, or state, goes on living, and therefore a man must sacrifice his own individuality for the life of the family or the state. In exactly the same way the Christian doctrine says to the man of the social, state conception of life, Repent ye--[GREEK WORD]-i. e., bethink yourself, or you will be ruined. Understand that this casual, personal life which now comes into being and to-morrow is no more can have no permanence, that no external means, no construction of it can give it consecutiveness and permanence. Take thought and understand that the life you are living is not real life--the life of the family, of society, of the state will not save you from annihilation. The true, the rational life is only possible for man according to the measure in which he can participate, not in the family or the state, but in the source of life--the Father; according to the measure in which he can merge his life in the life of the Father. Such is undoubtedly the Christian conception of life, visible in every utterance of the Gospel.

[TRANSCRIBIST'S NOTE: The GREEK WORD above used Greek letters, spelled: mu-epsilon-tau-alpha-nu-omicron-zeta-epsilon-tau-epsilon]

One may not share this view of life, one may reject it, one may show its inaccuracy and its erroneousness, but we cannot judge of the Christian teaching without mastering this view of life. Still less can one criticise a subject on a higher plane from a lower point of view. From the basement one cannot judge of the effect of the spire. But this is just what the learned critics of the day try to do. For they share the erroneous idea of the orthodox believers that they are in possession of certain infallible means for investigating a subject. They fancy if they apply their so-called scientific methods of criticism, there can be no doubt of their conclusion being correct.

This testing the subject by the fancied infallible method of science is the principal obstacle to understanding the Christian religion for unbelievers, for so-called educated people. From this follow all the mistakes made by scientific men about the Christian religion, and especially two strange misconceptions which, more than everything else, hinder them from a correct understanding of it. One of these misconceptions is that the Christian moral teaching cannot be carried out, and that therefore it has either no force at all--that is, it should not be accepted as the rule of conduct--or it must be transformed, adapted to the limits within which its fulfillment is possible in our society. Another misconception is that the Christian doctrine of love of God, and therefore of his service, is an obscure, mystic principle, which gives no definite object for love, and should therefore be replaced by the more exact and comprehensible principles of love for men and the service of humanity.

The first misconception in regard to the impossibility of following the principle is the result of men of the state conception of life unconsciously taking that conception as the standard by which the Christian religion directs men, and taking the Christian principle of perfection as the rule by which that life is to be ordered; they think and say that to follow Christ's teaching is impossible, because the complete fulfillment of all that is required by this teaching would put an end to life. "If a man were to carry out all that Christ teaches, he would destroy his own life; and if all men carried it out, then the human race would come to an end," they say.

"If we take no thought for the morrow, what we shall eat and what we shall drink, and wherewithal we shall be clothed, do not defend our life, nor resist evil by force, lay down our life for others, and observe perfect chastity, the human race cannot exist," they say.

And they are perfectly right if they take the principle of perfection given by Christ's teaching as a rule which everyone is bound to fulfill, just as in the state principles of life everyone is bound to carry out the rule of paying taxes, supporting the law, and so on.

The misconception is based precisely on the fact that the teaching of Christ guides men differently from the way in which the precepts founded on the lower conception of life guide men. The precepts of the state conception of life only guide men by requiring of them an exact fulfillment of rules or laws. Christ's teaching guides men by pointing them to the infinite perfection of their heavenly Father, to which every man independently and voluntarily struggles, whatever the degree of his imperfection in the present.

The misunderstanding of men who judge of the Christian principle from the point of view of the state principle, consists in the fact that on the supposition that the perfection which Christ points to, can be fully attained, they ask themselves (just as they ask the same question on the supposition that state laws will be carried out) what will be the result of all this being carried out? This supposition cannot be made, because the perfection held up to Christians is infinite and can never be attained; and Christ lays down his principle, having in view the fact that absolute perfection can never be attained, but that striving toward absolute, infinite perfection will continually increase the blessedness of men, and that this blessedness may be increased to infinity thereby.

Christ is teaching not angels, but men, living and moving in the animal life. And so to this animal force of movement Christ, as it were, applies the new force-the recognition of Divine perfection-and thereby directs the movement by the resultant of these two forces..

To suppose that human life is going in the direction to which Christ pointed it, is just like supposing that a little boat afloat on a rabid river, and directing its course almost exactly against the current, will progress in that direction.

Christ recognizes the existence of both sides of the parallelogram, of both eternal indestructible forces of which the life of man is compounded: the force of his animal nature and the force of the consciousness of Kinship to God. Saying nothing of the animal force which asserts itself, remains always the same, and is therefore independent of human will, Christ speaks only of the Divine force, calling upon a man to know it more closely, to set it more free from all that retards it, and to carry it to a higher degree of intensity.

In the process of liberating, of strengthening this force, the true life of man, according to Christ's teaching, consists. The true life, according to preceding religions, consists in carrying out rules, the law; according to Christ's teaching it consists in an ever closer approximation to the divine perfection held up before every man, and recognized within himself by every man, in an ever closer and closer approach to the perfect fusion of his will in the will of God, that fusion toward which man strives, and the attainment of which would be the destruction of the life me know.

The divine perfection is the asymptote of human life to which it is always striving, and always approaching, though it can only be reached in infinity.

The Christian religion seems to exclude the possibility of life only when men mistake the pointing to an ideal as the laying down of a rule. It is only then that the principles presented in Christ's teaching appear to be destructive of life. These principles, on the contrary, are the only ones that make true life possible. Without these principles true life could not be possible.

"One ought not to expect so much," is what people usually say in discussing the requirements of the Christian religion. "One cannot expect to take absolutely no thought for the morrow, as is said in the Gospel, but only not to take too much thought for it; one cannot give away all to the poor, but one must give away a certain definite part; one need not aim at virginity, but one must avoid debauchery; one need not forsake wife and children, but one must not give too great a place to them in one's heart," and so on.

But to speak like this is just like telling a man who is struggling on a swift river and is directing his course against the current, that it is impossible to cross the river rowing against the current, and that to cross it he must float in the direction of the point he wants to reach.

In reality, in order to reach the place to which he wants to go, he must row with all his strength toward a point much higher up.

To let go the requirements of the ideal means not only to diminish the possibility of perfection, but to make an end of the ideal itself. The ideal that has power over men is not an ideal invented by someone, but the ideal that every man carries within his soul. Only this ideal of complete infinite perfection has power over men, and stimulates them to action. A moderate perfection loses its power of influencing men's hearts.

Christ's teaching only has power when it demands absolute perfection--that is, the fusion of the divine nature which exists in every man's soul with the will of God--the union of the Son with the Father. Life according to Christ's teaching consists of nothing but this setting free of the Son of God, existing in every man, from the animal, and in bringing him closer to the Father.

The animal existence of a man does not constitute human life alone. Life, according to the will of God only, is also not human life. Human life is a combination of the animal life and the divine life. And the more this combination approaches to the divine life, the more life there is in it.

Life, according to the Christian religion, is a progress toward the divine perfection. No one condition, according to this doctrine, can be higher or lower than another. Every condition, according to this doctrine, is only a particular stage, of no consequence in itself, on the way toward unattainable perfection, and therefore in itself it does not imply a greater or lesser degree of life. Increase of life, according to this, consists in nothing but the quickening of the progress toward perfection. And therefore the progress toward perfection of the publican Zaccheus, of the woman that was a sinner, and of the robber on the cross, implies a higher degree of life than the stagnant righteousness of the Pharisee. And therefore for this religion there cannot be rules which it is obligatory to obey. The man who is at a lower level but is moving onward toward perfection is living a more moral, a better life, is more fully carrying out Christ's teaching, than the man on a much higher level of morality who is not moving onward toward perfection.

It is in this sense that the lost sheep is dearer to the Father than those that were not lost. The prodigal son, the piece of money lost and found again, were more precious than those that were not lost.

The fulfillment of Christ's teaching consists in moving away from self toward God. It is obvious that there cannot be definite laws and rules for this fulfillment of the teaching. Every degree of perfection and every degree of imperfection are equal in it; no obedience to laws constitutes a fulfillment of this doctrine, and therefore for it there can be no binding rules and laws.

From this fundamental distinction between the religion of Christ and all preceding religions based on the state conception of life, follows a corresponding difference in the special precepts of the state theory and the Christian precepts. The precepts of the state theory of life insist for the most part on certain practical prescribed acts, by which men are justified and secure of being right. The Christian precepts (the commandment of love is not a precept in the strict sense of the word, but the expression of the very essence of the religion) are the five commandments of the Sermon on the Mount--all negative in character. They show only what at a certain stage of development of humanity men may not do.

These commandments are, as it were, signposts on the endless road to perfection, toward which humanity is moving, showing the point of perfection which is possible at a certain period in the development of humanity.

Christ has given expression in the Sermon on the Mount to the eternal ideal toward which men are spontaneously struggling, and also the degree of attainment of it to which men may reach in our times.

The ideal is not to desire to do ill to anyone, not to provoke ill will, to love all men. The precept, showing the level below which we cannot fall in the attainment of this ideal, is the prohibition of evil speaking. And that is the first command.

The ideal is perfect chastity, even in thought. The precept, showing the level below which we cannot fall in the attainment of this ideal, is that of purity of married life, avoidance of debauchery. That is the second command.

The ideal is to take no thought for the future, to live in the present moment. The precept, showing the level below which we cannot fall, is the prohibition of swearing, of promising anything in the future. And that is the third command.

The ideal is never for any purpose to use force. The precept, showing the level below which we cannot fall is that of returning good for evil, being patient under wrong, giving the cloak also. That is the fourth command.

The ideal is to love the enemies who hate us. The precept, showing the level below which we cannot fall, is not to do evil to our enemies, to speak well of them, and to make no difference between them and our neighbors.

All these precepts are indications of what, on our journey to perfection, we are already fully able to avoid, and what we must labor to attain now, and what we ought by degrees to translate into instinctive and unconscious habits. But these precepts, far from constituting the whole of Christ's teaching and exhausting it, are simply stages on the way to perfection. These precepts must and will be followed by higher and higher precepts on the way to the perfection held up by the religion.

And therefore it is essentially a part of the Christian religion to make demands higher than those expressed in its precepts; and by no means to diminish the demands either of the ideal itself, or of the precepts, as people imagine who judge it from the standpoint of the social conception of life.

So much for one misunderstanding of the scientific men, in relation to the import and aim of Christ's teaching. Another misunderstanding arising from the same source consists in substituting love for men, the service of humanity, for the Christian principles of love for God and his service.

The Christian doctrine to love God and serve him, and only as a result of that love to love and serve one's neighbor, seems to scientific men obscure, mystic, and arbitrary. And they would absolutely exclude the obligation of love and service of God, holding that the doctrine of love for men, for humanity alone, is far more clear, tangible, and reasonable.

Scientific men teach in theory that the only good and rational life is that which is devoted to the service of the whole of humanity. That is for them the import of the Christian doctrine, and to that they reduce Christ's teaching. They seek confirmation of their own doctrine in the Gospel, on the supposition that the two doctrines are really the same.

This idea is an absolutely mistaken one. The Christian doctrine has nothing in common with the doctrine of the Positivists, Communists, and all the apostles of the universal brotherhood of mankind, based on the general advantage of such a brotherhood. They differ from one another especially in Christianity's having a firm and clear basis in the human soul, while love for humanity is only a theoretical deduction from analogy.

The doctrine of love for humanity alone is based on the social conception of life.

The essence of the social conception of life consists in the transference of the aim of the individual life to the life of societies of individuals: family, clan, tribe, or state. This transference is accomplished easily and naturally in its earliest forms, in the transference of the aim of life from the individual to the family and the clan. The transference to the tribe or the nation is more difficult and requires special training. And the transference of the sentiment to the state is the furthest limit which the process can reach.

To love one's self is natural to everyone, and no one needs any encouragement to do so. To love one's clan who support and protect one, to love one's wife, the joy and help of one's existence, one's children, the hope and consolation of one's life, and one's parents, who have given one life and education, is natural. And such love, though far from being so strong as love of self, is met with pretty often.

To love--for one's own sake, through personal pride--one's tribe, one's nation, though not so natural, is nevertheless common. Love of one's own people who are of the same blood, the same tongue, and the same religion as one's self is possible, though far from being so strong as love of self, or even love of family or clan. But love for a state, such as Turkey, Germany, England, Austria, or Russia is a thing almost impossible. And though it is zealously inculcated, it is only an imagined sentiment; it has no existence in reality. And at that limit man's power of transferring his interest ceases, and he cannot feel any direct sentiment for that fictitious entity. The Positivists, however, and all the apostles of fraternity on scientific principles, without taking into consideration the weakening of sentiment in proportion to the extension of its object, draw further deductions in theory in the same direction. "Since," they say, "it was for the advantage of the individual to extend his personal interest to the family, the tribe, and subsequently to the nation and the state, it would be still more advantageous to extend his interest in societies of men to the whole of mankind, and so all to live for humanity just as men live for the family or the state."

Theoretically it follows, indeed, having extended the love and interest for the personality to the family, the tribe, and thence to the nation and the state, it would be perfectly logical for men to save themselves the strife and calamities which result from the division of mankind into nations and states by extending their love to the whole of humanity. This would be most logical, and theoretically nothing would appear more natural to its advocates, who do not observe that love is a sentiment which may or may not be felt, but which it is useless to advocate; and moreover, that love must have an object, and that humanity is not an object. It is nothing but a fiction.

The family, the tribe, even the state were not invented by men, but formed themselves spontaneously, like ant-hills or swarms of bees, and have a real existence. The man who, for the sake of his own animal personality, loves his family, knows whom he loves: Anna, Dolly, John, Peter, and so on. The man who loves his tribe and takes pride in it, knows that he loves all the Guelphs or all the Ghibellines; the man who loves the state knows that he loves France bounded by the Rhine, and the Pyrenees, and its principal city Paris, and its history and so on. But the man who loves humanity--what does he love? There is such a thing as a state, as a nation; there is the abstract conception of man; but humanity as a concrete idea does not, and cannot exist.

Humanity! Where is the definition of humanity? Where does it end and where does it begin? Does humanity end with the savage, the idiot, the dipsomaniac, or the madman? If we draw a line excluding from humanity its lowest representatives, where are we to draw the line? Shall we exclude the negroes like the Americans, or the Hindoos like some Englishmen, or the Jews like some others? If we include all men without exception, why should we not include also the higher animals, many of whom are superior to the lowest specimens of the human race.

We know nothing of humanity as an eternal object, and we know nothing of its limits. Humanity is a fiction, and it is impossible to love it. It would, doubtless, be very advantageous if men could love humanity just as they love their family. It would be very advantageous, as Communists advocate, to replace the competitive, individualistic organization of men's activity by a social universal organization, so that each would be for all and all for each.

Only there are no motives to lead men to do this. The Positivists, the Communists, and all the apostles of fraternity on scientific principles advocate the extension to the whole of humanity of the love men feel for themselves, their families, and the state. They forget that the love which they are discussing is a personal love, which might expand in a rarefied form to embrace a man's native country, but which disappears before it can embrace an artificial state such as Austria, England, or Turkey, and which we cannot even conceive of in relation to all humanity, an absolutely mystic conception.

"A man loves himself (his animal personality), he loves his family, he even loves his native country. Why should he not love humanity? That would be such an excellent thing. And by the way, it is precisely what is taught by Christianity." So think the advocates of Positivist, Communistic, or Socialistic fraternity.

It would indeed be an excellent thing. But it can never be, for the love that is based on a personal or social conception of life can never rise beyond love for the state.

The fallacy of the argument lies in the fact that the social conception of life, on which love for family and nation is founded, rests itself on love of self, and that love grows weaker and weaker as it is extended from self to family, tribe, nationality, and slate; and in the state we reach the furthest limit beyond which it cannot go.

The necessity of extending the sphere of love is beyond dispute. But in reality the possibility of this love is destroyed by the necessity of extending its object indefinitely. And thus the insufficiency of personal human love is made manifest.

And here the advocates of Positivist, Communistic, Socialistic fraternity propose to draw upon Christian love to make up the default of this bankrupt human love; but Christian love only in its results, not in its foundations. They propose love for humanity alone, apart from love for God.

But such a love cannot exist. There is no motive to produce it. Christian love is the result only of the Christian conception of life, in which the aim of life is to love and serve God.

The social conception of life has led men, by a natural transition from love of self and then of family, tribe, nation, and state, to a consciousness of the necessity of love for humanity, a conception which has no definite limits and extends to all living things. And this necessity for love of what awakens no kind of sentiment in a man is a contradiction which cannot be solved by the social theory of life.

The Christian doctrine in its full significance can alone solve it, by giving a new meaning to life. Christianity recognizes love of self, of family, of nation, and of humanity, and not only of humanity, but of everything living, everything existing; it recognizes the necessity of an infinite extension of the sphere of love. But the object of this love is not found outside self in societies of individuals, nor in the external world, but within self, in the divine self whose essence is that very love, which the animal self is brought to feel the need of through its consciousness of its own perishable nature.

The difference between the Christian doctrine and those which preceded it is that the social doctrine said: "Live in opposition to your nature [understanding by this only the animal nature], make it subject to the external law of family, society, and state." Christianity says: "Live according to your nature [understanding by this the divine nature]; do not make it subject to anything--neither you (an animal self) nor that of others--and you will attain the very aim to which you are striving when you subject your external self."

The Christian doctrine brings a man to the elementary consciousness of self, only not of the animal self, but of the divine self, the divine spark, the self as the Son of God, as much God as the Father himself, though confined in an animal husk. The consciousness of being the Son of God, whose chief characteristic is love, satisfies the need for the extension of the sphere of love to which the man of the social conception of life had been brought. For the latter, the welfare of the personality demanded an ever-widening extension of the sphere of love; love was a necessity and was confined to certain objects--self, family, society. With the Christian conception of life, love is not a necessity and is confined to no object; it is the essential faculty of the human soul. Man loves not because it is his interest to love this or that, but because love is the essence of his soul, because he cannot but love.

The Christian doctrine shows man that the essence of his soul is love--that his happiness depends not on loving this or that object, but on loving the principle of the whole--God, whom he recognizes within himself as love, and therefore he loves all things and all men.

In this is the fundamental difference between the Christian doctrine and the doctrine of the Positivists, and all the theorizers about universal brotherhood on non-Christian principles.

Such are the two principal misunderstandings relating to the Christian religion, from which the greater number of false reasonings about it proceed. The first consists in the belief that Christ's teaching instructs men, like all previous religions, by rules, which they are bound to follow, and that these rules cannot be fulfilled. The second is the idea that the whole purport of Christianity is to teach men to live advantageously together, as one family, and that to attain this we need only follow the rule of love to humanity, dismissing all thought of love of God altogether.

The mistaken notion of scientific men that the essence of Christianity consists in the supernatural, and that its moral teaching is impracticable, constitutes another reason of the failure of men of the present day to understand

Christianity.

CHAPTER V.

CONTRADICTION BETWEEN OUR LIFE AND OUR CHRISTIAN CONSCIENCE.

Men Think they can Accept Christianity without Altering their Life--Pagan Conception of Life does not Correspond with Present Stage of Development of Humanity, and Christian Conception Alone Can Accord with it--Christian Conception of Life not yet Understood by Men, but the Progress of Life itself will Lead them Inevitably to Adopt it--The Requirements of a New Theory of Life Always Seem Incomprehensible, Mystic, and Supernatural--So Seem the Requirements of the Christian Theory of Life to the Majority of Men--The Absorption of the Christian Conception of Life will Inevitably be Brought About as the Result of Material and Spiritual Causes--The Fact of Men Knowing the Requirements of the Higher View of Life, and yet Continuing to Preserve Inferior Organizations of Life, Leads to Contradictions and Sufferings which Embitter Existence and Must Result in its Transformation--The Contradictions of our Life--The Economic Contradiction and the Suffering Induced by it for Rich and Poor Alike--The Political Contradiction and the Sufferings Induced by Obedience to the Laws of the State--The International Contradiction and the Recognition of it by Contemporaries: Komarovsky, Ferri, Booth, Passy, Lawson, Wilson, Bartlett, Defourney, Moneta--The Striking Character of the Military Contradiction.

There are many reasons why Christ's teaching is not understood.

One reason is that people suppose they have understood it when they have decided, as the Churchmen do, that it was revealed by supernatural means, or when they have studied, as the scientific men do, the external forms in which it has been manifested. Another reason is the mistaken notion that it is impracticable, and ought to be replaced by the doctrine of love for humanity. But the principal reason, which is the source of all the other mistaken ideas about it, is the notion that Christianity is a doctrine which can be accepted or rejected without any change of life.

Men who are used to the existing order of things, who like it and dread its being changed, try to take the doctrine as a collection of revelations and rules which one can accept without their modifying one's life. While Christ's teaching is not only a doctrine which gives rules which a man must follow, it unfolds a new meaning in life, and defines a whole world of human activity quite different from all that has preceded it and appropriate to the period on which man is entering.

The life of humanity changes and advances, like the life of the individual, by stages, and every stage has a theory of life appropriate to it, which is inevitably absorbed by men. Those who do not absorb it consciously, absorb it unconsciously. It is the same with the changes in the beliefs of peoples and of all humanity as it is with the changes of belief of individuals. If the father of a family continues to be guided in his conduct by his childish conceptions of life, life becomes so difficult for him that he involuntarily seeks another philosophy and readily absorbs that which is appropriate to his age.

That is just what is happening now to humanity at this time of transition through which we are passing, from the pagan conception of life to the Christian. The socialized man of the present day is brought by experience of life itself to the necessity of abandoning the pagan conception of life, which is inappropriate to the present stage of humanity, and of submitting to the obligation of the Christian doctrines, the truths of which, however corrupt and misinterpreted, are still known to him, and alone offer him a solution of the contradictions surrounding him.

If the requirements of the Christian doctrine seem strange and even alarming to the man of the social theory of life, no less strange, incomprehensible, and alarming to the savage of ancient times seemed the requirements of the social doctrine when it was not fully understood and could not be foreseen in its results.

"It is unreasonable," said the savage, "to sacrifice my peace of mind or my life in defense of something incomprehensible, impalpable, and conventional--family, tribe, or nation; and above all it is unsafe to put oneself at the disposal of the power of others."

But the time came when the savage, on one hand, felt, though vaguely, the value of the social conception of life, and of its chief motor power, social censure, or social approbation--glory, and when, on the other hand, the difficulties of his personal life became so great that he could not continue to believe in the value of his old theory of life. Then he accepted the social, state theory of life and submitted to it.

That is just what the man of the social theory of life is passing through now.

"It is unreasonable," says the socialized man, "to sacrifice my welfare and that of my family and my country in order to fulfill some higher law, which requires me to renounce my most natural and virtuous feelings of love of self, of family, of kindred, and of country; and above all, it is unsafe to part with the security of life afforded by the organization of government."

But the time is coming when, on one hand, the vague consciousness in his soul of the higher law, of love to God and his neighbor, and, on the other hand, the suffering, resulting from the contradictions of life, will force the man to reject the social theory and to assimilate the new one prepared ready for him, which solves all the contradictions and removes all his sufferings--the Christian theory of life. And this time has now come.

We, who thousands of years ago passed through the transition, from the personal, animal view of life to the socialized view, imagine that that transition was an inevitable and natural one; but this transition through which we have been passing for the last eighteen hundred years seems arbitrary, unnatural, and alarming. But we only fancy this because that first transition has been so fully completed that the practice attained by it has become unconscious and instinctive in us, while the present transition is not yet over and we have to complete it consciously.

It took ages, thousands of years, for the social conception of life to permeate men's consciousness. It went through various forms and has now passed into the region of the instinctive through inheritance, education, and habit. And therefore it seems natural to us. But five thousand years ago it seemed as unnatural and alarming to men as the Christian doctrine in its true sense seems to-day.

We think to-day that the requirements of the Christian doctrine--of universal brotherhood, suppression of national distinctions, abolition of private property, and the strange injunction of non-resistance to evil by force--demand what is impossible. But it was just the same thousands of years ago, with every social or even family duty, such as the duty of parents to support their children, of the young to maintain the old, of fidelity in marriage. Still more strange, and even unreasonable, seemed the state duties of submitting to the appointed authority, and paying taxes, and fighting in defense of the country, and so on. All such requirements seem simple, comprehensible, and natural to us to-day, and we see nothing mysterious or alarming in them. But three or five thousand years ago they seemed to require what was impossible.

The social conception of life served as the basis of religion because at the time when it was first presented to men it seemed to them absolutely incomprehensible, mystic, and supernatural. Now that we have outlived that phase of the life of humanity, we understand the rational grounds for uniting men in families, communities, and states. But in antiquity the duties involved by such association were presented under cover of the supernatural and were confirmed by it.

The patriarchal religions exalted the family, the tribe, the nation. State religions deified emperors and states. Even now most ignorant people--like our peasants, who call the Tzar an earthly god--obey state laws, not through any rational recognition of their necessity, nor because they have any conception of the meaning of state, but through a religious sentiment.

In precisely the same way the Christian doctrine is presented to men of the social or heathen theory of life to-day, in the guise of a supernatural religion, though there is in reality nothing mysterious, mystic, or supernatural about it. It is simply the theory of life which is appropriate to the present degree of material development, the present stage of growth of humanity, and which must therefore inevitably be accepted.

The time will come--it is already coming--when the Christian principles of equality and fraternity, community of property, non-resistance of evil by force, will appear just as natural and simple as the principles of family or social life seem to us now.

Humanity can no more go backward in its development than the individual man. Men have outlived the social, family, and state conceptions of life. Now they must go forward and assimilate the next and higher conception of life, which is what is now taking place. This change is brought about in two ways: consciously through spiritual causes, and unconsciously through material causes.

Just as the individual man very rarely changes his way of life at the dictates of his reason alone, but generally continues to live as before, in spite of the new interests and aims revealed to him by his reason, and only alters his way of living when it has become absolutely opposed to his conscience, and consequently intolerable to him; so, too, humanity, long after it has learnt through its religions the new interests and aims of life, toward which it must strive, continues in the majority of its representatives to live as before, and is only brought to accept the new conception by finding it impossible to go on living its old life as before.

Though the need of a change of life is preached by the religious leaders and recognized and realized by the most intelligent men, the majority, in spite of their reverential attitude to their leaders, that is, their faith in their teaching, continue to be guided by the old theory of life in their present complex existence. As though the father of a family, knowing how he ought to behave at his age, should yet continue through habit and thoughtlessness to live in the same childish way as he did in boyhood.

That is just what is happening in the transition of humanity from one stage to another, through which we are passing now. Humanity has outgrown its social stage and has entered upon a new period. It recognizes the doctrine which ought to be made the basis of life in this new period. But through inertia it continues to keep up the old forms of life. From this inconsistency between the new conception of life and practical life follows a whole succession of contradictions and sufferings which embitter our life and necessitate its alteration.

One need only compare the practice of life with the theory of it, to be dismayed at the glaring antagonism between our conditions of life and our conscience.

Our whole life is in flat contradiction with all we know, and with all we regard as necessary and right. This contradiction runs through everything, in economic life, in political life, and in international life. As though we had forgotten what we knew and put away for a time the principles we believe in (we cannot help still believing in them because they are the only foundation we have to base our life on) we do the very opposite of all that our conscience and our common sense require of us.

We are guided in economical, political, and international questions by the principles which were appropriate to men of three or five thousand years ago, though they are directly opposed to our conscience and the conditions of life in which we are placed to-day.

It was very well for the man of ancient times to live in a society based on the division of mankind into masters and slaves, because he believed that such a distinction was decreed by God and must always exist. But is such a belief possible in these days?

The man of antiquity could believe he had the right to enjoy the good things of this world at the expense of other men, and to keep them in misery for generations, since he believed that men came from different origins, were base or noble in blood, children of Ham or of Japhet. The greatest sages of the world, the teachers of humanity, Plato and Aristotle, justified the existence of slaves and demonstrated the lawfulness of slavery; and even three centuries ago, the men who described an imaginary society of the future, Utopia, could not conceive of it without slaves.

Men of ancient and medieval times believed, firmly believed, that men are not equal, that the only true men are Persians, or Greeks, or Romans, or Franks. But we cannot believe that now. And people who sacrifice themselves for the principles of aristocracy and of patriotism to-duty, don't believe and can't believe what they assert.

We all know and cannot help knowing--even though we may never have heard the idea clearly expressed, may never have read of it, and may never have put it into words, still through unconsciously imbibing the Christian sentiments that are in the air--with our whole heart we know and cannot escape knowing the fundamental truth of the Christian doctrine, that we are all sons of one Father, wherever we may live and whatever language we may speak; we are all brothers and are subject to the same law of love implanted by our common Father in our hearts.

Whatever the opinions and degree of education of a man of to-day, whatever his shade of liberalism, whatever his school of philosophy, or of science, or of economics, however ignorant or superstitious he may be, every man of the present day knows that all men have an equal right to life and the good things of life, and that one set of people are no better nor worse than another, that all are equal. Everyone knows this, beyond doubt; everyone feels it in his whole being. Yet at the same time everyone sees all round him the division of men into two castes--the one, laboring, oppressed, poor, and suffering, the other idle, oppressing, luxurious, and profligate. And everyone not only sees this, but voluntarily or involuntarily, in one way or another, he takes part in maintaining this distinction which his conscience condemns. And he cannot help suffering from the consciousness of this contradiction and his share in it.

Whether he be master or slave, the man of to-day cannot help constantly feeling the painful opposition between his conscience and actual life, and the miseries resulting from it.

The toiling masses, the immense majority of mankind who are suffering under the incessant, meaningless, and hopeless toil and privation in which their whole life is swallowed up, still find their keenest suffering in the glaring contrast between what is and what ought to be, according to all the beliefs held by themselves, and those who have brought them to that condition and keep them in it.

They know that they are in slavery and condemned to privation and darkness to minister to the lusts of the minority who keep them down. They know it, and they say so plainly. And this knowledge increases their sufferings and constitutes its bitterest sting.

The slave of antiquity knew that he was a slave by nature, but our laborer, while he feels he is a slave, knows that he ought not to be, and so he tastes the agony of Tantalus, forever desiring and never gaining what might and ought to be his.

The sufferings of the working classes, springing from the contradiction between what is and what ought to be, are increased tenfold by the envy and hatred engendered by their consciousness of it.

The laborer of the present day would not cease to suffer even if his toil were much lighter than that of the slave of ancient times, even if he gained an eight-hour working day and a wage of three dollars a day. For he is working at the manufacture of things which he will not enjoy, working not by his own will for his own benefit, but through necessity, to satisfy the desires of luxurious and idle people in general, and for the profit of a single rich man, the owner of a factory or workshop in particular. And he knows that all this is going on in a world in which it is a recognized scientific principle that labor alone creates wealth, and that to profit by the labor of others is immoral, dishonest, and punishable by law; in a world, moreover, which professes to believe Christ's doctrine that we are all brothers, and that true merit and dignity is to be found in serving one's neighbor, not in exploiting him. All this he knows, and he cannot but suffer keenly from the sharp contrast between what is and what ought to be.

"According to all principles, according to all I know, and what everyone professes," the workman says to himself. "I ought to be free, equal to everyone else, and loved; and I am--a slave, humiliated and hated." And he too is filled with hatred and tries to find means to escape from his position, to shake off the enemy who is over-riding him, and to oppress him in turn. People say, "Workmen have no business to try to become capitalists, the poor to try to put themselves in the place of the rich." That is a mistake. The workingmen and the poor would be wrong if they tried to do so in a world in which slaves and masters were regarded as different species created by God; but they are living in a world which professes the faith of the Gospel, that all are alike sons of God, and so brothers and equal. And however men may try to conceal it, one of the first conditions of Christian life is love, not in words but in deeds.

The man of the so-called educated classes lives in still more glaring inconsistency and suffering. Every educated man, if he believes in anything, believes in the brotherhood of all men, or at least he has a sentiment of humanity, or else of justice, or else he believes in science. And all the while he knows that his whole life is framed on principles in direct opposition to it all, to all the principles of Christianity, humanity, justice, and science.

He knows that all the habits in which he has been brought up, and which he could not give up without suffering, can only be satisfied through the exhausting, often fatal, toil of oppressed laborers, that is, through the most obvious and brutal violation of the principles of Christianity, humanity, and justice, and even of science (that is, economic science). He advocates the principles of fraternity, humanity, justice, and science, and yet he lives so that he is dependent on the oppression of the working classes, which he denounces, and his whole life is based on the advantages gained by their oppression. Moreover he is directing every effort to maintaining this state of things so flatly opposed to all his beliefs.

We are all brothers--and yet every morning a brother or a sister must empty the bedroom slops for me. We are all brothers, but every morning I must have a cigar, a sweetmeat, an ice, and such things, which my brothers and sisters have been wasting their health in manufacturing, and I enjoy these things and demand them. We are all brothers, yet I live by working in a bank, or mercantile house, or shop at making all goods dearer for my brothers. We are all brothers, but I live on a salary paid me for prosecuting, judging, and condemning the thief or the prostitute whose existence the whole tenor of my life tends to bring about, and who I know ought not to be punished but reformed. We are all brothers, but I live on the salary I gain by collecting taxes from needy laborers to be spent on the luxuries of the rich and idle. We are all brothers, but I take a stipend for preaching a false Christian religion, which I do not myself believe in, and which only serve's to hinder men from understanding true Christianity. I take a stipend as priest or bishop for deceiving men in the matter of the greatest importance to them. We are all brothers, but I will not give the poor the benefit of my educational, medical, or literary labors except for money. We are all brothers, yet I take a salary for being ready to commit murder, for teaching men to murder, or making firearms, gunpowder, or fortifications.

The whole life of the upper classes is a constant inconsistency. The more delicate a man's conscience is, the more painful this contradiction is to him.

A man of sensitive conscience cannot but suffer if he lives such a life. The only means by which he can escape from this suffering is by blunting his conscience, but even if some men succeed in dulling their conscience they cannot dull their fears.

The men of the higher dominating classes whose conscience is naturally not sensitive or has become blunted, if they don't suffer through conscience, suffer from fear and hatred. They are bound to suffer. They know all the hatred of them existing, and inevitably existing in the working classes. They are aware that the working classes know that they are deceived and exploited, and that they are beginning to organize themselves to shake off oppression and revenge themselves on their oppressors. The higher classes see the unions, the strikes, the May Day Celebrations, and feel the calamity that is threatening them, and their terror passes into an instinct of self-defense and hatred. They know that if for one instant they are worsted in the struggle with their oppressed slaves, they will perish, because the slaves are exasperated and their exasperation is growing more intense with every day of oppression. The oppressors, even if they wished to do so, could not make an end to oppression. They know that they themselves will perish directly they even relax the harshness of their oppression. And they do not relax it, in spite of all their pretended care for the welfare of the working classes, for the eight-hour day, for regulation of the labor of minors and of women, for savings banks and pensions. All that is humbug, or else simply anxiety to keep the slave fit to do his work. But the slave is still a slave, and the master who cannot live without a slave is less disposed to set him free than ever.

The attitude of the ruling classes to the laborers is that of a man who has felled his adversary to the earth and holds him down, not so much because he wants to hold him down, as because he knows that if he let him go, even for a second, he would himself be stabbed, for his adversary is infuriated and has a knife in his hand. And therefore, whether their conscience is tender or the reverse, our rich men cannot enjoy the wealth they have filched from the poor as the ancients did who believed in their right to it. Their whole life and all their enjoyments are embittered either by the stings of conscience or by terror.

So much for the economic contradiction. The political contradiction is even more striking.

All men are brought up to the habit of obeying the laws of the state before everything. The whole existence of modern times is defined by laws. A man marries and is divorced, educates his children, and even (in many countries) professes his religious faith in accordance with the law. What about the law then which defines our whole existence? Do men believe in it? Do they regard it as good? Not at all. In the majority of cases people of the present time do not believe in the justice of the law, they despise it, but still they obey it. It was very well for the men of the ancient world to observe their laws. They firmly believed that their law (it was generally of a religious character) was the only just law, which everyone ought to obey. But is it so with us? we know and cannot help knowing that the law of our country is not the one eternal law; that it is only one of the many laws of different countries, which are equally imperfect, often obviously wrong and unjust, and are criticised from every point of view in the newspapers. The Jew might well obey his laws, since he had not the slightest doubt that God had written them with his finger; the Roman too might well obey the laws which he thought had been dictated by the nymph Egeria. Men might well observe the laws if they believed the Tzars who made them were God's anointed, or even if they thought they were the work of assemblies of lawgivers who had the power and the desire to make them as good as possible. But we all know how our laws are made. We have all been behind the scenes, we know that they are the product of covetousness, trickery, and party struggles; that there is not and cannot be any real justice in them. And so modern men cannot believe that obedience to civic or political laws can satisfy the demands of the reason or of human nature. Men have long ago recognized that it is irrational to obey a law the justice of which is very doubtful, and so they cannot but suffer in obeying a law which they do not accept as judicious and binding.

A man cannot but suffer when his whole life is defined beforehand for him by laws, which he must obey under threat of punishment, though he does not believe in their wisdom or justice, and often clearly perceives their injustice, cruelty, and artificiality.

We recognize the uselessness of customs and import duties, and are obliged to pay them. We recognize the uselessness of the expenditure on the maintenance of the Court and other members of Government, and we regard the teaching of the Church as injurious, but we are obliged to bear our share of the expenses of these institutions. We regard the punishments inflicted by law as cruel and shameless, but we must assist in supporting them. We regard as unjust and pernicious the distribution of landed property, but we are obliged to submit to it. We see no necessity for wars and armies, but we must bear terribly heavy burdens in support of troops and war expenses.

But this contradiction is nothing in comparison with the contradiction which confronts us when we turn to international questions, and which demands a solution, under pain of the loss of the sanity and even the existence of the human race. That is the contradiction between the Christian conscience and war.

We are all Christian nations living the same spiritual life, so that every noble and pregnant thought, springing up at one end of the world, is at once communicated to the whole of Christian humanity and evokes everywhere the same emotion at pride and rejoicing without distinction of nationalities. We who love thinkers, philanthropists, poets, and scientific men of foreign origin, and are as proud of the exploits of Father Damien as if he were one of ourselves, we, who have a simple love for men of foreign nationalities, Frenchmen, Germans, Americans, and Englishmen, who respect their qualities, are glad to meet them and make them so warmly welcome, cannot regard war with them as anything heroic.

We cannot even imagine without horror the possibility of a disagreement between these people and ourselves which would call for reciprocal murder. Yet we are all bound to take a hand in this slaughter which is bound to come to pass to-morrow not to-day.

It was very well for the Jew, the Greek, and the Roman to defend the independence of his nation by murder. For he piously believed that his people was the only true, fine, and good people dear to God, and all the rest were Philistines, barbarians. Men of medieval times--even up to the end of the last and beginning of this century--might continue to hold this belief. But however much we work upon ourselves we cannot believe it. And this contradiction for men of the present day has become so full of horror that without its solution life is no longer possible.

"We live in a time which is full of inconsistencies," writes Count Komarovsky, the professor of international law, in his learned treatise.

> "The press of all countries is continually expressing the universal desire for peace, and the general sense of its necessity for all nations.
>
> "Representatives of governments, private persons, and official organs say the same thing; it is repeated in parliamentary debates, diplomatic correspondence, and even in state treaties.

At the same time governments are increasing the strength of their armies every year, levying fresh taxes, raising loans, and leaving as a bequest to future generations the duty of repairing the blunders of the senseless policy of the present. What a striking contrast between words and deeds! Of course governments will plead in justification of these measures that all their expenditure and armament are exclusively for purposes of defense. But it remains a mystery to every disinterested man whence they can expect attacks if all the great powers are single-hearted in their policy, in pursuing nothing but self defense. In reality it looks as if each of the great powers were every instant anticipating an attack on the part of the others. And this results in a general feeling of insecurity and superhuman efforts on the part of each government to increase their forces beyond those of the other powers. Such a competition of itself increases the danger of war. Nations cannot endure the constant increase of armies for long, and sooner or later they will prefer war to all the disadvantages of their present position and the constant menace of war. Then the most trifling pretext will be sufficient to throw the whole of Europe into the fire of universal war. And it is a mistaken idea that such a crisis might deliver us from the political and economical troubles that are crushing us. The experience of the wars of latter years teaches us that every war has only intensified national hatreds, made military burdens more crushing and insupportable, and rendered the political and

> economical grievous and insoluble."

"Modern Europe keeps under arms an active army of nine millions of men," writes Enrico Ferri,

> "besides fifteen millions of reserve, with an outlay of four hundred millions of francs per annum. By continual increase of the armed force, the sources of social and individual prosperity are paralyzed, and the state of the modern world may be compared to that of a man who condemns himself to wasting from lack of nutrition in order to provide himself with arms, losing thereby the strength to use the arms he provides, under the weight of which he will at last succumb."

Charles Booth, in his paper read in London before the Association for the Reform and Codification of the Law of Nations, June 26, 1887, says the same thing. After referring to the same number, nine millions of the active army and fifteen millions of reserve, and the enormous expenditure of governments on the support and arming of these forces, he says:

> "These figures represent only a small part of the real cost, because besides the recognized expenditure of the war budget of the various nations, we ought also to take into account the enormous loss to society involved in withdrawing from it such an immense number of its most vigorous men, who are taken from

industrial pursuits and every kind of labor, as well as the enormous interest on the sums expended on military preparations without any return. The inevitable result of this expenditure on war and preparations for war is a continually growing national debt. The greater number of loans raised by the governments of Europe were with a view to war. Their total sum amounts to four hundred millions sterling, and these debts are increasing every year."

The same Professor Komarovsky says in another place:

"We live in troubled times. Everywhere we hear complaints of the depression of trade and manufactures, and the wretchedness of the economic position generally, the miserable conditions of existence of the working classes, and the universal impoverishment of the masses. But in spite of this, governments in their efforts to maintain their independence rush to the greatest extremes of senselessness. New taxes and duties are being devised everywhere, and the financial oppression of the nations knows no limits. If we glance at the budgets of the states of Europe for the last hundred years, what strikes us most of all is their rapid and continually growing increase.

"How can we explain this extraordinary phenomenon which sooner or later threatens us all with inevitable bankruptcy?

> "It is caused beyond dispute by the expenditure for the maintenance of armaments which swallows up a third and even a half of all the expenditure of European states. And the most melancholy thing is that one can foresee no limit to this augmentation of the budget and impoverishment of the masses. What is socialism but a protest against this abnormal position in which the greater proportion of the population of our world is placed?

"We are ruining ourselves," says Frederick Passy in a letter read before the last Congress of Universal Peace (in 1890) in London,

> "we are ruining ourselves in order to be able to take part in the senseless wars of the future or to pay the interest on debts we have incurred by the senseless and criminal wars of the past. We are dying of hunger so as to secure the means of killing each other."

Speaking later on of the way the subject is looked at in France, he says:

> "We believe that, a hundred years after the Declaration of the Rights of Man and of the citizen, the time has come to recognize the rights of nations and to renounce at once and forever all those undertakings based on fraud and force, which, under the name of conquests, are veritable crimes against

> humanity, and which, whatever the vanity of monarchs and the pride of nations may think of them, only weaken even those who are triumphant over them."

"I am surprised at the way religion is carried on in this country," said Sir Wilfrid Lawson at the same congress.

> "You send a boy to Sunday school, and you tell him: 'Dear boy, you must love your enemies. If another boy strikes you, you mustn't hit him back, but try to reform him by loving him.' Well. The boy stays in the Sunday school till he is fourteen or fifteen, and then his friends send him into the army. What has he to do in the army? He certainly won't love his enemy; quite the contrary, if he can only get at him, he will run him through with his bayonet. That is the nature of all religious teaching in this country. I do not think that that is a very good way of carrying out the precepts of religion. I think if it is a good thing for a boy to love his enemy, it is good for a grown-up man."

"There are in Europe twenty-eight millions of men under arms," says Wilson,

> "to decide disputes, not by discussion, but by murdering one another. That is the accepted method for deciding disputes among Christian nations. This method is, at the same time,

very expensive, for, according to the statistics I have read, the nations of Europe spent in the year 1872 a hundred and fifty millions sterling on preparations for deciding disputes by means of murder. It seems to me, therefore, that in such a state of things one of two alternatives must be admitted: either Christianity is a failure, or those who have undertaken to expound it have failed in doing so. Until our warriors are disarmed and our armies disbanded, the have not the right to call ourselves a Christian nation."

In a conference on the subject of the duty of Christian ministers to preach against war, G. D. Bartlett said among other things:

"If I understand the Scriptures, I say that men are only playing with Christianity so long as they ignore the question of war. I have lived a longish life and have heard our ministers preach on universal peace hardly half a dozen times. Twenty years ago, in a drawing room, I dared in the presence of forty persons to moot the proposition that war was incompatible with Christianity; I was regarded as an arrant fanatic. The idea that we could get on without war was regarded as unmitigated weakness and folly."

The Catholic priest Defourney has expressed himself in the same spirit. "One of the first precepts of the eternal law inscribed in the consciences of all men," says the Abby Defourney, "is the prohibition of taking the life or shedding the blood of a fellow-creature without sufficient cause, without being forced into the necessity of it. This is one of the commandments which is most deeply stamped in the heart of man. But so soon as it is a question of war, that is, of shedding blood in torrents, men of the present day do not trouble themselves about a sufficient cause. Those who take part in wars do not even think of asking themselves whether there is any justification for these innumerable murders, whether they are justifiable or unjustifiable, lawful or unlawful, innocent or criminal; whether they are breaking that fundamental commandment that forbids killing without lawful cause. But their conscience is mute. War has ceased to be something dependent on moral considerations. In warfare men have in all the toil and dangers they endure no other pleasure than that of being conquerors, no sorrow other than that of being conquered. Don't tell me that they are serving their country. A great genius answered that long ago in the words that have become a proverb: 'Without justice, what is an empire but a great band of brigands?' And is not every band of brigands a little empire? They too have their laws; and they too make war to gain booty, and even for honor.

"The aim of the proposed institution [the institution of an international board of arbitration] is that the nations of

Europe may cease to be nations of robbers, and their armies, bands of brigands. And one must add, not only brigands, but slaves. For our armies are simply gangs of slaves at the disposal of one or two commanders or ministers, who exercise a despotic control over them without any real responsibility, as we very well know.

"The peculiarity of a slave is that he is a mere tool in the hands of his master, a thing, not a man. That is just what soldiers, officers, and generals are, going to murder and be murdered at the will of a ruler or rulers. Military slavery is an actual fact, and it is the worst form of slavery, especially now when by means of compulsory service it lays its fetters on the necks of all the strong and capable men of a nation, to make them instruments of murder, butchers of human flesh, for that is all they are taken and trained to do.

"The rulers, two or three in number, meet together in cabinets, secretly deliberate without registers, without publicity, and consequently without responsibility, and send men to be murdered."

"Protests against armaments, burdensome to the people, have not originated in our times," says Signor E. G. Moneta.

"Hear what Montesquieu wrote in his day. 'France [and one

might say, Europe] will be ruined by soldiers. A new plague is spreading throughout Europe. It attacks sovereigns and forces them to maintain an incredible number of armed men. This plague is infectious and spreads, because directly one government increases its armament, all the others do likewise. So that nothing is gained by it but general ruin.

"'Every government maintains as great an army as it possibly could maintain if its people were threatened with extermination, and people call peace this state of tension of all against all. And therefore Europe is so ruined that if private persons were in the position of the governments of our continent, the richest of them would not have enough to live on. We are poor though we have the wealth and trade of the whole world.'

"That was written almost 150 years ago. The picture seems drawn from the world of to-day. One thing only has changed-the form of government. In Montesquieu's time it was said that the cause of the maintenance of great armaments was the despotic power of kings, who made war in the hope of augmenting by conquest their personal revenues and gaining glory. People used to say then: 'Ah, if only people could elect those who would have the right to refuse governments the soldiers and the money--then there would be an end to military politics.' Now there are representative governments in almost the whole of

Europe, and in spite of that, war expenditures and the preparations for war have increased to alarming proportions.

"It is evident that the insanity of sovereigns has gained possession of the ruling classes. War is not made now because one king has been wanting in civility to the mistress of another king, as it was in Louis XIV.'s time. But the natural and honorable sentiments of national honor and patriotism are so exaggerated, and the public opinion of one nation so excited against another, that it is enough for a statement to be made (even though it may be a false report) that the ambassador of one state was not received by the principal personage of another state to cause the outbreak of the most awful and destructive war there has ever been seen. Europe keeps more soldiers under arms to-day than in the time of the great Napoleonic wars. All citizens with few exceptions are forced to spend some years in barracks. Fortresses, arsenals, and ships are built, new weapons are constantly being invented, to be replaced in a short time by fresh ones, for, sad to say, science, which ought always to be aiming at the good of humanity, assists in the work of destruction, and is constantly inventing new means for killing the greatest number of men in the shortest time. And to maintain so great a multitude of soldiers and to make such vast preparations for murder, hundreds of millions are spent annually, sums which would be sufficient for the education of the people and for immense works of public utility, and which would make it possible to find a peaceful solution of the social question.

"Europe, then, is, in this respect, in spite of all the conquests of science, in the same position as in the darkest and most barbarous days of the Middle Ages. All deplore this state of things--neither peace nor war--and all would be glad to escape from it. The heads of governments all declare that they all wish for peace, and vie with one another in the most solemn protestations of peaceful intentions. But the same day or the next they will lay a scheme for the increase of the armament before their legislative assembly, saying that these are the preventive measures they take for the very purpose of securing peace.

"But this is not the kind of peace we want. And the nations are not deceived by it. True peace is based on mutual confidence, while these huge armaments show open and utter lack of confidence, if not concealed hostility, between states. What should we say of a man who, wanting to show his friendly feelings for his neighbor, should invite him to discuss their differences with a loaded revolver in his hand?

"It is just this flagrant contradiction between the peaceful professions and the warlike policy of governments which all good citizens desire to put an end to, at any cost."

People are astonished that every year there are sixty thousand cases of suicide in Europe, and those only the recognized and recorded cases--and excluding Russia and Turkey; but one ought rather to be surprised that there are so few. Every man of the present day, if we go deep enough into the contradiction between his conscience and his life, is in a state of despair.

Not to speak of all the other contradictions between modern life and the conscience, the permanently armed condition of Europe together with its profession of Christianity is alone enough to drive any man to despair, to doubt of the sanity of mankind, and to terminate an existence in this senseless and brutal world. This contradiction, which is a quintessence of all the other contradictions, is so terrible that to live and to take part in it is only possible if one does not think of it--if one is able to forget it.

What! all of us, Christians, not only profess to love one another, but do actually live one common life; we whose social existence beats with one common pulse--we aid one another, learn from one another, draw ever closer to one another to our mutual happiness, and find in this closeness the whole meaning of life!--and to-morrow some crazy ruler will say some stupidity, and another will answer in the same spirit, and then I must go expose myself to being murdered, and murder men--who have done me no harm--and more than that, whom I love. And this is not a remote contingency, but the very thing we are all preparing for, which is not only probable, but an inevitable certainty.

To recognize this clearly is enough to drive a man out of his senses or to make him shoot himself. And this is just what does happen, and especially often among military men. A man need only come to himself for an instant to be impelled inevitably to such an end.

And this is the only explanation of the dreadful intensity with which men of modern times strive to stupefy themselves, with spirits, tobacco, opium, cards, reading newspapers, traveling, and all kinds of spectacles and amusements. These pursuits are followed up as an important, serious business. And indeed they are a serious business. If there were no external means of dulling their sensibilities, half of mankind would shoot themselves without delay, for to live in opposition to one's reason is the most intolerable condition. And that is the condition of all men of the present day. All men of the modern world exist in a state of continual and flagrant antagonism between their conscience and their way of life. This antagonism is apparent in economic as well as political life. But most striking of all is the contradiction between the Christian law of the brotherhood of men existing in the conscience and the necessity under which all men are placed by compulsory military service of being prepared for hatred and murder--of being at the same time a Christian and a gladiator.

CHAPTER VI.

ATTITUDE OF MEN OF THE PRESENT DAY TO WAR.

People do not Try to Remove the Contradiction between Life and Conscience by a Change of Life, but their Cultivated Leaders Exert Every Effort to Obscure the Demands of Conscience, and justify their Life; in this Way they Degrade Society below Paganism to a State of Primeval Barbarism--Undefined Attitude of Modern Leaders of Thought to War, to Universal Militarism, and to Compulsory Service in Army--One Section Regards War as an Accidental Political Phenomenon, to be Avoided by External Measures only--Peace Congress--The Article in the REVUE DES REVUES--Proposition of Maxime du Camp--Value of Boards of Arbitration and Suppression of Armies--Attitude of Governments to Men of this Opinion and What they Do--Another Section Regards War as Cruel, but Inevitable--Maupassant--Rod--A Third Section Regard War as Necessary, and not without its Advantages--Doucet-Claretie-Zola-Vogüé.

The antagonism between life and the conscience may be removed in two ways: by a change of life or by a change of conscience. And there would seem there can be no doubt as to these alternatives.

A man may cease to do what he regards as wrong, but he cannot cease to consider wrong what is wrong. Just in the same way all humanity may cease to do what it regards as wrong, but far from being able to change, it cannot even retard for a time the continual growth of a clearer recognition of what is wrong and therefore ought not to be. And therefore it would seem inevitable for Christian men to abandon the pagan forms of society which they condemn, and to reconstruct their social existence on the Christian principles they profess.

So it would be were it not for the law of inertia, as immutable a force in men and nations as in inanimate bodies. In men it takes the form of the psychological principle, so truly expressed in the words of the Gospel, "They have loved darkness better than light because their deeds were evil." This principle shows itself in men not trying to recognize the truth, but to persuade themselves that the life they are leading, which is what they like and are used to, is a life perfectly consistent with truth.

Slavery was opposed to all the moral principles advocated by Plato and Aristotle, yet neither of them saw that, because to renounce slavery would have meant the break up of the life they were living. We see the same thing in our modern world.

The division of men into two castes, as well as the use of force in government and war, are opposed to every moral principle professed by our modern society. Yet the cultivated and advanced men of the day seem not to see it.

The majority, if not all, of the cultivated men of our day try unconsciously to maintain the old social conception of life, which justifies their position, and to hide from themselves and others its insufficiency, and above all the necessity of adopting the Christian conception of life, which will mean the break up of the whole existing social order. They struggle to keep up the organization based on the social conception of life, but do not believe in it themselves, because it is extinct and it is impossible to believe in it.

All modern literature--philosophical, political, and artistic--is striking in this respect. What wealth of idea, of form, of color, what erudition, what art, but what a lack of serious matter, what dread of any exactitude of thought or expression! Subtleties, allegories, humorous fancies, the widest generalizations, but nothing simple and clear, nothing going straight to the point, that is, to the problem of life.

But that is not all; besides these graceful frivolities, our literature is full of simple nastiness and brutality, of arguments which would lead men back in the most refined way to primeval barbarism, to the principles not only of the pagan, but even of the animal life, which we have left behind us five thousand years ago.

And it could not be otherwise. In their dread of the Christian conception of life which will destroy the social order, which some cling to only from habit, others also from interest, men cannot but be thrown back upon the pagan conception of life and the principles based on it. Nowadays we see advocated not only patriotism and aristocratic principles just as they were advocated two thousand years ago, but even the coarsest epicureanism and animalism, only with this difference, that the men who then professed those views believed in them, while nowadays even the advocates of such views do not believe in them, for they have no meaning for the present day. No one can stand still when the earth is shaking under his feet. If we do not go forward we must go back. And strange and terrible to say, the cultivated men of our day, the leaders of thought, are in reality with their subtle reasoning drawing society back, not to paganism even, but to a state of primitive barbarism.

This tendency on the part of the leading thinkers of the day is nowhere more apparent than in their attitude to the phenomenon in which all the insufficiency of the social conception of life is presented in the most concentrated form--in their attitude, that is, to war, to the general arming of nations, and to universal compulsory service.

The undefined, if not disingenuous, attitude of modern thinkers to this phenomenon is striking. It takes three forms in cultivated society. One section look at it as an incidental phenomenon, arising out of the special political situation of Europe, and consider that this state of things can be reformed without a revolution in the whole internal social order of nations, by external measures of international diplomacy. Another section regard it as something cruel and hideous, but at the same time fated and inevitable, like disease and death. A third party with cool indifference consider war as an inevitable phenomenon, beneficial in its effects and therefore desirable.

Men look at the subject from different points of view, but all alike talk of war as though it were something absolutely independent of the will of those who take part in it. And consequently they do not even admit the natural question which presents itself to every simple man: "How about me--ought I to take any part in it?" In their view no question of this kind even exists, and every man, however he may regard war from a personal standpoint, must slavishly submit to the requirements of the authorities on the subject.

The attitude of the first section of thinkers, those who see a way out of war in international diplomatic measures, is well expressed in the report of the last Peace Congress in London, and the articles and letters upon war that appeared in No. 8 of the REVUE DES REVUES, 1891. The congress after gathering together from various quarters the verbal and written opinion of learned men opened the proceedings by a religious service, and after listening to addresses for five whole days, concluded them by a public dinner and speeches. They adopted the following resolutions:

"1. The congress affirms its belief that the brotherhood of man involves as a necessary consequence a brotherhood of nations.

"2. The congress recognizes the important influence that Christianity exercises on the moral and political progress of mankind, and earnestly urges upon ministers of the Gospel and other religious teachers the duty of setting forth the principles of peace and good will toward men. AND IT RECOMMENDS THAT THE THIRD SUNDAY IN DECEMBER BE SET APART FOR THAT PURPOSE.

"3. The congress expresses the opinion that all teachers of history should call the attention of the young to the grave evils inflicted on mankind in all ages by war, and to the fact that such war has been waged for most inadequate causes.

"4. The congress protests against the use of military drill in schools by way of physical exercise, and suggests the formation of brigades for saving life rather than of a quasi-military character; and urges the desirability of impressing on the Board of Examiners who formulate the questions for examination the propriety of guiding the minds of children in the principles of peace.

"5. The congress holds that the doctrine of the Rights of Man requires that the aboriginal and weaker races, their territories and liberties, shall be guarded from injustice and fraud, and that these races shall be shielded against the vices so prevalent among the so-called advanced races of men. It further expresses its conviction that there should be concert of action among the nations for the accomplishment of these ends. The congress expresses its hearty appreciation of the resolutions of the Anti-slavery Conference held recently at Brussels for the amelioration of the condition of the peoples of Africa.

"6. The congress believes that the warlike prejudices and traditions which are still fostered in the various nationalities, and the misrepresentations by leaders of public opinion in legislative assemblies or through the press, are often indirect causes of war, and that these evils should be counteracted by the publication of accurate information tending to the removal of misunderstanding between nations, and recommends the importance of considering the question of commencing an international newspaper with such a purpose.

"7. The congress proposes to the Inter-parliamentary Conference that the utmost support should be given to every project for unification of weights and measures, coinage, tariff, postage, and telegraphic arrangements, etc., which would assist in constituting a commercial, industrial, and scientific union of the peoples.

"8. The congress, in view of the vast social and moral influence of woman, urges upon every woman to sustain the things that make for peace, as otherwise she incurs grave responsibility for the continuance of the systems of militarism.

"9. The congress expresses the hope that the Financial Reform Association and other similar societies in Europe and America should unite in considering means for establishing equitable commercial relations between states, by the reduction of import duties. The congress feels that it can affirm that the whole of Europe desires peace, and awaits with impatience the suppression of armaments, which, under the plea of defense, become in their turn a danger by keeping alive mutual distrust, and are, at the same time, the cause of that general economic disturbance which stands in the way of settling in a satisfactory manner the problems of labor and poverty, which ought to take precedence of all others.

"10. The congress, recognizing that a general disarmament would be the best guarantee of peace and would lead to the solution of the questions which now most divide states, expresses the wish that a congress of representatives of all the states of Europe may be assembled as soon as possible to consider the means of effecting a gradual general disarmament.

"11. The congress, in consideration of the fact that the timidity of a single power might delay the convocation of the above-mentioned congress, is of opinion that the government which should first dismiss any considerable number of soldiers would confer a signal benefit on Europe and mankind, because it would, by public opinion, oblige other governments to follow its example, and by the moral force of this accomplished fact would have increased rather than diminished the conditions of its national defense.

"12. The congress, considering the question of disarmament, as of peace in general, depends on public opinion, recommends the peace societies, as well as all friends of peace, to be active in its propaganda, especially at the time of parliamentary elections, in order that the electors should give their votes to candidates who are pledged to support Peace, Disarmament, and Arbitration.

"13. The congress congratulates the friends of peace on the resolution adopted by the International American Conference, held at Washington in April last, by which it was recommended that arbitration should be obligatory in all controversies, whatever their origin, except only those which may imperil the independence of one of the nations involved.

"14. The congress recommends this resolution to the attention of European statesmen, and expresses the ardent desire that similar treaties may speedily be entered into between the other nations of the world.

"15. The congress expresses its satisfaction at the adoption by the Spanish Senate on June 16 last of a project of law authorizing the government to negotiate general or special treaties of arbitration for the settlement of all disputes except those relating to the independence or internal government of the states affected; also at the adoption of resolutions to a like effect by the Norwegian Storthing and by the Italian Chamber.

"16. The congress resolves that a committee be appointed to address communications to the principal political, religious, commercial, and labor and peace organizations, requesting them to send petitions to the governmental authorities praying that measures be taken for the formation of suitable tribunals for the adjudicature of international questions so as to avoid the resort to war.

"17. Seeing (1) that the object pursued by all peace societies is the establishment of judicial order between nations, and (2) that neutralization by international treaties constitutes a step toward this judicial state and lessens the number of districts in which war can be carried on, the congress recommends a larger extension of the rule of neutralization, and expresses the wish, (1) that all treaties which at present assure to certain states the benefit of neutrality remain in force, or if necessary be amended in a manner to render the neutrality more effective, either by extending neutralization

to the whole of the state or by ordering the demolition of fortresses, which constitute rather a peril than a guarantee for neutrality; (2) that new treaties in harmony with the wishes of the populations concerned be concluded for establishing the neutralization of other states.

"18. The sub-committee proposes, (1) that the annual Peace Congress should be held either immediately before the meeting of the annual Sub-parliamentary Conference, or immediately after it in the same town; (2) that the question of an international peace emblem be postponed SINE DIE; (3) that the following resolutions be adopted:

"a. To express satisfaction at the official overtures of the Presbyterian Church in the United States addressed to the highest representatives of each church organization in

Christendom to unite in a general conference to promote the substitution of international arbitration for war.

"b. To express in the name of the congress its profound reverence for the memory of Aurelio Saffi, the great Italian jurist, a member of the committee of the International League of Peace and Liberty.

"(4) That the memorial adopted by this congress and signed by the president to the heads of the civilized states should, as far as practicable, be presented to each power by influential deputations.

"(5) That the following resolutions be adopted:

"a. A resolution of thanks to the presidents of the various sittings of the congress.

"b. A resolution of thanks to the chairman, the secretaries, and the members of the bureau of the congress.

"c. A resolution of thanks to the conveners and members of the sectional committees.

"d. A resolution of thanks to Rev. Canon Scott Holland, Rev. Dr. Reuen Thomas, and Rev. J. Morgan Gibbon for their pulpit addresses before the congress, and also to the authorities of St. Paul's Cathedral, the City Temple, and Stamford Hill Congregational Church for the use of those buildings for public services.

"e. A letter of thanks to her Majesty for permission to visit Windror Castle.

"f. And also a resolution of thanks to the Lord Mayor and Lady Mayoress, to Mr. Passmore Edwards, and other friends who have extended their hospitality to the members of the congress.

"19. The congress places on record a heartfelt expression of gratitude to Almighty God for the remarkable harmony and concord which have characterized the meetings of the assembly, in which so many men and women of varied nations, creeds, tongues, and races have gathered in closest co-operation, and for the conclusion of the labors of the congress; and expresses its firm and unshaken belief in the ultimate triumph of the cause of peace and of the principles advocated at these meetings."

The fundamental idea of the congress is the necessity (1) of diffusing among all people by all means the conviction of the disadvantages of war and the great blessing of peace, and (2) of rousing governments to the sense of the superiority of international arbitration over war and of the consequent advisability and necessity of disarmament. To attain the first aim the congress has recourse to teachers of history, to women, and to the clergy, with the advice to the latter to preach on the evil of war and the blessing of peace every third Sunday in December. To attain the second object the congress appeals to governments with the suggestion that they should disband their armies and replace war by arbitration.

To preach to men of the evil of war and the blessing of peace! But the blessing of peace is so well known to men that, ever since there have been men at all, their best wish has been expressed in the greeting, "Peace be with you." So why preach about it?

Not only Christians, but pagans, thousands of years ago, all recognized the evil of war and the blessing of peace. So that the recommendation to ministers of the Gospel to preach on the evil of war and the blessing of peace every third Sunday in December is quite superfluous.

The Christian cannot but preach on that subject every day of his life. If Christians and preachers of Christianity do not do so, there must be reasons for it. And until these have been removed no recommendations will be effective. Still less effective will be the recommendations to governments to disband their armies and replace them by international boards of arbitration. Governments, too, know very well the difficulty and the burdensomeness of raising and maintaining forces, and if in spite of that knowledge they do, at the cost of terrible strain and effort, raise and maintain forces, it is evident that they cannot do otherwise, and the recommendation of the congress can never change it. But the learned gentlemen are unwilling to see that, and keep hoping to find a political combination, through which governments shall be induced to limit their powers themselves.

"Can we get rid of war"? asks a learned writer in the REVUE DES REVUES.

> "All are agreed that if it were to break out in Europe, its consequences would be like those of the great inroads of barbarians. The existence of whole nationalities would be at stake, and therefore the war would be desperate, bloody, atrocious.
>
> "This consideration, together with the terrible engines of destruction invented by modern science, retards the moment of declaring war, and maintains the present temporary situation, which might continue for an indefinite period, except for the fearful cost of maintaining armaments which are exhausting the European states and threatening to reduce nations to a state of misery hardly less than that of war itself.

"Struck by this reflection, men of various countries have tried to find means for preventing, or at least for softening, the results of the terrible slaughter with which we are threatened.

"Such are the questions brought forward by the Peace Congress shortly to be held in Rome, and the publication of a pamphlet, Sur le Désarmement.'

"It is unhappily beyond doubt that with the present organization of the majority of European states, isolated from one another and guided by distinct interests, the absolute suppression of war is an illusion with which it would be dangerous to cheat ourselves. Wiser rules and regulations imposed on these duels between nations might, however, at least limit its horrors.

"It is equally chimerical to reckon on projects of disarmament, the execution of which is rendered almost impossible by considerations of a popular character present to the mind of all our readers. [This probably means that France cannot disband its army before taking its revenge.] Public opinion is not prepared to accept them, and moreover, the international relations between different peoples are not such as to make their acceptance possible. Disarmament imposed on one nation by another in circumstances threatening its security would be equivalent to a declaration of war.

"However, one may admit that an exchange of ideas between the nations interested could aid, to a certain degree, in bringing about the good understanding indispensable to any negotiations, and would render possible a considerable reduction of the military expenditure which is crushing the nations of Europe and greatly hindering the solution of the social question, which each individually must solve on pain of having internal war as the price for escaping it externally.

"We might at least demand the reduction of the enormous expenses of war organized as it is at present with a view to the power of invasion within twenty-four hours and a decisive battle within a week of the declaration of war.

"We ought to manage so that states could not make the attack suddenly and invade each other's territories within twenty-four hours."

This practical notion has been put forth by Maxime du Camp, and his article concludes with it.

The propositions of M. du Camp are as follows:

1. A diplomatic congress to be held every year.

2. No war to be declared till two months after the incident which provoked it. (The difficulty here would be to decide precisely what incident did provoke the war, since whenever war is declared there are very many such incidents, and one would have to decide from which to reckon the two months' interval.)

3. No war to be declared before it has been submitted to a plebiscitum of the nations preparing to take part in it.

4. No hostilities to be commenced till a month after the official declaration of war.

"No war to be declared. No hostilities to be commenced," etc. But who is to arrange that no war is to be declared? Who is to compel people to do this and that? Who is to force states to delay their operations for a certain fixed time? All the other states. But all these others are also states which want holding in check and keeping within limits, and forcing, too. Who is to force them, and how? Public opinion. But if there is a public opinion which can force governments to delay their operations for a fixed period, the same public opinion can force governments not to declare war at all.

But, it will be replied, there may be such a balance of power, such a PONDÉRATION DE FORCES, as would lead states to hold back of their own accord. Well, that has been tried and is being tried even now. The Holy Alliance was nothing but that, the League of Peace was another attempt at the same thing, and so on.

But, it will be answered, suppose all were agreed. If all were agreed there would be no more war certainly, and no need for arbitration either.

"A court of arbitration! Arbitration shall replace war. Questions shall be decided by a court of arbitration. The Alabama question was decided by a court of arbitration, and the question of the Caroline Islands was submitted to the decision of the Pope. Switzerland, Belgium, Denmark, and Holland have all declared that they prefer arbitration to war."

I dare say Monaco has expressed the same preference. The only unfortunate thing is that Germany, Russia, Austria, and France have not so far shown the same inclination. It is amazing how men can deceive themselves when they find it necessary! Governments consent to decide their disagreements by arbitration and to disband their armies! The differences between Russia and Poland, between England and Ireland, between Austria and Bohemia, between Turkey and the Slavonic states, between France and Germany, to be soothed away by amiable conciliation!

One might as well suggest to merchants and bankers that they should sell nothing for a greater price than they gave for it, should undertake the distribution of wealth for no profit, and should abolish money, as it would thus be rendered unnecessary.

But since commercial and banking operations consist in nothing but selling for more than the cost price, this would be equivalent to an invitation to suppress themselves. It is the same in regard to governments. To suggest to governments that they should not have recourse to violence, but should decide their misunderstandings in accordance with equity, is inviting them to abolish themselves as rulers, and that no government can ever consent to do.

The learned men form societies (there are more than a hundred such societies), assemble in congresses (such as those recently held in London and Paris, and shortly to be held in Rome), deliver addresses, eat public dinners and make speeches, publish journals, and prove by every means possible that the nations forced to support millions of troops are strained to the furthest limits of their endurance, that the maintenance of these huge armed forces is in opposition to all the aims, the interests, and the wishes of the people, and that it is possible, moreover, by writing numerous papers, and uttering a great many words, to bring all men into agreement and to arrange so that they shall have no antagonistic interests, and then there will be no more war.

When I was a little boy they told me if I wanted to catch a bird I must put salt on its tail. I ran after the birds with the salt in my hand, but I soon convinced myself that if I could put salt on a bird's tail, I could catch it, and realized that I had been hoaxed.

People ought to realize the same fact when they read books and articles on arbitration and disarmament.

If one could put salt on a bird's tail, it would be because it could not fly and there would be no difficulty in catching it. If the bird had wings and did not want to be caught, it would not let one put salt on its tail, because the specialty of a bird is to fly. In precisely the same way the specialty of government is not to obey, but to enforce obedience. And a government is only a government so long as it can make itself obeyed, and therefore it always strives for that and will never willingly abandon its power. But since it is on the army that the power of government rests, it will never give up the army, and the use of the army in war.

The error arises from the learned jurists deceiving themselves and others, by asserting that government is not what it really is, one set of men banded together to oppress another set of men, but, as shown by science, is the representation of the citizens in their collective capacity. They have so long been persuading other people of this that at last they have persuaded themselves of it;

and thus they often seriously suppose that government can be bound by considerations of justice. But history shows that from Caesar to Napoleon, and from Napoleon to Bismarck, government is in its essence always a force acting in violation of justice, and that it cannot be otherwise. Justice can have no binding force on a ruler or rulers who keep men, deluded and drilled in readiness for acts of violence--soldiers, and by means of them control others. And so governments can never be brought to consent to diminish the number of these drilled slaves, who constitute their whole power and importance.

Such is the attitude of certain learned men to the contradiction under which our society is being crushed, and such are their methods of solving it. Tell these people that the whole matter rests on the personal attitude of each man to the moral and religious question put nowadays to everyone, the question, that is, whether it is lawful or unlawful for him to take his share of military service, and these learned gentlemen will shrug their shoulders and not condescend to listen or to answer you. The solution of the question in their idea is to be found in reading addresses, writing books, electing presidents, vice-presidents, and secretaries, and meeting and speaking first in one town and then in another. From all this speechifying and writing it will come to pass, according to their notions, that governments will cease to levy the soldiers, on whom their whole strength depends, will listen to their discourses, and will disband their forces, leaving themselves without any defense, not only against their neighbors, but also against their own subjects. As though a band of brigands, who have some unarmed travelers bound and ready to be plundered, should be so touched by their complaints of the pain caused by the cords they are fastened with as to let them go again.

Still there are people who believe in this, busy themselves over peace congresses, read addresses, and write books. And governments, we may be quite sure, express their sympathy and make a show of encouraging them. In the same way they pretend to support temperance societies, while they are living principally on the drunkenness of the people; and pretend to encourage education, when their whole strength is based on ignorance; and to support constitutional freedom, when their strength rests on the absence of freedom; and to be anxious for the improvement of the condition of the working classes, when their very existence depends on their oppression; and to support Christianity, when Christianity destroys all government.

To be able to do this they have long ago elaborated methods encouraging temperance, which cannot suppress drunkenness; methods of supporting education, which not only fail to prevent ignorance, but even increase it; methods of aiming at freedom and constitutionalism, which are no hindrance to despotism; methods of protecting the working classes, which will not free them from slavery; and a Christianity, too, they have elaborated, which does not destroy, but supports governments.

Now there is something more for the government to encourage--peace. The sovereigns, who nowadays take counsel with their ministers, decide by their will alone whether the butchery of millions is to be begun this year or next. They know very well that all these discourses upon peace will not hinder them from sending millions of men to butchery when it seems good to them. They listen even with satisfaction to these discourses, encourage them, and take part in them.

All this, far from being detrimental, is even of service to governments, by turning people's attention from the most important and pressing question: Ought or ought not each man called upon for military service to submit to serve in the army?

"Peace will soon be arranged, thanks to alliances and congresses, to books and pamphlets; meantime go and put on your uniform, and prepare to cause suffering and to endure it for our benefit," is the government's line of argument. And the learned gentlemen who get up congresses and write articles are in perfect agreement with it.

This is the attitude of one set of thinkers. And since it is that most beneficial to governments, it is also the most encouraged by all intelligent governments.

Another attitude to war has something tragical in it. There are men who maintain that the love for peace and the inevitability of war form a hideous contradiction, and that such is the fate of man. These are mostly gifted and sensitive men, who see and realize all the horror and imbecility and cruelty of war, but through some strange perversion of mind neither see nor seek to find any way out of this position, and seem to take pleasure in teasing the wound by dwelling on the desperate position of humanity. A notable example of such an attitude to war is to be found in the celebrated French writer Guy de Maupassant. Looking from his yacht at the drill and firing practice of the French soldiers the following reflections occur to him:

"When I think only of this word war, a kind of terror seizes upon me, as though I were listening to some tale of sorcery, of the Inquisition, some long past, remote abomination, monstrous, unnatural.

"When cannibalism is spoken of, we smile with pride, proclaiming our superiority to these savages. Which are the savages, the real savages? Those who fight to eat the conquered, or those who fight to kill, for nothing but to kill?

"The young recruits, moving about in lines yonder, are destined to death like the flocks of sheep driven by the butcher along the road. They will fall in some plain with a saber cut in the head, or a bullet through the breast. And these are young men who might work, be productive and useful. Their fathers are old and poor. Their mothers, who have loved them for twenty years, worshiped them as none but mothers can, will learn in six months' time, or a year perhaps, that their son, their boy, the big boy reared with so much labor, so much expense, so much love, has been thrown in a hole like some dead dog, after being disemboweled by a bullet, and trampled, crushed, to a mass of pulp by the charges of cavalry. Why have they killed her boy, her handsome boy, her one hope, her pride, her life? She does not know. Ah, why?

"War! fighting! slaughter! massacres of men! And we have now, in our century, with our civilization, with the spread of science, and the degree of philosophy which the genius of man is supposed to have attained, schools for training to kill, to kill very far off, to perfection, great numbers at once, to kill poor devils of innocent men with families and without any kind of trial.

"AND WHAT IS MOST BEWILDERING IS THAT THE PEOPLE DO NOT RISE AGAINST THEIR GOVERNMENTS. FOR WHAT DIFFERENCE IS THERE BETWEEN MONARCHIES AND REPUBLICS? THE MOST BEWILDERING THING IS THAT THE WHOLE OF SOCIETY IS NOT IN REVOLT AT THE WORD WAR."

"Ah! we shall always live under the burden of the ancient and odious customs, the criminal prejudices, the ferocious ideas of our barbarous ancestors, for we are beasts, and beasts we shall remain, dominated by instinct and changed by nothing. Would not any other man than Victor Hugo have been exiled for that mighty cry of deliverance and truth? 'To-day force is called violence, and is being brought to judgment; war has been put on its trial. At the plea of the human race, civilization arraigns warfare, and draws up the great list of crimes laid at the charge of conquerors and generals. The nations are coming to understand that the magnitude of a crime cannot be its extenuation; that if killing is a crime, killing many can be no extenuating circumstance; that if robbery is disgraceful, invasion cannot be glorious. Ah! let us proclaim these absolute truths; let us dishonor war!'

"Vain wrath," continues Maupassant, "a poet's indignation. War is held in more veneration than ever.

"A skilled proficient in that line, a slaughterer of genius, Von Moltke, in reply to the peace delegates, once uttered these strange words:

"'War is holy, war is ordained of God. It is one of the most sacred laws of the world. It maintains among men all the great and noble sentiments--honor, devotion, virtue, and courage, and saves them in short from falling into the most hideous materialism.'

"So, then, bringing millions of men together into herds, marching by day and by night without rest, thinking of nothing, studying nothing, learning nothing, reading nothing, being useful to no one, wallowing in filth, sleeping in mud, living like brutes in a continual state of stupefaction, sacking towns, burning villages, ruining whole populations, then meeting another mass of human flesh, falling upon them, making pools of blood, and plains of flesh mixed with trodden mire and red with heaps of corpses, having your arms or legs carried off, your brains blown out for no advantage to anyone, and dying in some corner of a field while your old parents, your wife and children are perishing of hunger--that is what is meant by not falling into the most hideous materialism!

"Warriors are the scourge of the world. We struggle against nature and ignorance and obstacles of all kinds to make our wretched life less hard. Learned men--benefactors of all--spend their lives in working, in seeking what can aid, what be of use, what can alleviate the lot of their fellows. They devote themselves unsparingly to their task of usefulness, making one discovery after another, enlarging the sphere of human intelligence, extending the bounds of science, adding each day some new store to the sum of knowledge, gaining each day prosperity, ease, strength for their country.

"War breaks out. In six months the generals have destroyed the work of twenty years of effort, of patience, and of genius.

"That is what is meant by not falling into the most hideous materialism.

"We have seen it, war. "We have seen men turned to brutes, frenzied, killing for fun, for terror, for bravado, for ostentation. Then when right is no more, law is dead, every notion of justice has disappeared. We have seen men shoot innocent creatures found on the road, and suspected because they were afraid. We have seen them kill dogs chained at their masters' doors to try their new revolvers, we have seen them fire on cows lying in a field for no reason whatever, simply for the sake of shooting, for a joke.

"That is what is meant by not falling into the most hideous materialism.

"Going into a country, cutting the man's throat who defends his house because he wears a blouse and has not a military cap on his head, burning the dwellings of wretched beings who have nothing to eat, breaking furniture and stealing goods, drinking the wine found in the cellars, violating the women in the streets, burning thousands of francs' worth of powder, and leaving misery and cholera in one's track--

"That is what is meant by not falling into the most hideous materialism.

"What have they done, those warriors, that proves the least intelligence? Nothing. What have they invented? Cannons and muskets. That is all.

"What remains to us from Greece? Books and statues. Is Greece great from her conquests or her creations?

"Was it the invasions of the Persians which saved Greece from falling into the most hideous materialism?

"Were the invasions of the barbarians what saved and regenerated Rome?

"Was it Napoleon I. who carried forward the great intellectual movement started by the philosophers of the end of last century?

"Yes, indeed, since government assumes the right of annihilating peoples thus, there is nothing surprising in the fact that the peoples assume the right of annihilating governments.

"They defend themselves. They are right. No one has an absolute right to govern others. It ought only to be done for the benefit of those who are governed. And it is as much the duty of anyone who governs to avoid war as it is the duty of a captain of a ship to avoid shipwreck.

"When a captain has let his ship come to ruin, he is judged and condemned, if he is found guilty of negligence or even incapacity.

"Why should not the government be put on its trial after every declaration of war? IF THE PEOPLE UNDERSTOOD THAT, IF THEY THEMSELVES PASSED JUDGMENT ON MURDEROUS GOVERNMENTS, IF THEY REFUSED TO LET THEMSELVES BE KILLED FOR NOTHING, IF THEY WOULD ONLY TURN THEIR ARMS AGAINST THOSE WHO HAVE GIVEN THEM TO THEM FOR MASSACRE, ON THAT DAY WAR WOULD BE NO MORE. BUT THAT DAY WILL NEVER COME" [Footnote: "Sur l'Eau," pp. 71-80].

The author sees all the horror of war. He sees that it is caused by governments forcing men by deception to go out to slaughter and be slain without any advantage to themselves. And he sees, too, that the men who make up the armies could turn their arms against the governments and bring them to judgment. But he thinks that that will never come to pass, and that there is, therefore, no escape from the present position.

> "I think war is terrible, but that it is inevitable; that compulsory military service is as inevitable as death, and that since government will always desire it, war will always exist."

So writes this talented and sincere writer, who is endowed with that power of penetrating to the innermost core of the subjects which is the essence of the poetic faculty. He brings before us all the cruelty of the inconsistency between men's moral sense and their actions, but without trying to remove it; seems to admit that this inconsistency must exist and that it is the poetic tragedy of life.

Another no less gifted writer, Edouard Rod, paints in still more vivid colors the cruelty and madness of the present state of things. He too only aims at presenting its tragic features, without suggesting or forseeing any issue from the position.

> "What is the good of doing anything? What is the good of undertaking any enterprise? And how are we to love men in these troubled times when every fresh day is a menace of danger?... All we have begun, the plans we are developing, our schemes of work, the little good we may have been able to do,

will it not all be swept away by the tempest that is in preparation?... Everywhere the earth is shaking under our feet and storm-clouds are gathering on our horizon which will have no pity on us.

"Ah! if all we had to dread were the revolution which is held up as a specter to terrify us! Since I cannot imagine a society more detestable than ours, I feel more skeptical than alarmed in regard to that which will replace it. If I should have to suffer from the change, I should be consoled by thinking that the executioners of that day were the victims of the previous time, and the hope of something better would help us to endure the worst. But it is not that remote peril which frightens me. I see another danger, nearer and far more cruel; more cruel because there is no excuse for it, because it is absurd, because it can lead to no good. Every day one balances the chances of war on the morrow, every day they become more merciless.

"The imagination revolts before the catastrophe which is coming at the end of our century as the goal of the progress of our era, and yet we must get used to facing it. For twenty years past every resource of science has been exhausted in the invention of engines of destruction, and soon a few charges of cannon will suffice to annihilate a whole army. No longer a few thousands of poor devils, who were paid a price for their blood, are kept under arms, but whole nations are under arms to cut each other's throats. They are robbed of their time now (by compulsory service) that they may be robbed of their lives later. To prepare them for the work of massacre, their hatred is kindled by persuading them that they are hated. And peaceable men let themselves be played on thus and go and fall on one another with the ferocity of wild beasts; furious troops of peaceful citizens taking up arms at an empty word of command, for some ridiculous question of frontiers or colonial trade interests--Heaven only knows what... They will go like sheep to the slaughter, knowing all the while where they are going, knowing that they are leaving their wives, knowing that their children will want for food, full of misgivings, yet intoxicated by the fine-sounding lies that are dinned into their ears. THEY WILL MARCH WITHOUT REVOLT, PASSIVE, RESIGNED--THOUGH THE NUMBERS AND THE STRENGTH ARE THEIRS, AND THEY MIGHT, IF THEY KNEW HOW TO CO-OPERATE TOGETHER, ESTABLISH THE REIGN OF GOOD SENSE AND FRATERNITY, instead of the barbarous trickery of diplomacy. They will march to battle so deluded, so duped, that they will believe slaughter to be a duty, and will ask the benediction of God on their lust for blood. They will march to battle trampling underfoot the harvests they have sown, burning the towns they have built--with songs of triumph, festive music, and cries of jubilation. And their sons will raise statues to those who have done most in their slaughter.

"The destiny of a whole generation depends on the hour in which some ill-fated politician may give the signal that will be followed. We know that the best of us will be cut down and our work will be destroyed in embryo. WE KNOW IT AND TREMBLE WITH RAGE, BUT WE CAN DO NOTHING. We are held fast in the toils of officialdom and red tape, and too rude a shock would be needed to set us free. We are enslaved by the laws we set up for our protection, which have become our oppression. WE ARE BUT THE TOOLS OF THAT AUTOCRATIC ABSTRACTION THE STATE, WHICH ENSLAVES EACH INDIVIDUAL IN THE NAME OF THE WILL OF ALL, WHO WOULD ALL, TAKEN INDIVIDUALLY, DESIRE EXACTLY THE OPPOSITE OF WHAT THEY WILL BE MADE TO DO.

"And if it were only a generation that must be sacrificed! But there are graver interests at stake.

"The paid politicians, the ambitious statesmen, who exploit the evil passions of the populace, and the imbeciles who are deluded by fine-sounding phrases, have so embittered national feuds that the existence of a whole race will be at stake in the war of the morrow. One of the elements that constitute the modern world is threatened, the conquered people will be wiped out of existence, and whichever it may be, we shall see a moral force annihilated, as if there were too many forces to work for good--we shall have a new Europe formed on foundations so unjust, so brutal, so sanguinary, stained with so monstrous a crime, that it cannot but be worse than the Europe of to-day--more iniquitous, more barbarous, more violent.

"Thus one feels crushed under the weight of an immense discouragement. We are struggling in a CUL DE SAC with muskets aimed at us from the housetops. Our labor is like that of sailors executing their last task as the ship begins to sink. Our pleasures are those of the condemned victim, who is offered his choice of dainties a quarter of an hour before his execution. Thought is paralyzed by anguish, and the most it is capable of is to calculate--interpreting the vague phrases of ministers, spelling out the sense of the speeches of sovereigns, and ruminating on the words attributed to diplomatists reported on the uncertain authority of the newspapers--whether it is to be to-morrow or the day after, this year or the next, that we are to be murdered. So that one might seek in vain in history an epoch more insecure, more crushed under the weight of suffering" [footnote: "Le Sens de la Vie," pp. 208-13].

Here it is pointed out that the force is in the hands of those who work their own destruction, in the hands of the individual men who make up the masses; it is pointed out that the source of the evil is the government. It would seem evident that the contradiction between life and conscience had reached the limit beyond which it cannot go, and after reaching this limit some solution of it must be found.

But the author does not think so. He sees in this the tragedy of human life, and after depicting all the horror of the position he concludes that human life must be spent in the midst of this horror.

So much for the attitude to war of those who regard it as something tragic and fated by destiny.

The third category consists of men who have lost all conscience and, consequently, all common sense and feeling of humanity.

To this category belongs Moltke, whose opinion has been quoted above by Maupassant, and the majority of military men, who have been educated in this cruel superstition, live by it, and consequently are often in all simplicity convinced that war is not only an inevitable, but even a necessary and beneficial thing. This is also the view of some civilians, so-called educated and cultivated people.

Here is what the celebrated academician Camille Doucet writes in reply to the editor of the REVUE DES REVUES, where several letters on war were published together:

"Dear Sir: When you ask the least warlike of academicians whether he is a partisan of war, his answer is known beforehand.

"Alas! sir, you yourself speak of the pacific ideal inspiring your generous compatriots as a dream.

"During my life I have heard a great many good people protest against this frightful custom of international butchery, which all admit and deplore; but how is it to be remedied?

"Often, too, there have been attempts to suppress dueling; one would fancy that seemed an easy task: but not at all! All that has been done hitherto with that noble object has never been and never will be of use.

"All the congresses of both hemispheres may vote against war, and against dueling too, but above all arbitrations, conventions, and legislations there will always be the personal honor of individual men, which has always demanded dueling, and the interests of nations, which will always demand war.

"I wish none the less from the depths of my heart that the Congress of Universal Peace may succeed at last in its very honorable and difficult enterprise.

"I am, dear sir, etc.,

"CAMILLE DOUCET."

The upshot of this is that personal honor requires men to fight, and the interests of nations require them to ruin and exterminate each other. As for the efforts to abolish war, they call for nothing but a smile.

The opinion of another well-known academician, Jules Claretie, is of the same kind.

"Dear Sir [he writes]: For a man of sense there can be but one opinion on the subject of peace and war.

"Humanity is created to live, to live free, to perfect and ameliorate its fate by peaceful labor. The general harmony preached by the Universal Peace Congress is but a dream perhaps, but at least it is the fairest of all dreams. Man is always looking toward the Promised Land, and there the harvests are to ripen with no fear of their being torn up by shells or crushed by cannon wheels... But! Ah! but----since philosophers and philanthropists are not the controlling powers, it is well for our soldiers to guard our frontier and homes, and their arms, skillfully used, are perhaps the surest guarantee of the peace we all love.

"Peace is a gift only granted to the strong and the resolute.

"I am, dear sir, etc.,

"JULES CLARETIE."

The upshot of this letter is that there is no harm in talking about what no one intends or feels obliged to do. But when it comes to practice, we must fight.

And here now is the view lately expressed by the most popular novelist in Europe, Émile Zola:

"I regard war as a fatal necessity, which appears inevitable for us from its close connection with human nature and the whole constitution of the world. I should wish that war could be put off for the longest possible time. Nevertheless, the moment will come when we shall be forced to go to war. I am considering it at this moment from the standpoint of universal humanity, and making no reference to our misunderstanding with Germany--a most trivial incident in the history of mankind. I say that war is necessary and beneficial, since it seems one of the conditions of existence for humanity. War confronts us everywhere, not only war between different races and peoples, but war too, in private and family life. It seems one of the principal elements of progress, and every step in advance that humanity has taken hitherto has been attended by bloodshed.

"Men have talked, and still talk, of disarmament, while disarmament is something impossible, to which, even if it were possible, we ought not to consent. I am convinced that a general disarmament throughout the world would involve something like a moral decadence, which would show itself in general feebleness, and would hinder the progressive advancement of humanity. A warlike nation has always been strong and flourishing. The art of war has led to the development of all the other arts. History bears witness to it. So in Athens and in Rome, commerce, manufactures, and literature never attained so high a point of development as when those cities were masters of the whole world by force of arms. To take an example from times nearer our own, we may recall the age of Louis XIV. The wars of the Grand Monarque were not only no hindrance to the progress of the arts and sciences, but even, on the contrary, seem to have promoted and favored their development."

So war is a beneficial thing!

But the best expression of this attitude is the view of the most gifted of the writers of this school, the academician de Vogüé. This is what he writes in an article on the Military Section of the Exhibition of 1889:

"On the Esplanade des Invalides, among the exotic and colonial encampments, a building in a more severe style overawes the picturesque bazaar; all these fragments of the globe have come to gather round the Palace of War, and in turn our guests mount guard submissively before the mother building, but for whom they would not be here. Fine subject for the antithesis of rhetoric, of humanitarians who could not fail to whimper over this juxtaposition, and to say that 'CECI TUERA CELA,' [footnote: Phrase quoted from Victor-Hugo, "Notre-Dame de Paris."] that the union of the nations through science and labor will overcome the instinct of war. Let us leave them to cherish the chimera of a golden age, which would soon become, if it could be realized, an age of mud. All history teaches us that the one is created for the other, that blood is needed to hasten and cement the union of the nations. Natural science has ratified in our day the mysterious law revealed to Joseph de Maistre by the intuition of his genius and by meditation on fundamental truths; he saw the world redeeming itself from hereditary degenerations by sacrifice; science shows it advancing to perfection through struggle and violent selection; there is the statement of the same law in both, expressed in different formulas. The statement is disagreeable, no doubt; but the laws of the world are not made for our pleasure, they are made for our progress. Let us enter this inevitable, necessary palace of war; we shall be able to observe there how the most tenacious of our instincts, without losing any of its vigor, is transformed and adapted to the varying exigencies of historical epochs."

M. de Vogüé finds the necessity for war, according to his views, well expressed by the two great writers, Joseph de Maistre and Darwin, whose statements he likes so much that he quotes them again.

"Dear Sir [he writes to the editor of the REVUE DES REVUES]: You ask me my view as to the possible success of the Universal Congress of Peace. I hold with Darwin that violent struggle is a law of nature which overrules all other laws; I hold with Joseph de Maistre that it is a divine law; two different ways of describing the same thing. If by some impossible chance a fraction of human society--all the civilized West, let us suppose--were to succeed in suspending the action of this law, some races of stronger instincts would undertake the task of putting it into action against us: those races would vindicate nature's reasoning against human reason; they would be successful, because the certainty of peace--I do not say PEACE, I say the CERTAINTY OF PEACE--would, in half a century, engender a corruption and a decadence more destructive for mankind than the worst of wars. I believe that we must do with war--the criminal law of humanity--as with all our criminal laws, that is, soften them, put them in force as rarely as possible; use every effort to make their application unnecessary. But all the experience of history teaches us that they cannot be altogether suppressed so long as two men are left on earth, with bread, money, and a woman between them.

"I should be very happy if the Congress would prove me in error. But I doubt if it can prove history, nature, and God in error also.

"I am, dear sir, etc.
"E. M. DE VOGÜÉ."

This amounts to saying that history, human nature, and God show us that so long as there are two men, and bread, money and a woman--there will be war. That is to say that no progress will lead men to rise above the savage conception of life, which regards no participation of bread, money (money is good in this context) and woman possible without fighting.

They are strange people, these men who assemble in Congresses, and make speeches to show us how to catch birds by putting salt on their tails, though they must know it is impossible to do it. And amazing are they too, who, like Maupassant, Rod, and many others, see clearly all the horror of war, all the inconsistency of men not doing what is needful, right, and beneficial for them to do; who lament over the tragedy of life, and do not see that the whole tragedy is at an end directly men, ceasing to take account of any unnecessary considerations, refuse to do what is hateful and disastrous to them. They are amazing people truly, but those who, like De Vogüé and others, who, professing the doctrine of evolution, regard war as not only inevitable, but beneficial and therefore desirable--they are terrible, hideous, in their moral perversion. The others, at least, say that they hate evil, and love good, but these openly declare that good and evil do not exist.

All discussion of the possibility of re-establishing peace instead of everlasting war--is the pernicious sentimentality of phrasemongers. There is a law of evolution by which it follows that I must live and act in an evil way; what is to be done? I am an educated man, I know the law of evolution, and therefore I will act in an evil way. "ENTRONS AU PALAIS DE LA GUERRE." There is the law of evolution, and therefore there is neither good nor evil, and one must live for the sake of one's personal existence, leaving the rest to the action of the law of evolution. This is the last word of refined culture, and with it, of that overshadowing of conscience which has come upon the educated classes of our times. The desire of the educated classes to support the ideas they prefer, and the order of existence based on them, has attained its furthest limits. They lie, and delude themselves, and one another, with the subtlest forms of deception, simply to obscure, to deaden conscience.

Instead of transforming their life into harmony with their conscience, they try by every means to stifle its voice. But it is in darkness that the light begins to shine, and so the light is rising upon our epoch.

CHAPTER VII.

SIGNIFICANCE OF COMPULSORY SERVICE.

Universal Compulsory Service is not a Political Accident, but the Furthest Limit of the Contradiction Inherent in the Social Conception of Life--Origin of Authority in Society--Basis of Authority is Physical Violence--To be Able to Perform its Acts of Violence Authority Needs a Special Organization--The Army--Authority, that is, Violence, is the Principle which is Destroying the Social Conception of Life--Attitude of Authority to the Masses, that is, Attitude of Government to Working Oppressed Classes--Governments Try to Foster in Working Classes the Idea that State Force is Necessary to Defend Them from External Enemies--But the Army is Principally Needed to Preserve Government from its own Subjects--The Working Classes--Speech of M. de Caprivi--All Privileges of Ruling Classes Based on Violence--The Increase of Armies up to Point of Universal Service--Universal Compulsory Service Destroys all the Advantages of Social Life, which Government is Intended to Preserve--Compulsory Service is the Furthest Limit of Submission, since in Name of the State it Requires Sacrifice of all that can be Precious to a Man--Is Government Necessary?--The Sacrifices Demanded by Government in Compulsory Service have No Longer any Reasonable Basis--And there is More Advantage to be Gained by not Submitting to the Demands of the State than by Submitting to Them.

Educated people of the upper classes are trying to stifle the ever-growing sense of the necessity of transforming the existing social order. But life, which goes on growing more complex, and developing in the same direction, and increases the inconsistencies and the sufferings of men, brings them to the limit beyond which they cannot go. This furthest limit of inconsistency is universal compulsory military service.

It is usually supposed that universal military service and the increased armaments connected with it, as well as the resulting increase of taxes and national debts, are a passing phenomenon, produced by the particular political situation of Europe, and that it may be removed by certain political combinations without any modification of the inner order of life.

This is absolutely incorrect. Universal military service is only the internal inconsistency inherent in the social conception of life, carried to its furthest limits, and becoming evident when a certain stage of material development is reached.

The social conception of life, we have seen, consists in the transfer of the aim of life from the individual to groups and their maintenance--to the tribe, family, race, or state.

In the social conception of life it is supposed that since the aim of life is found in groups of individuals, individuals will voluntarily sacrifice their own interests for the interests of the group. And so it has been, and still is, in fact, in certain groups, the distinction being that they are the most primitive forms of association in the family or tribe or race, or even in the patriarchal state. Through tradition handed down by education and supported by religious sentiment, individuals without compulsion merged their interests in the interest of the group and sacrificed their own good for the general welfare.

But the more complex and the larger societies become, and especially the more often conquest becomes the cause of the amalgamation of people into a state, the more often individuals strive to attain their own aims at the public expense, and the more often it becomes necessary to restrain these insubordinate individuals by recourse to authority, that is, to violence. The champions of the social conception of life usually try to connect the idea of authority, that is, of violence, with the idea of moral influence, but this connection is quite impossible.

The effect of moral influence on a man is to change his desires and to bend them in the direction of the duty required of him. The man who is controlled by moral influence acts in accordance with his own desires. Authority, in the sense in which the word is ordinarily understood, is a means of forcing a man to act in opposition to his desires. The man who submits to authority does not do as he chooses but as he is obliged by authority. Nothing can oblige a man to do what he does not choose except physical force, or the threat of it, that is--deprivation of freedom, blows, imprisonment, or threats--easily carried out--of such punishments. This is what authority consists of and always has consisted of.

In spite of the unceasing efforts of those who happen to be in authority to conceal this and attribute some other significance to it, authority has always meant for man the cord, the chain with which he is bound and fettered, or the knout with which he is to be flogged, or the ax with which he is to have hands, ears, nose, or head cut off, or at the very least, the threat of these terrors. So it was under Nero and Ghenghis Khan, and so it is to-day, even under the most liberal government in the Republics of the United States or of France. If men submit to authority, it is only because they are liable to these punishments in case of non-submission. All state obligations, payment of taxes, fulfillment of state duties, and submission to punishments, exile, fines, etc., to which people appear to submit voluntarily, are always based on bodily violence or the threat of it.

The basis of authority is bodily violence. The possibility of applying bodily violence to people is provided above all by an organization of armed men, trained to act in unison in submission to one will. These bands of armed men, submissive to a single will, are what constitute the army. The army has always been and still is the basis of power. Power is always in the hands of those who control the army, and all men in power--from the Roman Caesars to the Russian and German Emperors--take more interest in their army than in anything, and court popularity in the army, knowing that if that is on their side their power is secure.

The formation and aggrandizement of the army, indispensable to the maintenance of authority, is what has introduced into the social conception of life the principle that is destroying it.

The object of authority and the justification for its existence lie in the restraint of those who aim at attaining their personal interests to the detriment of the interests of society.

But however power has been gained, those who possess it are in no way different from other men, and therefore no more disposed than others to subordinate their own interests to those of the society. On the contrary, having the power to do so at their disposal, they are more disposed than others to subordinate the public interests to their own. Whatever means men have devised for preventing those in authority from over-riding public interests for their own benefit, or for intrusting power only to the most faultless people, they have not so far succeeded in either of those aims.

All the methods of appointing authorities that have been tried, divine right, and election, and heredity, and balloting, and assemblies and parliaments and senate--have all proved ineffectual. Everyone knows that not one of these methods attains the aim either of intrusting power only to the incorruptible, or of preventing power from being abused. Everyone knows on the contrary that men in authority--be they emperors, ministers, governors, or police officers--are always, simply from the possession of power, more liable to be demoralized, that is, to subordinate public interests to their personal aims than those who have not the power to do so. Indeed, it could not be otherwise.

The state conception of life could be justified only so long as all men voluntarily sacrificed their personal interests to the public welfare. But so soon as there were individuals who would not voluntarily sacrifice their own interests, and authority, that is, violence, was needed to restrain them, then the disintegrating principle of the coercion of one set of people by another set entered into the social conception of the organization based on it.

For the authority of one set of men over another to attain its object of restraining those who override public interests for their personal ends, power ought only to be put into the hands of the impeccable, as it is supposed to be among the Chinese, and as it was supposed to be in the Middle Ages, and is even now supposed to be by those who believe in the consecration by anointing. Only under those conditions could the social organization be justified.

But since this is not the case, and on the contrary men in power are always far from being saints, through the very fact of their possession of power, the social organization based on power has no justification.

Even if there was once a time when, owing to the low standard of morals, and the disposition of men to violence, the existence of an authority to restrain such violence was an advantage, because the violence of government was less than the violence of individuals, one cannot but see that this advantage could not be lasting. As the disposition of individuals to violence diminished, and as the habits of the people became more civilized, and as power grew more social organization demoralized through lack of restraint, this advantage disappeared.

The whole history of the last two thousand years is nothing but the history of this gradual change of relation between the moral development of the masses on the one hand and the demoralization of governments on the other.

This, put simply, is how it has come to pass.

Men lived in families, tribes, and races, at feud with one another, plundering, outraging, and killing one another. These violent hostilities were carried on on a large and on a small scale: man against man, family against family, tribe against tribe, race against race, and people against people. The larger and stronger groups conquered and absorbed the weaker, and the larger and stronger they became, the more internal feuds disappeared and the more the continuity of the group seemed assured.

The members of a family or tribe, united into one community, are less hostile among themselves, and families and tribes do not die like one man, but have a continuity of existence. Between the members of one state, subject to a single authority, the strife between individuals seems still less and the life of the state seems even more secure.

Their association into larger and larger groups was not the result of the conscious recognition of the benefits of such associations, as it is said to be in the story of the Varyagi. It was produced, on one hand, by the natural growth of population, and, on the other, by struggle and conquest.

After conquest the power of the emperor puts an end to internal dissensions, and so the state conception of life justifies itself. But this justification is never more than temporary. Internal dissensions disappear only in proportion to the degree of oppression exerted by the authority over the dissentient individuals. The violence of internal feud crushed by authority reappears in authority itself, which falls into the hands of men who, like the rest, are frequently or always ready to sacrifice the public welfare to their personal interest, with the difference that their subjects cannot resist them, and thus they are exposed to all the demoralizing influence of authority. And thus the evil of violence, when it passes into the hands of authority, is always growing and growing, and in time becomes greater than the evil it is supposed to suppress, while, at the same time, the tendency to violence in the members of the society becomes weaker and weaker, so that the violence of authority is less and less needed.

Government authority, even if it does suppress private violence, always introduces into the life of men fresh forms of violence, which tend to become greater and greater in proportion to the duration and strength of the government.

So that though the violence of power is less noticeable in government than when it is employed by members of society against one another, because it finds expression in submission, and not in strife, it nevertheless exists, and often to a greater degree than in former days.

And it could not be otherwise, since, apart from the demoralizing influence of power, the policy or even the unconscious tendency of those in power will always be to reduce their subjects to the extreme of weakness, for the weaker the oppressed, the less effort need be made to keep him in subjection.

And therefore the oppression of the oppressed always goes on growing up to the furthest limit, beyond which it cannot go without killing the goose with the golden eggs. And if the goose lays no more eggs, like the American Indians, negroes, and Fijians, then it is killed in spite of the sincere protests of philanthropists.

The most convincing example of this is to be found in the condition of the working classes of our epoch, who are in reality no better than the slaves of ancient times subdued by conquest.

In spite of the pretended efforts of the higher classes to ameliorate the position of the workers, all the working classes of the present day are kept down by the inflexible iron law by which they only get just what is barely necessary, so that they are forced to work without ceasing while still retaining strength enough to labor for their employers, who are really those who have conquered and enslaved them.

So it has always been. In ratio to the duration and increasing strength of authority its advantages for its subjects disappear and its disadvantages increase.

And this has been so, independently of the forms of government under which nations have lived. The only difference is that under a despotic form of government the authority is concentrated in a small number of oppressors and violence takes a cruder form; under constitutional monarchies and republics as in France and America authority is divided among a great number of oppressors and the forms assumed by violence is less crude, but its effect of making the disadvantages of authority greater than its advantages, and of enfeebling the oppressed to the furthest extreme to which they can be reduced with advantage to the oppressors, remains always the same.

Such has been and still is the condition of all the oppressed, but hitherto they have not recognized the fact. In the majority of instances they have believed in all simplicity that governments exist for their benefit; that they would be lost without a government; that the very idea of living without a government is a blasphemy which one hardly dare put into words; that this is the--for some reason terrible--doctrine of anarchism, with which a mental picture of all kinds of horrors is associated.

People have believed, as though it were something fully proved, and so needing no proof, that since all nations have hitherto developed in the form of states, that form of organization is an indispensable condition of the development of humanity.

And in that way it has lasted for hundreds and thousands of years, and governments--those who happened to be in power--have tried it, and are now trying more zealously than ever to keep their subjects in this error.

So it was under the Roman emperors and so it is now. In spite of the fact that the sense of the uselessness and even injurious effects of state violence is more and more penetrating into men's consciousness, things might have gone on in the same way forever if governments were not under the necessity of constantly increasing their armies in order to maintain their power.

It is generally supposed that governments strengthen their forces only to defend the state from other states, in oblivion of the fact that armies are necessary, before all things, for the defense of governments from their own oppressed and enslaved subjects.

That has always been necessary, and has become more and more necessary with the increased diffusion of education among the masses, with the improved communication between people of the same and of different nationalities. It has become particularly indispensable now in the face of communism, socialism, anarchism, and the labor movement generally. Governments feel that it is so, and strengthen the force of their disciplined armies. [See Footnote]

[Footnote: The fact that in America the abuses of authority exist in spite of the small number of their troops not only fails to disprove this position, but positively confirms it. In America there are fewer soldiers than in other states. That is why there is nowhere else so little oppression of the working classes, and no country where the end of the abuses of government and of government itself seems so near. Of late as the combinations of laborers gain in strength, one hears more and more frequently the cry raised for the increase of the army, though the United States are not threatened with any attack from without. The upper classes know that an army of fifty thousand will soon be insufficient, and no longer relying on Pinkerton's men, they feel that the security of their position depends on the increased strength of the army.]

In the German Reichstag not long ago, in reply to a question why funds were needed for raising the salaries of the under-officers, the German Chancellor openly declared that trustworthy under-officers were necessary to contend against socialism. Caprivi only said aloud what every statesman knows and assiduously conceals from the people. The reason to which he gave expression is essentially the same as that which made the French kings and the popes engage Swiss and Scotch guards, and makes the Russian authorities of to-day so carefully distribute the recruits, so that the regiments from the frontiers are stationed in central districts, and the regiments from the center are stationed on the frontiers. The meaning of Caprivi's speech, put into plain language, is that funds are needed, not to resist foreign foes, but to BUY UNDER-OFFICERS to be ready to act against the enslaved toiling masses.

Caprivi incautiously gave utterance to what everyone knows perfectly well, or at least feels vaguely if he does not recognize it, that is, that the existing order of life is as it is, not, as would be natural and right, because the people wish it to be so, but because it is so maintained by state violence, by the army with its BOUGHT UNDER-OFFICERS and generals.

If the laborer has no land, if he cannot use the natural right of every man to derive subsistence for himself and his family out of the land, that is not because the people wish it to be so, but because a certain set of men, the land-owners, have appropriated the right of giving or refusing admittance to the land to the laborers. And this abnormal order of things is maintained by the army. If the immense wealth produced by the labor of the working classes is not regarded as the property of all, but as the property of a few exceptional persons; if labor is taxed by authority and the taxes spent by a few on what they think fit; if strikes on the part of laborers are repressesd, while on the part of capitalists they are encouraged; if certain persons appropriate the right of choosing the form of the education, religious and secular, of children, and certain persons monopolize the right of making the laws all must obey, and so dispose of the lives and properties of other people--all this is not done because the people wish it and because it is what is natural and right, but because the government and ruling classes wish this to be so for their own benefit, and insist on its being so even by physical violence.

Everyone, if he does not recognize this now, will know that it is so at the first attempt at insubordination or at a revolution of the existing order.

Armies, then, are needed by governments and by the ruling classes above all to support the present order, which, far from being the result of the people's needs, is often in direct antagonism to them, and is only beneficial to the government and ruling classes.

To keep their subjects in oppression and to be able to enjoy the fruits of their labor the government must have armed forces.

But there is not only one government. There are other governments, exploiting their subjects by violence in the same way, and always ready to pounce down on any other government and carry off the fruits of the toil of its enslaved subjects. And so every government needs an army also to protect its booty from its neighbor brigands. Every government is thus involuntarily reduced to the necessity of emulating one another in the increase of their armies. This increase is contagious, as Montesquieu pointed out 150 years ago.

Every increase in the army of one state, with the aim of self-defense against its subjects, becomes a source of danger for neighboring states and calls for a similar increase in their armies.

The armed forces have reached their present number of millions not only through the menace of danger from neighboring states, but principally through the necessity of subduing every effort at revolt on the part of the subjects.

Both causes, mutually dependent, contribute to the same result at once; troops are required against internal forces and also to keep up a position with other states. One is the result of the other. The despotism of a government always increases with the strength of the army and its external successes, and the aggressiveness of a government increases with its internal despotism.

The rivalry of the European states in constantly increasing their forces has reduced them to the necessity of having recourse to universal military service, since by that means the greatest possible number of soldiers is obtained at the least possible expense. Germany first hit on this device. And directly one state adopted it the others were obliged to do the same. And by this means all citizens are under arms to support the iniquities practiced upon them; all citizens have become their own oppressors.

Universal military service was an inevitable logical necessity, to which we were bound to come. But it is also the last expression of the inconsistency inherent in the social conception of life, when violence is needed to maintain it. This inconsistency has become obvious in universal military service. In fact, the whole significance of the social conception of life consists in man's recognition of the barbarity of strife between individuals, and the transitoriness of personal life itself, and the transference of the aim of life to groups of persons. But with universal military service it comes to pass that men, after making every sacrifice to get rid of the cruelty of strife and the insecurity of existence, are called upon to face all the perils they had meant to avoid. And in addition to this the state, for whose sake individuals renounced their personal advantages, is exposed again to the same risks of insecurity and lack of permanence as the individual himself was in previous times.

Governments were to give men freedom from the cruelty of personal strife and security in the permanence of the state order of existence. But instead of doing that they expose the individuals to the same necessity of strife, substituting strife with individuals of other states for strife with neighbors. And the danger of destruction for the individual, and the state too, they leave just as it was.

Universal military service may be compared to the efforts of a man to prop up his falling house who so surrounds it and fills it with props and buttresses and planks and scaffolding that he manages to keep the house standing only by making it impossible to live in it.

In the same way universal military service destroys all the benefits of the social order of life which it is employed to maintain.

The advantages of social organization are security of property and labor and associated action for the improvement of existence--universal military service destroys all this.

The taxes raised from the people for war preparations absorb the greater part of the produce of labor which the army ought to defend.

The withdrawing of all men from the ordinary course of life destroys the possibility of labor itself. The danger of war, ever ready to break out, renders all reforms of life social life vain and fruitless.

In former days if a man were told that if he did not acknowledge the authority of the state, he would be exposed to attack from enemies domestic and foreign, that he would have to resist them alone, and would be liable to be killed, and that therefore it would be to his advantage to put up with some hardships to secure himself from these calamities, he might well believe it, seeing that the sacrifices he made to the state were only partial and gave him the hope of a tranquil existence in a permanent state. But now, when the sacrifices have been increased tenfold and the promised advantages are disappearing, it would be a natural reflection that submission to authority is absolutely useless.

But the fatal significance of universal military service, as the manifestation of the contradiction inherent in the social conception of life, is not only apparent in that. The greatest manifestation of this contradiction consists in the fact that every citizen in being made a soldier becomes a prop of the government organization, and shares the responsibility of everything the government does, even though he may not admit its legitimacy.

Governments assert that armies are needed above all for external defense, but that is not true. They are needed principally against their subjects, and every man, under universal military service, becomes an accomplice in all the acts of violence of the government against the citizens without any choice of his own.

To convince oneself of this one need only remember what things are done in every state, in the name of order and the public welfare, of which the execution always falls to the army. All civil outbreaks for dynastic or other party reasons, all the executions that follow on such disturbances, all repression of insurrections, and military intervention to break up meetings and to suppress strikes, all forced extortion of taxes, all the iniquitous distributions of land, all the restrictions on labor--are either carried out directly by the military or by the police with the army at their back. Anyone who serves his time in the army shares the responsibility of all these things, about which he is, in some cases, dubious, while very often they are directly opposed to his conscience. People are unwilling to be turned out of the land they have cultivated for generations, or they are unwilling to disperse when the government authority orders them, or they are unwilling to pay the taxes required of them, or to recognize laws as binding on them when they have had no hand in making them, or

to be deprived of their nationality--and I, in the fulfillment of my military duty, must go and shoot them for it. How can I help asking myself when I take part in such punishments, whether they are just, and whether I ought to assist in carrying them out?

Universal service is the extreme limit of violence necessary for the support of the whole state organization, and it is the extreme limit to which submission on the part of the subjects can go. It is the keystone of the whole edifice, and its fall will bring it all down.

The time has come when the ever-growing abuse of power by governments and their struggles with one another has led to their demanding such material and even moral sacrifices from their subjects that everyone is forced to reflect and ask himself, "Can I make these sacrifices? And for the sake of what am I making them? I am expected for the sake of the state to make these sacrifices, to renounce everything that can be precious to man--peace, family, security, and human dignity." What is this state, for whose sake such terrible sacrifices have to be made? And why is it so indispensably necessary? "The state," they tell us, "is indispensably needed, in the first place, because without it we should not be protected against the attacks of evil-disposed persons; and secondly, except for the state we should be savages and should have neither religion, culture, education, nor commerce, nor means of communication, nor other social institutions; and thirdly, without the state to defend us we should be liable to be conquered and enslaved by neighboring peoples."

"Except for the state," they say, "we should be exposed to the attacks of evil-disposed persons in our own country."

But who are these evil-disposed persons in our midst from whose attacks we are preserved by the state and its army? Even if, three or four centuries ago, when men prided themselves on their warlike prowess, when killing men was considered an heroic achievement, there were such persons; we know very well that there are no such persons now, that we do not nowadays carry or use firearms, but everyone professes humane principles and feels sympathy for his fellows, and wants nothing more than we all do--that is, to be left in peace to enjoy his existence undisturbed. So that nowadays there are no special malefactors from whom the state could defend us. If by these evil disposed persons is meant the men who are punished as criminals, we know very well that they are not a different kind of being like wild beasts among sheep, but are men just like ourselves, and no more naturally inclined to crimes than those against whom they commit them. We know now that threats and punishments cannot diminish their number; that that can only be done by change of environment and moral influence. So that the justification of state violence on the ground of the protection it gives us from evil-disposed persons, even if it had some foundation three or four centuries ago, has none whatever now. At present one would rather say on the contrary that the action of the state with its cruel methods of punishment, behind the general moral standard of the age, such as prisons, galleys, gibbets, and guillotines, tends rather to brutalize the people than to civilize them, and consequently rather to increase than diminish the number of malefactors.

"Except for the state," they tell us, "we should not have any religion, education, culture, means of communication, and so on. Without the state men would not have been able to form the social institutions needed for doing any thing." This argument too was well founded only some centuries ago.

If there was a time when people were so disunited, when they had so little means of communication and interchange of ideas, that they could not co-operate and agree together in any common action in commerce, economics, or education without the state as a center, this want of common action exists no longer. The great extension of means of communication and interchange of ideas has made men completely able to dispense with state aid in forming societies, associations, corporations, and congresses for scientific, economic, and political objects. Indeed government is more often an obstacle than an assistance in attaining these aims.

From the end of last century there has hardly been a single progressive movement of humanity which has not been retarded by the government. So it has been with abolition of corporal punishment, of trial by torture, and of slavery, as well as with the establishment of the liberty of the press and the right of public meeting. In our day governments not only fail to encourage, but directly hinder every movement by which people try to work out new forms of life for themselves. Every attempt at the solution of the problems of labor, land, politics, and religion meets with direct opposition on the part of government.

"Without governments nations would be enslaved by their neighbors." It is scarcely necessary to refute this last argument. It carries its refutation on the face of it. The government, they tell us, with its army, is necessary to defend us from neighboring states who might enslave us. But we know this is what all governments say of one another, and yet we know that all the European nations profess the same principles of liberty and fraternity, and therefore stand in no need of protection against one another. And if defense against barbarous nations is meant, one-thousandth part of the troops now under arms would be amply sufficient for that purpose. We see that it is really the very opposite of what we have been told. The power of the state, far from being a security against the attacks of our neighbors, exposes us, on the contrary, to much greater danger of such attacks. So that every man who is led, through his compulsory service in the army, to reflect on the value of the state for whose sake he is expected to be ready to sacrifice his peace, security, and life, cannot fail to perceive that there is no kind of justification in modern times for such a sacrifice.

And it is not only from the theoretical standpoint that every man must see that the sacrifices demanded by the state have no justification. Even looking at it practically, weighing, that is to say, all the burdens laid on him by the state, no man can fail to see that for him personally to comply with state demands and serve in the army, would, in the majority of cases, be more disadvantageous than to refuse to do so.

If the majority of men choose to submit rather than to refuse, it is not the result of sober balancing of advantages and disadvantages, but because they are induced by a kind of hypnotizing process practiced upon them. In submitting they simply yield to the suggestions given them as orders, without thought or effort of will. To resist would need independent thought and effort of which every man is not capable. Even apart from the moral significance of compliance or non-compliance, considering material advantage only, non-compliance will be more advantageous in general.

Whoever I may be, whether I belong to the well-to-do class of the oppressors, or the working class of the oppressed, in either case the disadvantages of non-compliance are less and its advantages greater than those of compliance. If I belong to the minority of oppressors the disadvantages of non-compliance will consist in my being brought to judgment for refusing to perform my duties to the state, and if I am lucky, being acquitted or, as is done in the case of the Mennonites in Russia, being set to work out my military service at some civil occupation for the state; while if I am unlucky, I may be condemned to exile or imprisonment for two or three years (I judge by the cases that have occurred in Russia), possibly to even longer imprisonment, or possibly to death, though the probability of that latter is very remote.

So much for the disadvantages of non-compliance. The

disadvantages of compliance will be as follows: if I am lucky I shall not be sent to murder my fellow-creatures, and shall not be exposed to great danger of being maimed and killed, but shall only be enrolled into military slavery. I shall be dressed up like a clown, I shall be at the beck and call of every man of a higher grade than my own from corporal to field-marshal, shall be put through any bodily contortions at their pleasure, and after being kept from one to five years I shall have for ten years afterward to be in readiness to undertake all of it again at any minute. If I am unlucky I may, in addition, be sent to war, where I shall be forced to kill men of foreign nations who have done me no harm, where I may be maimed or killed, or sent to certain destruction as in the case of the garrison of Sevastopol, and other cases in every war, or what would be most terrible of all, I may be sent against my own compatriots and have to kill my own brothers for some dynastic or other state interests which have absolutely nothing to do with me. So much for the comparative disadvantages.

The comparative advantages of compliance and non-compliance are as follows:

For the man who submits, the advantages will be that, after exposing himself to all the humiliation and performing all the barbarities required of him, he may, if he escapes being killed, get a decoration of red or gold tinsel to stick on his clown's dress; he may, if he is very lucky, be put in command of hundreds of thousands of others as brutalized as himself; be called a field-marshal, and get a lot of money.

The advantages of the man who refuses to obey will consist in preserving his dignity as a man, gaining the approbation of good men, and above all knowing that he is doing the work of God, and so undoubtedly doing good to his fellow-men.

So much for the advantages and disadvantages of both lines of conduct for a man of the wealthy classes, an oppressor. For a man of the poor working class the advantages and disadvantages will be the same, but with a great increase of disadvantages. The disadvantages for the poor man who submits will be aggravated by the fact that he will by taking part in it, and, as it were, assenting to it strengthen the state of subjection in which he is held himself.

But no considerations as to how far the state is useful or beneficial to the men who help to support it by serving in the army, nor of the advantages or disadvantages for the individual of compliance or non-compliance with state demands, will decide the question of the continued existence or the abolition of government. This question will be finally decided beyond appeal by the religious consciousness or conscience of every man who is forced, whether he will or no, through universal conscription, to face the question whether the state is to continue to exist or not.

CHAPTER VIII.

DOCTRINE OF NON-RESISTANCE TO EVIL BY FORCE MUST INEVITABLY BE ACCEPTED BY MEN OF THE PRESENT DAY.

Christianity is Not a System of Rules, but a New Conception of Life, and therefore it was Not Obligatory and was Not Accepted in its True Significance by All, but only by a Few--Christianity is, Moreover, Prophetic of the Destruction of the Pagan Life, and therefore of Necessity of the Acceptance of the Christian Doctrines--Non-resistance of Evil by Force is One Aspect of the Christian Doctrine, which must Inevitably in Our Times be Accepted by Men--Two Methods of Deciding Every Quarrel--First Method is to Find a Universal Definition of Evil, which All Must Accept, and to Resist this Evil by Force--Second Method is the Christian One of Complete Non-resistance by Force--Though the Failure of the First Method was Recognized since the Early Days of Christianity, it was Still Proposed, and only as Mankind has Progressed it has Become More and More Evident that there Cannot be any Universal Definition of Evil--This is Recognized by All at the Present Day, and if Force is Still Used to Resist Evil, it is Not Because it is Now Regarded as Right, but Because People Don't Know How to Avoid It--The Difficulty of Avoiding It is the Result of the Subtle and Complex Character of the Government Use of Force--Force is Used in Four Ways: Intimidation, Bribery, Hypnotism, and Coercion by Force of Arms--State Violence Can Never be Suppressed by the Forcible Overthrow of the Government--Men are Led by the Sufferings of the Pagan Mode of Life to the Necessity of Accepting Christ's Teaching with its Doctrine of Non-resistance by Force--The Consciousness of its Truth which is Diffused Throughout Our Society, Will also Bring About its Acceptance--This Consciousness is in Complete Contradiction with Our Life--This is Specially Obvious in Compulsory Military Service, but Through Habit and the Application of the Four Methods of Violence by the State, Men do not See this Inconsistency of Christianity with Life of a Soldier--They do Not even See It, though the Authorities Themselves Show all the Immorality of a Soldier's Duties with Perfect Clearness--The Call to Military Service is the Supreme Test for Every Man, when the Choice is Offered Him, between Adopting the Christian Doctrine of Non-resistance, or Slavishly Submitting to the Existing State Organization--Men Usually Renounce All They Hold Sacred, and Submit to the Demands of Government, Seeming to See No Other Course Open to Them--For Men of the Pagan Conception of Life there is No Other Course Open, and Never Will Be, in Spite of the Growing Horrors of War--Society, Made Up of Such Men, Must Perish, and No Social Reorganization Can Save It--Pagan Life Has Reached Its Extreme Limit, and Will Annihilate Itself.

It is often said that if Christianity is a truth, it ought to have been accepted by everyone directly it appeared, and ought to have transformed men's lives for the better. But this is like saying that if the seed were ripe it ought at once to bring forth stalls, flower, and fruit.

The Christian religion is not a legal system which, being imposed by violence, may transform men's lives. Christianity is a new and higher conception of life. A new conception of life cannot be imposed on men; it can only be freely assimilated. And it can only be freely assimilated in two ways: one spiritual and internal, the other experimental and external.

Some people--a minority--by a kind of prophetic instinct divine the truth of the doctrine, surrender themselves to it and adopt it. Others--the majority--only through a long course of mistakes, experiments, and suffering are brought to recognize the truth of the doctrine and the necessity of adopting it.

And by this experimental external method the majority of Christian men have now been brought to this necessity of assimilating the doctrine. One sometimes wonders what necessitated the corruption of Christianity which is now the greatest obstacle to its acceptance in its true significance.

If Christianity had been presented to men in its true, uncorrupted form, it would not have been accepted by the majority, who would have been as untouched by it as the nations of Asia are now. The peoples who accepted it in its corrupt form were subjected to its slow but certain influence, and by a long course of errors and experiments and their resultant sufferings have now been brought to the necessity of assimilating it in its true significance.

The corruption of Christianity and its acceptance in its corrupt form by the majority of men was as necessary as it is that the seed should remain hidden for a certain time in the earth in order to germinate.

Christianity is at once a doctrine of truth and a prophecy. Eighteen centuries ago Christianity revealed to men the truth in which they ought to live, and at the same time foretold what human life would become if men would not live by it but continued to live by their previous principles, and what it would become if they accepted the Christian doctrine and carried it out in their lives.

Laying down in the Sermon on the Mount the principles by which to guide men's lives, Christ said: "Whosoever heareth these sayings of mine, and doeth them, I will liken him unto a wise man, who built his house upon a rock; and the rain descended, and the floods came, and the winds blew, and beat upon that house; and it fell not, for it was founded upon a rock. And everyone that heareth these sayings, and doeth them not, shall be likened unto a foolish man, who built his house upon the sand; and the rain descended, and the floods came, and the winds blew, and beat upon that house; and it fell: and great was the fall of it" (Matt. vii. 24-27).

And now after eighteen centuries the prophecy has been fulfilled. Not having followed Christ's teaching generally and its application to social life in non-resistance to evil, men have been brought in spite of themselves to the inevitable destruction foretold by Christ for those who do not fulfill his teaching.

People often think the question of non-resistance to evil by force is a theoretical one, which can be neglected. Yet this question is presented by life itself to all men, and calls for some answer from every thinking man. Ever since Christianity has been outwardly professed, this question is for men in their social life like the question which presents itself to a traveler when the road on which he has been journeying divides into two branches. He must go on and he cannot say: I will not think about it, but will go on just as I did before. There was one road, now there are two, and he must make his choice.

In the same way since Christ's teaching has been known by men they cannot say: I will live as before and will not decide the question of resistance or non-resistance to evil by force. At every new struggle that arises one must inevitably decide; am I, or am I not, to resist by force what I regard as evil.

The question of resistance or non-resistance to evil arose when the first conflict between men took place, since every conflict is nothing else than resistance by force to what each of the combatants regards as evil. But before Christ, men did not see that resistance by force to what each regards as evil, simply because one thinks evil what the other thinks good, is only one of the methods of settling the dispute, and that there is another method, that of not resisting evil by force at all.

Before Christ's teaching, it seemed to men that the one only means of settling a dispute was by resistance to evil by force. And they acted accordingly, each of the combatants trying to convince himself and others that what each respectively regards as evil, is actually, absolutely evil.

And to do this from the earliest time men have devised definitions of evil and tried to make them binding on everyone. And such definitions of evil sometimes took the form of laws, supposed to have been received by supernatural means, sometimes of the commands of rulers or assemblies to whom infallibility was attributed. Men resorted to violence against others, and convinced themselves and others that they were directing their violence against evil recognized as such by all.

This means was employed from the earliest times, especially by those who had gained possession of authority, and for a long while its irrationality was not detected.

But the longer men lived in the world and the more complex their relations became, the more evident it was that to resist by force what each regarded as evil was irrational, that conflict was in no way lessened thereby, and that no human definitions can succeed in making what some regard as evil be accepted as such by others.

Already at the time Christianity arose, it was evident to a great number of people in the Roman Empire where it arose, that what was regarded as evil by Nero and Caligula could not be regarded as evil by others. Even at that time men had begun to understand that human laws, though given out for divine laws, were compiled by men, and cannot be infallible, whatever the external majesty with which they are invested, and that erring men are not rendered infallible by assembling together and calling themselves a senate or any other name. Even at that time this was felt and understood by many. And it was then that Christ preached his doctrine, which consisted not only of the prohibition of resistance to evil by force, but gave a new conception of life and a means of putting an end to conflict between all men, not by making it the duty of one section only of mankind to submit without conflict to what is prescribed to them by certain authorities, but by making it the duty of all--and consequently of those in authority--not to resort to force against anyone in any circumstances.

This doctrine was accepted at the time by only a very small number of disciples. The majority of men, especially all who were in power, even after the nominal acceptance of Christianity, continued to maintain for themselves the principle of resistance by force to what they regarded as evil. So it was under the Roman and Byzantine emperors, and so it continued to be later.

The insufficiency of the principle of the authoritative definition of evil and resistance to it by force, evident as it was in the early ages of Christianity, becomes still more obvious through the division of the Roman Empire into many states of equal authority, through their hostilities and the internal conflicts that broke out within them.

But men were not ready to accept the solution given by Christ, and the old definitions of evil, which ought to be resisted, continued to be laid down by means of making laws binding on all and enforced by forcible means. The authority who decided what ought to be regarded as evil and resisted by force was at one time the Pope, at another an emperor or king, an elective assembly or a whole nation. But both within and without the state there were always men to be found who did not accept as binding on themselves the laws given out as the decrees of a god, or made by men invested with a sacred character, or the institutions supposed to represent the will of the nation; and there were men who thought good what the existing authorities regarded as bad, and who struggled against the authorities with the same violence as was employed against them.

The men invested with religious authority regarded as evil what the men and institutions invested with temporal authority regarded as good and vice versa, and the struggle grew more and more intense. And the longer men used violence as the means of settling their disputes, the more obvious it became that it was an unsuitable means, since there could be no external authority able to define evil recognized by all.

Things went on like this for eighteen centuries, and at last reached the present position in which it is absolutely obvious that there is, and can be, no external definition of evil binding upon all. Men have come to the point of ceasing to believe in the possibility or even desirability of finding and establishing such a general definition. It has come to men in power ceasing to attempt to prove that what they regard as evil is evil, and simply declaring that they regard as evil what they don't like, while their subjects no longer obey them because they accept the definition of evil laid down by them, but simply obey because they cannot help themselves. It was not because it was a good thing, necessary and beneficial to men, and the contrary course would have been an evil, but simply because it was the will of those in power that Nice was incorporated into France, and Lorraine into

Germany, and Bohemia into Austria, and that Poland was divided, and Ireland and India ruled by the English government, and that the Chinese are attacked and the Africans slaughtered, and the Chinese prevented from immigrating by the Americans, and the Jews persecuted by the Russians, and that landowners appropriate lands they do not cultivate and capitalists enjoy the fruits of the labor of others. It has come to the present state of things; one set of men commit acts of violence no longer on the pretext of resistance to evil, but simply for their profit or their caprice, and another set submit to violence, not because they suppose, as was supposed in former times, that this violence was practised upon them for the sake of securing them from evil, but simply because they cannot avoid it.

If the Roman, or the man of mediaeval times, or the average Russian of fifty years ago, as I remember him, was convinced without a shade of doubt that the violence of authority was indispensable to preserve him from evil; that taxes, dues, serfage, prisons, scourging, knouts, executions, the army and war were what ought to be--we know now that one can seldom find a man who believes that all these means of violence preserve anyone from any evil whatever, and indeed does not clearly perceive that most of these acts of violence to which he is exposed, and in which he has some share, are in themselves a great and useless evil.

There is no one to-day who does not see the uselessness and injustice of collecting taxes from the toiling masses to enrich idle officials; or the senselessness of inflicting punishments on weak or depraved persons in the shape of transportation from one place to another, or of imprisonment in a fortress where, living in security and indolence, they only become weaker and more depraved; or the worse than uselessness and injustice, the positive insanity and barbarity of preparations for war and of wars, causing devastation and ruin, and having no kind of justification. Yet these forms of violence continue and are supported by the very people who see their uselessness, injustice, and cruelty, and suffer from them. If fifty years ago the idle rich man and the illiterate laborer were both alike convinced that their state of everlasting holiday for one and everlasting toil for the other was ordained by God himself, we know very well that nowadays, thanks to the growth of population and the diffusion of books and education, it would be hard to find in Europe or even in Russia, either among rich or poor, a man to whom in one shape or another a doubt as to the justice of this state of things had never presented itself. The rich know that they are guilty in the very fact of being rich, and try to expiate their guilt by sacrifices to art and science, as of old they expiated their sins by sacrifices to the Church. And even the larger half of the working people openly declare that the existing order is iniquitous and bound to be destroyed or reformed. One set of religious people of whom there are millions in Russia, the so-called sectaries, consider the existing social order as unjust and to be destroyed on the ground of the Gospel teaching taken in its true sense. Others regard it as unjust on the ground of the socialistic, communistic, or anarchistic theories, which are springing up in the lower strata of the working people. Violence no longer rests on the belief in its utility, but only on the fact of its having existed so long, and being organized by the ruling classes who profit by it, so that those who are under their authority cannot extricate themselves from it. The governments of our day--all of them, the most despotic and the liberal alike--have become what Herzen so well called "Ghenghis Khan with the telegraph;" that is to say, organizations of violence based on no principle but the grossest tyranny, and at the same time taking advantage of all the means invented by science for the peaceful collective social activity of free and equal men, used by them to enslave and oppress their fellows.

Governments and the ruling classes no longer take their stand on right or even on the semblance of justice, but on a skillful organization carried to such a point of perfection by the aid of science that everyone is caught in the circle of violence and has no chance of escaping from it. This circle is made up now of four methods of working upon men, joined together like the limes of a chain ring.

The first and oldest method is intimidation. This consists in representing the existing state organization--whatever it may be, free republic or the most savage despotism--as something sacred and immutable, and therefore following any efforts to alter it with the cruellest punishments. This method is in use now--as it has been from olden times--wherever there is a government: in

Russia against the so-called Nihilists, in America against Anarchists, in France against Imperialists, Legitimists, Communards, and Anarchists.

Railways, telegraphs, telephones, photographs, and the great perfection of the means of getting rid of men for years, without killing them, by solitary confinement, where, hidden from the world, they perish and are forgotten, and the many other modern inventions employed by government, give such power that when once authority has come into certain hands, the police, open and secret, the administration and prosecutors, jailers and executioners of all kinds, do their work so zealously that there is no chance of overturning the government, however cruel and senseless it may be.

The second method is corruption. It consists in plundering the industrious working people of their wealth by means of taxes and distributing it in satisfying the greed of officials, who are bound in return to support and keep up the oppression of the people. These bought officials, from the highest ministers to the poorest copying clerks, make up an unbroken network of men bound together by the same interest--that of living at the expense of the people. They become the richer the more submissively they carry out the will of the government; and at all times and places, sticking at nothing, in all departments support by word and deed the violence of government, on which their own prosperity also rests.

The third method is what I can only describe as hypnotizing the people. This consists in checking the moral development of men, and by various suggestions keeping them back in the ideal of life, outgrown by mankind at large, on which the power of government rests. This hypnotizing process is organized at the present in the most complex manner, and starting from their earliest childhood, continues to act on men till the day of their death. It begins in their earliest years in the compulsory schools, created for this purpose, in which the children have instilled into them the ideas of life of their ancestors, which are in direct antagonism with the conscience of the modern world. In countries where there is a state religion, they teach the children the senseless blasphemies of the Church catechisms, together with the duty of obedience to their superiors. In republican states they teach them the savage superstition of patriotism and the same pretended obedience to the governing authorities.

The process is kept up during later years by the encouragement of religious and patriotic superstitions.

The religious superstition is encouraged by establishing, with money taken from the people, temples, processions, memorials, and festivals, which, aided by painting, architecture, music, and incense, intoxicate the people, and above all by the support of the clergy, whose duty consists in brutalizing the people and keeping them in a permanent state of stupefaction by their teaching, the solemnity of their services, their sermons, and their interference in private life--at births, deaths, and marriages. The patriotic superstition is encouraged by the creation, with money taken from the people, of national fêtes, spectacles, monuments, and festivals to dispose men to attach importance to their own nation, and to the aggrandizement of the state and its rulers, and to feel antagonism and even hatred for other nations. With these objects under despotic governments there is direct prohibition against printing and disseminating books to enlighten the people, and everyone who might rouse the people from their lethargy is exiled or imprisoned. Moreover, under every government without exception everything is kept back that might emancipate and everything encouraged that tends to corrupt the people, such as literary works tending to keep them in the barbarism of religious and patriotic superstition, all kinds of sensual amusements, spectacles, circuses, theaters, and even the physical means of inducing stupefaction, as tobacco and alcohol, which form the principal source of revenue of states. Even prostitution is encouraged, and not only recognized, but even organized by the government in the majority of states. So much for the third method.

The fourth method consists in selecting from all the men who have been stupefied and enslaved by the three former methods a certain number, exposing them to special and intensified means of stupefaction and brutalization, and so making them into a passive instrument for carrying out all the cruelties and brutalities needed by the government. This result is attained by taking them at the youthful age when men have not had time to form clear and definite principles of morals, and removing them from all natural and human conditions of life, home, family and kindred, and useful labor. They are shut up together in barracks, dressed in special clothes, and worked upon by cries, drums, music, and shining objects to go through certain daily actions invented for this purpose, and by this means are brought into an hypnotic condition in which they cease to be men and become mere senseless machines, submissive to the hypnotizer. These physically vigorous young men (in these days of universal conscription, all young men), hypnotized, armed with murderous weapons, always obedient to the governing authorities and ready for any act of violence at their command, constitute the fourth and principal method of enslaving men.

By this method the circle of violence is completed.

Intimidation, corruption, and hypnotizing bring people into a condition in which they are willing to be soldiers; the soldiers give the power of punishing and plundering them (and purchasing officials with the spoils), and hypnotizing them and converting them in time into these same soldiers again.

The circle is complete, and there is no chance of breaking through it by force.

Some persons maintain that freedom from violence, or at least a great diminution of it, may be gained by the oppressed forcibly overturning the oppressive government and replacing it by a new one under which such violence and oppression will be unnecessary, but they deceive themselves and others, and their efforts do not better the position of the oppressed, but only make it worse. Their conduct only tends to increase the despotism of government. Their efforts only afford a plausible pretext for government to strengthen their power.

Even if we admit that under a combination of circumstances specially unfavorable for the government, as in France in 1870, any government might be forcibly overturned and the power transferred to other hands, the new authority would rarely be less oppressive than the old one; on the contrary, always having to defend itself against its dispossessed and exasperated enemies, it would be more despotic and cruel, as has always been the rule in all revolutions.

While socialists and communists regard the individualistic, capitalistic organization of society as an evil, and the anarchists regard as an evil all government whatever, there are royalists, conservatives, and capitalists who consider any socialistic or communistic organization or anarchy as an evil, and all these parties have no means other than violence to bring men to agreement. Whichever of these parties were successful in bringing their schemes to pass, must resort to support its authority to all the existing methods of violence, and even invent new ones.

The oppressed would be another set of people, and coercion would take some new form; but the violence and oppression would be unchanged or even more cruel, since hatred would be intensified by the struggle, and new forms of oppression would have been devised. So it has always been after all revolutions and all attempts at revolution, all conspiracies, and all violent changes of government. Every conflict only strengthens the means of oppression in the hands of those who happen at a given moment to be in power.

The position of our Christian society, and especially the ideals most current in it, prove this in a strikingly convincing way.

There remains now only one sphere of human life not encroached upon by government authority--that is the domestic, economic sphere, the sphere of private life and labor. And even this is now--thanks to the efforts of communists and socialists--being gradually encroached upon by government, so that labor and recreation, dwellings, dress, and food will gradually, if the hopes of the reformers are successful, be prescribed and regulated by government.

The slow progress of eighteen centuries has brought the Christian nations again to the necessity of deciding the question they have evaded--the question of the acceptance or non-acceptance of Christ's teaching, and the question following upon it in social life of resistance or non-resistance to evil by force. But there is this difference, that whereas formerly men could accept or refuse to accept the solution given by Christ, now that solution cannot be avoided, since it alone can save men from the slavery in which they are caught like a net.

But it is not only the misery of the position which makes this inevitable.

While the pagan organization has been proved more and more false, the truth of the Christian religion has been growing more and more evident.

Not in vain have the best men of Christian humanity, who apprehended the truth by spiritual intuition, for eighteen centuries testified to it in spite of every menace, every privation, and every suffering. By their martyrdom they passed on the truth to the masses, and impressed it on their hearts.

Christianity has penetrated into the consciousness of humanity, not only negatively by the demonstration of the impossibility of continuing in the pagan life, but also through its simplification, its increased clearness and freedom from the superstitions intermingled with it, and its diffusion through all classes of the population.

Eighteen centuries of Christianity have not passed without an effect even on those who accepted it only externally. These eighteen centuries have brought men so far that even while they continue to live the pagan life which is no longer consistent with the development of humanity, they not only see clearly all the wretchedness of their position, but in the depths of their souls they believe (they can only live through this belief) that the only salvation from this position is to be found in fulfilling the Christian doctrine in its true significance. As to the time and manner of salvation, opinions are divided according to the intellectual development and the prejudices of each society. But every man of the modern world recognizes that our salvation lies in fulfilling the law of Christ. Some believers in the supernatural character of Christianity hold that salvation will come when all men are brought to believe in Christ, whose second coming is at hand. Other believers in supernatural Christianity hold that salvation will come through the Church, which will draw all men into its fold, train them in the Christian virtues, and transform their life. A third section, who do not admit the divinity of Christ, hold that the salvation of mankind will be brought about by slow and gradual progress, through which the pagan principles of our existence will be replaced by the principles of liberty, equality, and fraternity--that is, by Christian principles. A fourth section, who believe in the social revolution, hold that salvation will come when through a violent revolution men are forced into community of property, abolition of government, and collective instead of individual industry--that is to say, the realization of one side of the Christian doctrine. In one way or another all men of our day in their inner consciousness condemn the existing effete pagan order, and admit, often unconsciously and while regarding themselves as hostile to Christianity, that our salvation is only to be found in the application of the Christian doctrine, or parts of it, in its true significance to our daily life.

Christianity cannot, as its Founder said, be realized by the majority of men all at once; it must grow like a huge tree from a tiny seed. And so it has grown, and now has reached its full development, not yet in actual life, but in the conscience of men of to-day.

Now not only the minority, who have always comprehended Christianity by spiritual intuition, but all the vast majority who seem so far from it in their social existence recognize its true significance.

Look at individual men in their private life, listen to their standards of conduct in their judgment of one another; hear not only their public utterances, but the counsels given by parents and guardians to the young in their charge; and you will see that, far as their social life based on violence may be from realizing Christian truth, in their private life what is considered good by all without exception is nothing but the Christian virtues; what is considered as bad is nothing but the antichristian vices. Those who consecrate their lives self-sacrificingly to the service of humanity are regarded as the best men. The selfish, who make use of the misfortunes of others for their own advantage, are regarded as the worst of men.

Though some non-Christian ideals, such as strength, courage, and wealth, are still worshiped by a few who have not been penetrated by the Christian spirit, these ideals are out of date and are abandoned, if not by all, at least by all those regarded as the best people. There are no ideals, other than the Christian ideals, which are accepted by all and regarded as binding on all.

The position of our Christian humanity, if you look at it from the outside with all its cruelty and degradation of men, is terrible indeed. But if one looks at it within, in its inner consciousness, the spectacle it presents is absolutely different.

All the evil of our life seems to exist only because it has been so for so long; those who do the evil have not had time yet to learn how to act otherwise, though they do not want to act as they do.

All the evil seems to exist through some cause independent of the conscience of men.

Strange and contradictory as it seems, all men of the present day hate the very social order they are themselves supporting.

I think it is Max Müller who describes the amazement of an Indian convert to Christianity, who after absorbing the essence of the Christian doctrine came to Europe and saw the actual life of Christians. He could not recover from his astonishment at the complete contrast between the reality and what he had expected to find among Christian nations. If we feel no astonishment at the contrast between our convictions and our conduct, that is because the influences, tending to obscure the contrast, produce an effect upon us too. We need only look at our life from the point of view of that Indian, who understood Christianity in its true significance, without any compromises or concessions, we need but look at the savage brutalities of which our life is full, to be appalled at the contradictions in the midst of which we live often without observing them.

We need only recall the preparations for war, the mitrailleuses, the silver-gilt bullets, the torpedoes, and--the Red Cross; the solitary prison cells, the experiments of execution by electricity--and the care of the hygienic welfare of prisoners; the philanthropy of the rich, and their life, which produces the poor they are benefiting.

And these inconsistencies are not, as it might seem, because men pretend to be Christians while they are really pagans, but because of something lacking in men, or some kind of force hindering them from being what they already feel themselves to be in their consciousness, and what they genuinely wish to be. Men of the present day do not merely pretend to hate oppression, inequality, class distinction, and every kind of cruelty to animals as well as human beings. They genuinely detest all this, but they do not know how to put a stop to it, or perhaps cannot decide to give up what preserves it all, and seems to them necessary.

Indeed, ask every man separately whether he thinks it laudable and worthy of a man of this age to hold a position from which he receives a salary disproportionate to his work; to take from the people--often in poverty--taxes to be spent on constructing cannon, torpedoes, and other instruments of butchery, so as to make war on people with whom we wish to be at peace, and who feel the same wish in regard to us; or to receive a salary for devoting one's whole life to constructing these instruments of butchery, or to preparing oneself and others for the work of murder. And ask him whether it is laudable and worthy of a man, and suitable for a Christian, to employ himself, for a salary, in seizing wretched, misguided, often illiterate and drunken, creatures because they appropriate the property of others--on a much smaller scale than we do--or because they kill men in a different fashion from that in which we undertake to do it--and shutting them in prison for it, ill treating them and killing them; and whether it is laudable and worthy of a man and a Christian to preach for a salary to the people not Christianity, but superstitions which one knows to be stupid and pernicious; and whether it is laudable and worthy of a man to rob his neighbor for his gratification of what he wants to satisfy his simplest needs, as the great landowners do; or to force him to exhausting labor beyond his strength to augment one's wealth, as do factory owners and manufacturers; or to profit by the poverty of men to increase one's gains, as merchants do. And everyone taken separately, especially if one's remarks are directed at someone else, not himself, will answer, No! And yet the very man who sees all the baseness of those actions, of his own free will, uncoerced by anyone, often even for no pecuniary profit, but only from childish vanity, for a china cross, a scrap of ribbon, a bit of fringe he is allowed to wear, will enter military service, become a magistrate or justice of the peace, commissioner, archbishop, or beadle, though in fulfilling these offices he must commit acts the baseness and shamefulness of which he cannot fail to recognize.

I know that many of these men will confidently try to prove that they have reasons for regarding their position as legitimate and quite indispensable. They will say in their defense that authority is given by God, that the functions of the state are indispensable for the welfare of humanity, that property is not opposed to Christianity, that the rich young man was only commanded to sell all he had and give to the poor if he wished to be perfect, that the existing distribution of property and our commercial system must always remain as they are, and are to the advantage of all, and so on. But, however much they try to deceive themselves and others, they all know that what they are doing is opposed to all the beliefs which they profess, and in the depths of their souls, when they are left alone with their conscience, they are ashamed and miserable at the recollection of it, especially if the baseness of their action has been pointed out to them. A man of the present day, whether he believes in the divinity of Christ or not, cannot fail to see that to assist in the capacity of tzar, minister, governor, or commissioner in taking from a poor family its last cow for taxes to be spent on cannons, or on the pay and pensions of idle officials, who live in luxury and are worse than useless; or in putting into prison some man we have ourselves corrupted, and throwing his family on the streets; or in plundering and butchering in war; or in inculcating savage and idolatrous superstitious in the place of the law of

Christ; or in impounding the cow found on one's land, though it belongs to a man who has no land; or to cheat the workman in a factory, by imposing fines for accidentally spoiled articles; or making a poor man pay double the value for anything simply because he is in the direst poverty;--not a man of the present day can fail to know that all these actions are base and disgraceful, and that they need not do them. They all know it. They know that what they are doing is wrong, and would not do it for anything in the world if they had the power of resisting the forces which shut their eyes to the criminality of their actions and impel them to commit them.

In nothing is the pitch of inconsistency modern life has attained to so evident as in universal conscription, which is the last resource and the final expression of violence.

Indeed, it is only because this state of universal armament has been brought about gradually and imperceptibly, and because governments have exerted, in maintaining it, every resource of intimidation, corruption, brutalization, and violence, that we do not see its flagrant inconsistency with the Christian ideas and sentiments by which the modern world is permeated.

We are so accustomed to the inconsistency that we do not see all the hideous folly and immorality of men voluntarily choosing the profession of butchery as though it were an honorable career, of poor wretches submitting to conscription, or in countries where compulsory service has not been introduced, of people voluntarily abandoning a life of industry to recruit soldiers and train them as murderers. We know that all of these men are either Christians, or profess humane and liberal principles, and they know that they thus become partly responsible--through universal conscription, personally responsible--for the most insane, aimless, and brutal murders. And yet they all do it.

More than that, in Germany, where compulsory service first originated, Caprivi has given expression to what had been hitherto so assiduously concealed--that is, that the men that the soldiers will have to kill are not foreigners alone, but their own countrymen, the very working people from whom they themselves are taken. And this admission has not opened people's eyes, has not horrified them! They still go like sheep to the slaughter, and submit to everything required of them.

And that is not all: the Emperor of Germany has lately shown still more clearly the duties of the army, by thanking and rewarding a soldier for killing a defenseless citizen who made his approach incautiously. By rewarding an action always regarded as base and cowardly even by men on the lowest level of morality, William has shown that a soldier's chief duty--the one most appreciated by the authorities--is that of executioner; and not a professional executioner who kills only condemned criminals, but one ready to butcher any innocent man at the word of command.

And even that is not all. In 1892, the same William, the ENFANT TERRIBLE of state authority, who says plainly what other people only think, in addressing some soldiers gave public utterance to the following speech, which was reported next day in thousands of newspapers: "Conscripts!" he said, "you have sworn fidelity to ME before the altar and the minister of God! You are still too young to understand all the importance of what has been said here; let your care before all things be to obey the orders and instructions given you. You have sworn fidelity TO ME, lads of my guard; THAT MEANS THAT YOU ARE NOW MY SOLDIERS, that YOU HAVE GIVEN YOURSELVES TO ME BODY AND SOUL. For you there is now but one enemy, MY enemy. IN THESE DAYS OF SOCIALISTIC SEDITION IT MAY COME TO PASS THAT I COMMAND YOU TO FIRE ON YOUR OWN KINDRED, YOUR BROTHERS, EVEN YOUR OWN FATHERS AND MOTHERS--WHICH GOD FORBID!--even then you are bound to obey my orders without hesitation."

This man expresses what all sensible rulers think, but studiously conceal. He says openly that the soldiers are in HIS service, at HIS disposal, and must be ready for HIS advantage to murder even their brothers and fathers.

In the most brutal words he frankly exposes all the horrors and criminality for which men prepare themselves in entering the army, and the depths of ignominy to which they fall in promising obedience. Like a bold hypnotizer, he tests the degree of insensibility of the hypnotized subject. He touches his skin with a red-hot iron; the skin smokes and scorches, but the sleeper does not awake.

This miserable man, imbecile and drunk with power, outrages in this utterance everything that can be sacred for a man of the modern world. And yet all the Christians, liberals, and cultivated people, far from resenting this outrage, did not even observe it.

The last, the most extreme test is put before men in its coarsest form. And they do not seem even to notice that it is a test, that there is any choice about it. They seem to think there is no course open but slavish submission. One would have thought these insane words, which outrage everything a man of the present day holds sacred, must rouse indignation. But there has been nothing of the kind.

All the young men through the whole of Europe are exposed year after year to this test, and with very few exceptions they renounce all that a man can hold sacred, all express their readiness to kill their brothers, even their fathers, at the bidding of the first crazy creature dressed up in a livery with red and gold trimming, and only wait to be told where and when they are to kill. And they actually are ready.

Every savage has something he holds sacred, something for which he is ready to suffer, something he will not consent to do. But what is it that is sacred to the civilized man of to-day? They say to him: "You must become my slave, and this slavery may force you to kill even your own father;" and he, often very well educated, trained in all the sciences at the university, quietly puts his head under the yoke. They dress him up in a clown's costume, and order him to cut capers, turn and twist and bow, and kill--he does it all submissively. And when they let him go, he seems to shake himself and go back to his former life, and he continues to discourse upon the dignity of man, liberty, equality, and fraternity as before.

"Yes, but what is one to do?" people often ask in genuine perplexity. "If everyone would stand out it would be something, but by myself, I shall only suffer without doing any good to anyone."

And that is true. A man with the social conception of life cannot resist. The aim of his life is his personal welfare. It is better for his personal welfare for him to submit, and he submits.

Whatever they do to him, however they torture or humiliate him, he will submit, for, alone, he can do nothing; he has no principle for the sake of which he could resist violence alone. And those who control them never allow them to unite together. It is often said that the invention of terrible weapons of destruction will put an end to war. That is an error. As the means of extermination are improved, the means of reducing men who hold the state conception of life to submission can be improved to correspond. They may slaughter them by thousands, by millions, they may tear them to pieces, still they will march to war like senseless cattle. Some will want beating to make them move, others will be proud to go if they are allowed to wear a scrap of ribbon or gold lace.

And of this mass of men so brutalized as to be ready to promise to kill their own parents, the social reformers--conservatives, liberals, socialists, and anarchists--propose to form a rational and moral society. What sort of moral and rational society can be formed out of such elements? With warped and rotten planks you cannot build a house, however you put them together. And to form a rational moral society of such men is just as impossible a task. They can be formed into nothing but a herd of cattle, driven by the shouts and whips of the herdsmen. As indeed they are.

So, then, we have on one side men calling themselves Christians, and professing the principles of liberty, equality, and fraternity, and along with that ready, in the name of liberty, to submit to the most slavish degradation; in the name of equality, to accept the crudest, most senseless division of men by externals merely into higher and lower classes, allies and enemies; and, in the name of fraternity, ready to murder their brothers [see footnote].

[Footnote: The fact that among certain nations, as the English and the American, military service is not compulsory (though already one hears there are some who advocate that it should be made so) does not affect the servility of the citizens to the government in principle. Here we have each to go and kill or be killed, there they have each to give the fruit of their toil to pay for the recruiting and training of soldiers.]

The contradiction between life and conscience and the misery resulting from it have reached the extreme limit and can go no further. The state organization of life based on violence, the aim of which was the security of personal, family, and social welfare, has come to the point of renouncing the very objects for which it was founded--it has reduced men to absolute renunciation and loss of the welfare it was to secure.

The first half of the prophecy has been fulfilled in the generation of men who have not accepted Christ's teaching, Their descendants have been brought now to the absolute necessity of patting the truth of the second half to the test of experience.

CHAPTER IX.

THE ACCEPTANCE OF THE CHRISTIAN CONCEPTION OF LIFE WILL EMANCIPATE MEN FROM THE MISERIES OF OUR PAGAN LIFE.

The External Life of Christian Peoples Remains Pagan Though they are Penetrated by Christian Consciousness--The Way Out of this Contradiction is by the Acceptance of the Christian Theory of Life--Only Through Christianity is Every Man Free, and Emancipated of All Human Authority--This Emancipation can be Effected by no Change in External Conditions of Life, but Only by a Change in the Conception of Life--The Christian Ideal of Life Requires Renunciation of all Violence, and in Emancipating the Man who Accepts it, Emancipates the Whole World from All External Authorities--The Way Out of the Present Apparently Hopeless Position is for Every Man who is Capable of Assimilating the Christian Conception of Life, to Accept it and Live in Accordance with it--But Men Consider this Way too Slow, and Look for Deliverance Through Changes in Material Conditions of Life Aided by Government--That Will Lead to No Improvement, as it is simply Increasing the Evil under which Men are Suffering--A Striking Instance of this is the Submission to Compulsory Military Service, which it would be More Advantageous for Every Man to Refuse than to Submit to--The Emancipation of Men Can Only be Brought About by each Individual Emancipating Himself, and the Examples of this Self-emancipation which are already Appearing Threaten the Destruction of Governmental Authority--Refusal to Comply with the Unchristian Demands of Government Undermines the Authority of the State and

Emancipates Men--And therefore Cases of such Non-compliance are Regarded with more Dread by State Authorities than any Conspiracies or Acts of Violence--Examples of Non-compliance in Russia, in Regard to Oath of Allegiance, Payment of Taxes, Passports, Police Duties, and Military Service--Examples of such Non-compliance in other States--Governments do not Know how to Treat Men who Refuse to Comply with their Demands on Christian Grounds--Such People, without Striking a Blow, Undermine the very Basis of Government from Within--To Punish them is Equivalent to Openly Renouncing Christianity, and Assisting in Diffusing the Very Principle by which these Men justify their Non-compliance--So Governments are in a Helpless Position--Men who Maintain the Uselessness of Personal Independence, only Retard the Dissolution of the Present State Organization Based on Force.

The position of the Christian peoples in our days has remained just as cruel as it was in the times of paganism. In many respects, especially in the oppression of the masses, it has become even more cruel than it was in the days of paganism.

But between the condition of men in ancient times and their condition in our days there is just the difference that we see in the world of vegetation between the last days of autumn and the first days of spring. In the autumn the external lifelessness in nature corresponds with its inward condition of death, while in the spring the external lifelessness is in sharp contrast with the internal state of reviving and passing into new forms of life.

In the same way the similarity between the ancient heathen life and the life of to-day is merely external: the inward condition of men in the times of heathenism was absolutely different from their inward condition at the present time.

Then the outward condition of cruelty and of slavery was in complete harmony with the inner conscience of men, and every step in advance intensified this harmony; now the outward condition of cruelty and of slavery is completely contradictory to the Christian consciousness of men, and every step in advance only intensifies this contradiction.

Humanity is passing through seemingly unnecessary, fruitless agonies. It is passing through something like the throes of birth. Everything is ready for the new life, but still the new life does not come.

There seems no way out of the position. And there would be none, except that a man (and thereby all men) is gifted with the power of forming a different, higher theory of life, which at once frees him from all the bonds by which he seems indissolubly fettered.

And such a theory is the Christian view of life made known to mankind eighteen hundred years ago.

A man need only make this theory of life his own, for the fetters which seemed so indissolubly forged upon him to drop off of themselves, and for him to feel himself absolutely free, just as a bird would feel itself free in a fenced-in place directly it tools to its wings.

People talk about the liberty of the Christian Church, about giving or not giving freedom to Christians. Underlying all these ideas and expressions there is some strange misconception. Freedom cannot be bestowed on or taken from a Christian or Christians. Freedom is an inalienable possession of the Christian.

If we talk of bestowing freedom on Christians or withholding it from them, we are obviously talking not of real Christians but of people who only call themselves Christians. A Christian cannot fail to be free, because the attainment of the aim he sets before himself cannot be prevented or even hindered by anyone or anything.

Let a man only understand his life as Christianity teaches him to understand it, let him understand, that is, that his life belongs not to him--not to his own individuality, nor to his family, nor to the state--but to him who has sent him into the world, and let him once understand that he must therefore fulfill not the law of his own individuality, nor his family, nor of the state, but the infinite law of him from whom he has come; and he will not only feel himself absolutely free from every human power, but will even cease to regard such power as at all able to hamper anyone.

Let a man but realize that the aim of his life is the fulfillment of God's law, and that law will replace all other laws for him, and he will give it his sole allegiance, so that by that very allegiance every human law will lose all binding and controlling power in his eyes.

The Christian is independent of every human authority by the fact that he regards the divine law of love, implanted in the soul of every man, and brought before his consciousness by Christ, as the sole guide of his life and other men's also.

The Christian may be subjected to external violence, he may be deprived of bodily freedom, he may be in bondage to his passions (he who commits sin is the slave of sin), but he cannot be in bondage in the sense of being forced by any danger or by any threat of external harm to perform an act which is against his conscience.

He cannot be compelled to do this, because the deprivations and sufferings which form such a powerful weapon against men of the state conception of life, have not the least power to compel him.

Deprivations and sufferings take from them the happiness for which they live; but far from disturbing the happiness of the Christian, which consists in the consciousness of fulfilling the will of God, they may even intensify it, when they are inflicted on him for fulfilling his will.

And therefore the Christian, who is subject only to the inner divine law, not only cannot carry out the enactments of the external law, when they are not in agreement with the divine law of love which he acknowledges (as is usually the case with state obligations), he cannot even recognize the duty of obedience to anyone or anything whatever, he cannot recognize the duty of what is called allegiance.

For a Christian the oath of allegiance to any government whatever --the very act which is regarded as the foundation of the existence of a state--is a direct renunciation of Christianity. For the man who promises unconditional obedience in the future to laws, made or to be made, by that very promise is in the most, positive manner renouncing Christianity, which means obeying in every circumstance of life only the divine law of love he recognizes within him.

Under the pagan conception of life it was possible to carry out the will of the temporal authorities, without infringing the law of God expressed in circumcisions, Sabbaths, fixed times of prayer, abstention from certain kinds of food, and so on. The one law was not opposed to the other. But that is just the distinction between the Christian religion and heathen religion. Christianity does not require of a man certain definite negative acts, but puts him in a new, different relation to men, from which may result the most diverse acts, which cannot be defined beforehand. And therefore the Christian not only cannot promise to obey the will of any other man, without knowing what will be required by that will; he not only cannot obey the changing laws of man, but he cannot even promise to do anything definite at a certain time, or to abstain from doing anything for a certain time. For he cannot know what at any time will be required of him by that Christian law of love, obedience to which constitutes the meaning of life for him. The Christian, in promising unconditional fulfillment of the laws of men in the future, would show plainly by that promise that the inner law of God does not constitute for him the sole law of his life.

For a Christian to promise obedience to men, or the laws of men, is just as though a workman bound to one employer should also promise to carry out every order that might be given him by outsiders. One cannot serve two masters.

The Christian is independent of human authority, because he acknowledges God's authority alone. His law, revealed by Christ, he recognizes in himself, and voluntarily obeys it.

And this independence is gained, not by means of strife, not by the destruction of existing forms of life, but only by a change in the interpretation of life. This independence results first from the Christian recognizing the law of love, revealed to him by his teacher, as perfectly sufficient for all human relations, and therefore he regards every use of force as unnecessary and unlawful; and secondly, from the fact that those deprivations and sufferings, or threats of deprivations and sufferings (which reduce the man of the social conception of life to the necessity of obeying) to the Christian from his different conception of life, present themselves merely as the inevitable conditions of existence. And these conditions, without striving against them by force, he patiently endures, like sickness, hunger, and every other hardship, but they cannot serve him as a guide for his actions. The only guide for the Christian's actions is to be found in the divine principle living within him, which cannot be checked or governed by anything.

The Christian acts according to the words of the prophecy applied to his teacher: "He shall not strive, nor cry; neither shall any man hear his voice in the streets. A bruised reed shall he not break, and smoking flax shall he not quench, till he send forth judgment unto victory." (Matt. xii. 19, 20.)

The Christian will not dispute with anyone, nor attack anyone, nor use violence against anyone. On the contrary, he will bear violence without opposing it. But by this very attitude to violence, he will not only himself be free, but will free the whole world from all external power.

"Ye shall know the truth, and the truth shall make you free." If there were any doubt of Christianity being the truth, the perfect liberty, that nothing can curtail, which a man experiences directly he makes the Christian theory of life his own, would be an unmistakable proof of its truth.

Men in their present condition are like a swarm of bees hanging in a cluster to a branch. The position of the bees on the branch is temporary, and must inevitably be changed. They must start off and find themselves a habitation. Each of the bees knows this, and desires to change her own and the others' position, but no one of them can do it till the rest of them do it. They cannot all start off at once, because one hangs on to another and hinders her from separating from the swarm, and therefore they all continue to hang there. It would seem that the bees could never escape from their position, just as it seems that worldly men, caught in the toils of the state conception of life, can never escape. And there would be no escape for the bees, if each of them were not a living, separate creature, endowed with wings of its own. Similarly there would be no escape for men, if each were not a living being endowed with the faculty of entering into the Christian conception of life.

If every bee who could fly, did not try to fly, the others, too, would never be stirred, and the swarm would never change its position. And if the man who has mastered the Christian conception of life would not, without waiting for other people, begin to live in accordance with this conception, mankind would never change its position. But only let one bee spread her wings, start off, and fly away, and after her another, and another, and the clinging, inert cluster would become a freely flying swarm of bees. Just in the same way, only let one man look at life as Christianity teaches him to look at it, and after him let another and another do the same, and the enchanted circle of existence in the state conception of life, from which there seemed no escape, will be broken through.

But men think that to set all men free by this means is too slow a process, that they must find some other means by which they could set all men free at once. It is just as though the bees who want to start and fly away should consider it too long a process to wait for all the swarm to start one by one; and should think they ought to find some means by which it would not be necessary for every separate bee to spread her wings and fly off, but by which the whole swarm could fly at once where it wanted to. But that is not possible; till a first, a second, a third, a hundredth bee spreads her wings and flies off of her own accord, the swarm will not fly off and will not begin its new life. Till every individual man makes the Christian conception of life his own, and begins to live in accord with it, there can be no solution of the problem of human life, and no establishment of a new form of life.

One of the most striking phenomena of our times is precisely this advocacy of slavery, which is promulgated among the masses, not by governments, in whom it is inevitable, but by men who, in advocating socialistic theories, regard themselves as the champions of freedom.

These people advance the opinion that the amelioration of life, the bringing of the facts of life into harmony with the conscience, will come, not as the result of the personal efforts of individual men, but of itself as the result of a certain possible reconstruction of society effected in some way or other. The idea is promulgated that men ought not to walk on their own legs where they want and ought to go, but that a kind of floor under their feet will be moved somehow, so that on it they can reach where they ought to go without moving their own legs. And, therefore, all their efforts ought to be directed, not to going so far as their strength allows in the direction they ought to go, but to standing still and constructing such a floor.

In the sphere of political economy a theory is propounded which amounts to saying that the worse things are the better they are; that the greater the accumulation of capital, and therefore the oppression of the workman, the nearer the day of emancipation, and, therefore, every personal effort on the part of a man to free himself from the oppression of capital is useless. In the sphere of government it is maintained that the greater the power of the government, which, according to this theory, ought to intervene in every department of private life in which it has not yet intervened, the better it will be, and that therefore we ought to invoke the interference of government in private life. In politics and international questions it is maintained that the improvement of the means of destruction, the multiplication of armaments, will lead to the necessity of making war by means of congresses, arbitration, and so on. And, marvelous to say, so great is the dullness of men, that they believe in these theories, in spite of the fact that the whole course of life, every step they take, shows how unworthy they are of belief.

The people are suffering from oppression, and to deliver them from this oppression they are advised to frame general measures for the improvement of their position, which measures are to be intrusted to the authorities, and themselves to continue to yield obedience to the authorities. And obviously all that results from this is only greater power in the hands of the authorities, and greater oppression resulting from it.

Not one of the errors of men carries them so far away from the aim toward which they are struggling as this very one. They do all kinds of different things for the attainment of their aim, but not the one simple obvious thing which is within reach of everyone. They devise the subtlest means for changing the position which is irksome to them, but not that simplest means, that everyone should refrain from doing what leads to that position.

I have been told a story of a gallant police officer, who came to a village where the peasants were in insurrection and the military had been called out, and he undertook to pacify the insurrection in the spirit of Nicholas I., by his personal influence alone. He ordered some loads of rods to be brought, and collecting all the peasants together into a barn, he went in with them, locking the door after him. To begin with, he so terrified the peasants by his loud threats that, reduced to submission by him, they set to work to flog one another at his command. And so they flogged one another until a simpleton was found who would not allow himself to be flogged, and shouted to his companions not to flog one another. Only then the fogging ceased, and the police officer made his escape. Well, this simpleton's advice would never be followed by men of the state conception of life, who continue to flog one another, and teach people that this very act of self-castigation is the last word of human wisdom.

Indeed, can one imagine a more striking instance of men flogging themselves than the submissiveness with which men of our times will perform the very duties required of them to keep them in slavery, especially the duty of military service? We see people enslaving themselves, suffering from this slavery, and believing that it must be so, that it does not matter, and will not hinder the emancipation of men, which is being prepared somewhere, somehow, in spite of the ever-increasing growth of slavery.

In fact, take any man of the present time whatever (I don't mean a true Christian, but an average man of the present day), educated or uneducated, believing or unbelieving, rich or poor, married or unmarried. Such a man lives working at his work, or enjoying his amusements, spending the fruits of his labors on himself or on those near to him, and, like everyone, hating every kind of restriction and deprivation, dissension and suffering. Such a man is going his way peaceably, when suddenly people come and say to him: First, promise and swear to us that you will slavishly obey us in everything we dictate to you, and will consider absolutely good and authoritative everything we plan, decide, and call law. Secondly, hand over a part of the fruits of your labors for us to dispose of--we will use the money to keep you in slavery, and to hinder you from forcibly opposing our orders. Thirdly, elect others, or be yourself elected, to take a pretended share in the government, knowing all the while that the government will proceed quite without regard to the foolish speeches you, and those like you, may utter, and knowing that its proceedings will be according to our will, the will of those who have the army in their hands. Fourthly, come at a certain time to the law courts and take your share in those senseless cruelties which we perpetrate on sinners, and those whom we have corrupted, in the shape of penal servitude, exile, solitary confinement, and death. And fifthly and lastly, more than all this, in spite of the fact that you maybe on the friendliest terms with people of other nations, be ready, directly we order you to do so, to regard those whom we indicate to you as your enemies; and be ready to assist, either in person or by proxy, in devastation, plunder, and murder of their men, women, children, and aged alike--possibly your own kinsmen or relations--if that is necessary to us.

One would expect that every man of the present day who has a grain of sense left, might reply to such requirements, "But why should I do all this?" One would think every right-minded man must say in amazement: "Why should I promise to yield obedience to everything that has been decreed first by Salisbury, then by Gladstone; one day by Boulanger, and another by Parliament; one day by Peter III., the next by Catherine, and the day after by Pougachef; one day by a mad king of Bavaria, another by William? Why should I promise to obey them, knowing them to be wicked or foolish people, or else not knowing them at all? Why am I to hand over the fruits of my labors to them in the shape of taxes, knowing that the money will be spent on the support of officials, prisons, churches, armies, on things that are harmful, and on my own enslavement? Why should I punish myself? Why should I go wasting my time and hoodwinking myself, giving to miscreant evildoers a semblance of legality, by taking part in elections, and pretending that I am taking part in the government, when I know very well that the real control of the government is in the hands of those who have got hold of the army? Why should I go to the law courts to take part in the trial and punishment of men because they have sinned, knowing, if I am a Christian, that the law of vengeance is replaced by the law of love, and, if I am an educated man, that punishments do not reform, but only deprave those on whom they are inflicted? And why, most of all, am I to consider as enemies the people of a neighboring nation, with whom I have hitherto lived and with whom I wish to live in love and harmony, and to kill and rob them, or to bring them to misery, simply in order that the keys of the temple at Jerusalem may be in the hands of one archbishop and not another, that one German and not another may be prince in Bulgaria, or that the English rather than the American merchants may capture seals?

And why, most of all, should I take part in person or hire others to murder my own brothers and kinsmen? Why should I flog myself? It is altogether unnecessary for me; it is hurtful to me, and from every point of view it is immoral, base, and vile. So why should I do this? If you tell me that if I do it not I shall receive some injury from someone, then, in the first place, I cannot anticipate from anyone an injury so great as the injury you bring on me if I obey you; and secondly, it is perfectly clear to me that if we our own selves do not flog ourselves, no one will flog us.

As for the government--that means the tzars, ministers, and officials with pens in their hands, who cannot force us into doing anything, as that officer of police compelled the peasants; the men who will drag us to the law court, to prison, and to execution, are not tzars or officials with pens in their hands, but the very people who are in the same position as we are. And it is just as unprofitable and harmful and unpleasant to them to be flogged as to me, and therefore there is every likelihood that if I open their eyes they not only would not treat me with violence, but would do just as I am doing.

Thirdly, even if it should come to pass that I had to suffer for it, even then it would be better for me to be exiled or sent to prison for standing up for common sense and right--which, if not to-day, at least within a very short time, must be triumphant--than to suffer for folly and wrong which must come to an end directly. And therefore, even in that case, it is better to run the risk of their banishing me, shutting me up in prison, or executing me, than of my living all my life in bondage, through my own fault, to wicked men. Better is this than the possibility of being destroyed by victorious enemies, and being stupidly tortured and killed by them, in fighting for a cannon, or a piece of land of no use to anyone, or for a senseless rag called a banner.

I don't want to flog myself and I won't do it. I have no reason to do it. Do it yourselves, if you want it done; but I won't do it.

One would have thought that not religious or moral feeling alone, but the simplest common sense and foresight should impel every man of the present day to answer and to act in that way. But not so. Men of the state conception of life are of the opinion that to act in that way is not necessary, and is even prejudicial to the attainment of their object, the emancipation of men from slavery. They hold that we must continue, like the police officer's peasants, to flog one another, consoling ourselves with the reflection that we are talking away in the assemblies and meetings, founding trades unions, marching through the streets on the 1st of May, getting up conspiracies, and stealthily teasing the government that is flogging us, and that through all this it will be brought to pass that, by enslaving ourselves in closer and closer bondage, we shall very soon be free.

Nothing hinders the emancipation of men from slavery so much as this amazing error. Instead of every man directing his energies to freeing himself, to transforming his conception of life, people seek for an external united method of gaining freedom, and continue to rivet their chains faster and faster.

It is much as if men were to maintain that to make up a fire there was no need to kindle any of the coals, but that all that was necessary was to arrange the coals in a certain order. Yet the fact that the freedom of all men will be brought about only through the freedom of individual persons, becomes more and more clear as time goes on. The freedom of individual men, in the name of the Christian conception of life, from state domination, which was formerly an exceptional and unnoticed phenomenon, has of late acquired threatening significance for state authorities.

If in a former age, in the Roman times, it happened that a Christian confessed his religion and refused to take part in sacrifices, and to worship the emperors or the gods; or in the Middle Ages a Christian refused to worship images, or to acknowledge the authority of the Pope--these cases were in the first place a matter of chance. A man might be placed under the necessity of confessing his faith, or he might live all his life without being placed under this necessity. But now all men, without exception, are subjected to this trial of their faith. Every man of the present day is under the necessity of taking part in the cruelties of pagan life, or of refusing all participation in them. And secondly, in those days cases of refusal to worship the gods or the images or the Pope were not incidents that had any material bearing on the state. Whether men worshiped or did not worship the gods or the images or the Pope, the state remained just as powerful. But now cases of refusing to comply with the unchristian demands of the government are striking at the very root of state authority, because the whole authority of the state is based on the compliance with these unchristian demands.

The sovereign powers of the world have in the course of time been brought into a position in which, for their own preservation, they must require from all men actions which cannot be performed by men who profess true Christianity.

And therefore in our days every profession of true Christianity, by any individual man, strikes at the most essential power of the state, and inevitably leads the way for the emancipation of all.

What importance, one might think, can one attach to such an incident as some dozens of crazy fellows, as people will call them, refusing to take the oath of allegiance to the government, refusing to pay taxes, to take part in law proceedings or in military service?

These people are punished and exiled to a distance, and life goes on in its old way. One might think there was no importance in such incidents; but yet, it is just those incidents, more than anything else, that will undermine the power of the state and prepare the way for the freedom of men. These are the individual bees, who are beginning to separate from the swarm, and are flying near it, waiting till the whole swarm can no longer be prevented from starting off after them. And the governments know this, and fear such incidents more than all the socialists, communists, and anarchists, and their plots and dynamite bombs.

A new reign is beginning. According to the universal rule and established order it is required that all the subjects should take the oath of allegiance to the new government. There is a general decree to that effect, and all are summoned to the council-houses to take the oath. All at once one man in Perm, another in Tula, a third in Moscow, and a fourth in Kalouga declare that they will not take the oath, and though there is no communication between them, they all explain their refusal on the same grounds--namely, that swearing is forbidden by the law of Christ, and that even if swearing had not been forbidden, they could not, in the spirit of the law of Christ, promise to perform the evil actions required of them in the oath, such as informing against all such as may act against the interests of the government, or defending their government with firearms or attacking its enemies. They are brought before rural police officers, district police captains, priests, and governors. They are admonished, questioned, threatened, and punished; but they adhere to their resolution, and do not take the oath. And among the millions of those who did take the oath, those dozens go on living who did not take the oath. And they are questioned:

"What, didn't you take the oath?"

"No, I didn't take the oath."

"And what happened--nothing?"

"Nothing."

The subjects of a state are all bound to pay taxes. And everyone pays taxes, till suddenly one man in Kharkov, another in Tver, and a third in Samara refuse to pay taxes--all, as though in collusion, saying the same thing. One says he will only pay when they tell him what object the money taken from him will be spent on. "If it is for good deeds," he says, "he will give it of his own accord, and more even than is required of him. If for evil deeds, then he will give nothing voluntarily, because by the law of Christ, whose follower he is, he cannot take part in evil deeds." The others, too, say the same in other words, and will not voluntarily pay the taxes.

Those who have anything to be taken have their property taken from them by force; as for those who have nothing, they are left alone.

"What, didn't you pay the tax?"

"No, I didn't pay it."

"And what happened-nothing?"

"Nothing."

There is the institution of passports. Everyone moving from his place of residence is bound to carry one, and to pay a duty on it. Suddenly people are to be found in various places declaring that to carry a passport is not necessary, that one ought not to recognize one's dependence on a state which exists by means of force; and these people do not carry passports, or pay the duty on them. And again, it's impossible to force those people by any means to do what is required. They send them to jail, and let them out again, and these people live without passports.

All peasants are bound to fill certain police offices--that of village constable, and of watchman, and so on. Suddenly in Kharkov a peasant refuses to perform this duty, justifying his refusal on the ground that by the law of Christ, of which he is a follower, he cannot put any man in fetters, lock him up, or drag him from place to place. The same declaration is made by a peasant in Tver, another in Tambov. These peasants are abused, beaten, shut up in prison, but they stick to their resolution and don't fill these offices against their convictions. And at last they cease to appoint them as constables. And again nothing happens.

All citizens are obliged to take a share in law proceedings in the character of jurymen. Suddenly the most different people--mechanics, professors, tradesmen, peasants, servants, as though by agreement refuse to fill this office, and not on the grounds allowed as sufficient by law, but because any process at law is, according to their views, unchristian. They fine these people, trying not to let them have an opportunity of explaining their motives in public, and replace them by others. And again nothing can be done.

All young men of twenty-one years of age are obliged to draw lots for service in the army. All at once one young man in Moscow, another in Tver, a third in Kharkov, and a fourth in Kiev present themselves before the authorities, and, as though by previous agreement, declare that they will not take the oath, they will not serve because they are Christians. I will give the details of one of the first cases, since they have become more frequent, which I happen to know about [footnote: All the details of this case, as well as those preceding it, are authentic]. The same treatment has been repeated in every other case. A young man of fair education refuses in the Moscow Townhall to take the oath. No attention is paid to what he says, and it is requested that he should pronounce the words of the oath like the rest. He declines, quoting a particular passage of the Gospel in which swearing is forbidden. No attention is paid to his arguments, and he is again requested to comply with the order, but he does not comply with it. Then it is supposed that he is a sectary and therefore does not understand Christianity in the right sense, that is to say, not in the sense in which the priests in the pay of the government understand it. And the young man is conducted under escort to the priests, that they may bring him to reason. The priests begin to reason with him, but their efforts in Christ's name to persuade him to renounce Christ obviously have no influence on him; he is pronounced incorrigible and sent back again to the army. He persists in not taking the oath and openly refuses to perform any military duties. It is a case that has not been provided for by the laws. To overlook such a refusal to comply with the demands of the authorities is out of the question, but to put such a case on a par with simple breach of discipline is also out of the question.

After deliberation among themselves, the military authorities decide to get rid of the troublesome young man, to consider him as a revolutionist, and they dispatch him under escort to the committee of the secret police. The police authorities and gendarmes cross-question him, but nothing that he says can be brought under the head of any of the misdemeanors which come under their jurisdiction. And there is no possibility of accusing him either of revolutionary acts or revolutionary plotting, since he declares that he does not wish to attack anything, but, on the contrary, is opposed to any use of force, and, far from plotting in secret, he seeks every opportunity of saying and doing all that he says and does in the most open manner. And the gendarmes, though they are bound by no hard-and-fast rules, still find no ground for a criminal charge in the young man, and, like the clergy, they send him back to the army. Again the authorities deliberate together, and decide to accept him though he has not taken the oath, and to enrol him among the soldiers. They put him into the uniform, enrol him, and send him under guard to the place where the army is quartered. There the chief officer of the division which he enters again expects the young man to perform his military duties, and again he refuses to obey, and in the presence of other soldiers explains the reason of his refusal, saying that he as a Christian cannot voluntarily prepare himself to commit murder, which is forbidden by the law of Moses.

This incident occurs in a provincial town. The case awakens the interest, and even the sympathy, not only of outsiders, but even of the officers. And the chief officers consequently do not decide to punish this refusal of obedience with disciplinary measures. To save appearances, though, they shut the young man up in prison, and write to the highest military authorities to inquire what they are to do. To refuse to serve in the army, in which the Tzar himself serves, and which enjoys the blessing of the Church, seems insanity from the official point of view. Consequently they write from Petersburg that, since the young man must be out of his mind, they must not use any severe treatment with him, but must send him to a lunatic asylum, that his mental condition may be inquired into and be scientifically treated.

They send him to the asylum in the hope that he will remain there, like another young man, who refused ten years ago at Tver to serve in the army, and who was tortured in the asylum till he submitted. But even this step does not rid the military authorities of the inconvenient man. The doctors examine him, interest themselves warmly in his case, and naturally finding in him no symptoms of mental disease, send him back to the army. There they receive him, and making believe to have forgotten his refusal, and his motives for it, they again request him to go to drill, and again in the presence of the other soldiers he refuses and explains the reason of his refusal. The affair continues to attract more and more attention, both among the soldiers and the inhabitants of the town. Again they write to Petersburg, and thence comes the decree to transfer the young man to some division of the army stationed on the frontier, in some place where the army is under martial law, where he can be shot for refusing to obey, and where the matter can proceed without attracting observation, seeing that there are few Russians and Christians in such a distant part, but the majority are foreigners and Mohammedans. This is accordingly done. They transfer him to a division stationed on the Zacaspian border, and in company with convicts send him to a chief officer who is notorious for his harshness and severity.

All this time, through all these changes from place to place, the young man is roughly treated, kept in cold, hunger, and filth, and life is made burdensome to him generally. But all these sufferings do not compel him to change his resolution. On the Zacaspian border, where he is again requested to go on guard fully armed, he again declines to obey. He does not refuse to go and stand near the haystacks where they place him, but refuses to take his arms, declaring that he will not use violence in any case against anyone. All this takes place in the presence of the other soldiers. To let such a refusal pass unpunished is impossible, and the young man is put on his trial for breach of discipline. The trial takes place, and he is sentenced to confinement in the military prison for two years. He is again transferred, in company with convicts, by étape, to Caucasus, and there he is shut up in prison and falls under the irresponsible power of the jailer. There he is persecuted for a year and a half, but he does not for all that alter his decision not to bear arms, and he explains why he will not do this to everyone with whom he is brought in contact. At the end of the second year they set him free, before the end of his term of imprisonment, reckoning it contrary to law to keep him in prison after his time of military service was over, and only too glad to get rid of him as soon as possible.

Other men in various parts of Russia behave, as though by agreement, precisely in the same way as this young man, and in all these cases the government has adopted the same timorous, undecided, and secretive course of action. Some of these men are sent to the lunatic asylum, some are enrolled as clerks and transferred to Siberia, some are sent to work in the forests, some are sent to prison, some are fined. And at this very time some men of this kind are in prison, not charged with their real offense--that is, denying the lawfulness of the action of the government, but for non-fulfillment of special obligations imposed by government. Thus an officer of reserve, who did not report his change of residence, and justified this on the ground that he would not serve in the army any longer, was fined thirty rubles for non-compliance with the orders of the superior authority. This fine he also declined voluntarily to pay. In the same way some peasants and soldiers who have refused to be drilled and to bear arms have been placed under arrest on a charge of breach of discipline and insolence.

And cases of refusing to comply with the demands of government when they are opposed to Christianity, and especially cases of refusing to serve in the army, are occurring of late not in Russia only, but everywhere. Thus I happen to know that in Servia men of the so-called sect of Nazarenes steadily refuse to serve in the army, and the Austrian Government has been carrying on a fruitless contest with them for years, punishing them with imprisonment. In the year 1885 there were 130 such cases. I know that in Switzerland in the year 1890 there were men in prison in the castle of Chillon for declining to serve in the army, whose resolution was not shaken by their punishment. There have been such cases in Sweden, and the men who refused obedience were sent to prison in exactly the same way, and the government studiously concealed these cases from the people. There have been similar cases also in Prussia. I know of the case of a sub-lieutenant of the Guards, who in 1891 declared to the authorities in Berlin that he would not, as a Christian, continue to serve, and in spite of all admonitions, threats, and punishments he stuck to his resolution. In the south of France a society has arisen of late bearing the name of the Hinschists (these facts are taken from the PEACE HERALD, July, 1891), the members of which refuse to enter military service on the grounds of their Christian principles. At first they were enrolled in the ambulance corps, but now, as their numbers increase, they are subjected to punishment for non-compliance, but they still refuse to bear arms just the same.

The socialists, the communists, the anarchists, with their bombs and riots and revolutions, are not nearly so much dreaded by governments as these disconnected individuals coming from different parts, and all justifying their non-compliance on the grounds of the same religion, which is known to all the world. Every government knows by what means and in what manner to defend itself from revolutionists, and has resources for doing so, and therefore does not dread these external foes. But what are governments to do against men who show the uselessness, superfluousness, and perniciousness of all governments, and who do not contend against them, but simply do not need them and do without them, and therefore are unwilling to take any part in them? The revolutionists say: The form of government is bad in this respect and that respect; we must overturn it and substitute this or that form of government. The Christian says: I know nothing about the form of government, I don't know whether it is good or bad, and I don't want to overturn it precisely because I don't know whether it is good or bad, but for the very same reason I don't want to support it either. And I not only don't want to, but I can't, because what it demands of me is against my conscience.

All state obligations are against the conscience of a Christian--the oath of allegiance, taxes, law proceedings, and military service. And the whole power of the government rests on these very obligations.

Revolutionary enemies attack the government from without. Christianity does not attack it at all, but, from within, it destroys all the foundations on which government rests.

Among the Russian people, especially since the age of Peter I., the protest of Christianity against the government has never ceased, and the social organization has been such that men emigrate in communes to Turkey, to China, and to uninhabited lands, and not only feel no need of state aid, but always regard the state as a useless burden, only to be endured as a misfortune, whether it happens to be Turkish, Russian, or Chinese. And so, too, among the Russian people more and more frequent examples have of late appeared of conscious Christian freedom from subjection to the state. And these examples are the more alarming for the government from the fact that these non-compliant persons often belong not to the so-called lower uneducated classes, but are men of fair or good education; and also from the fact that they do not in these days justify their position by any mystic and exceptional views, as in former times, do not associate themselves with any superstitious or fanatic rites, like the sects who practice self-immolation by fire, or the wandering pilgrims, but put their refusal on the very simplest and clearest grounds, comprehensible to all, and recognized as true by all.

Thus they refuse the voluntary payment of taxes, because taxes are spent on deeds of violence--on the pay of men of violence--soldiers, on the construction of prisons, fortresses, and cannons. They as Christians regard it as sinful and immoral to have any hand in such deeds.

Those who refuse to take the oath of allegiance refuse because to promise obedience to authorities, that is, to men who are given to deeds of violence, is contrary to the sense of Christ's teaching. They refuse to take the oath in the law courts, because oaths are directly forbidden by the Gospel. They refuse to perform police duties, because in the performance of these duties they must use force against their brothers and ill treat them, and a Christian cannot do that. They refuse to take part in trials at law, because they consider every appeal to law is fulfilling the law of vengeance, which is inconsistent with the Christian law of forgiveness and love. They refuse to take any part in military preparations and in the army, because they cannot be executioners, and they are unwilling to prepare themselves to be so.

The motives in all these cases are so excellent that, however despotic governments may be, they could hardly punish them openly. To punish men for refusing to act against their conscience the government must renounce all claim to good sense and benevolence. And they assure people that they only rule in the name of good sense and benevolence.

What are governments to do against such people?

Governments can of course flog to death or execute or keep in perpetual imprisonment all enemies who want to overturn them by violence, they can lavish gold on that section of the people who are ready to destroy their enemies. But what can they do against men who, without wishing to overturn or destroy anything, desire simply for their part to do nothing against the law of Christ, and who, therefore, refuse to perform the commonest state requirements, which are, therefore, the most indispensable to the maintenance of the state?

If they had been revolutionists, advocating and practicing violence and murder, their suppression would have been an easy matter; some of them could have been bought over, some could have been duped, some could have been overawed, and these who could not be bought over, duped, or overawed would have been treated as criminals, enemies of society, would have been executed or imprisoned, and the crowd would have approved of the action of the government. If they had been fanatics, professing some peculiar belief, it might have been possible, in disproving the superstitious errors mixed in with their religion, to attack also the truth they advocate. But what is to be done with men who profess no revolutionary ideas nor any peculiar religious dogmas, but merely because they are unwilling to do evil to any man, refuse to take the oath, to pay taxes, to take part in law proceedings, to serve in the army, to fulfill, in fact, any of the obligations upon which the whole fabric of a state rests? What is to done with such people? To buy them over with bribes is impossible; the very risks to which they voluntarily expose themselves show that they are incorruptible. To dupe them into believing that this is their duty to God is also impossible, since their refusal is based on the clear, unmistakable law of God, recognized even by those who are trying to compel men to act against it. To terrify them by threats is still less possible, because the deprivations and sufferings to which they are subjected only strengthen their desire to follow the faith by which they are commanded: to obey God rather than men, and not to fear those who can destroy the body, but to fear him who can destroy body and soul. To kill them or keep them in perpetual imprisonment is also impossible. These men have friends, and a past; their way of thinking and acting is well known; they are known by everyone for good, gentle, peaceable people, and they cannot be regarded as criminals who must be removed for the safety of society. And to put men to death who are regarded as good men is to provoke others to champion them and justify their refusal. And it is only necessary to explain the reasons of their refusal to make clear to everyone that these reasons have the same force for all other men, and that they all ought to have done the same long ago. These cases put the ruling powers into a desperate position. They see that the prophecy of Christianity is coming to pass, that it is loosening the fetters of those in chains, and setting free them that are in bondage, and that this must inevitably be the end of all oppressors. The ruling authorities see this, they know that their hours are numbered, and they can do nothing. All that they can do to save themselves is only deferring the hour of their downfall. And this they do, but their position is none the less desperate.

It is like the position of a conqueror who is trying to save a town which has been been set on fire by its own inhabitants. Directly he puts out the conflagration in one place, it is alight in two other places; directly he gives in to the fire and cuts off what is on fire from a large building, the building itself is alight at both ends. These separate fires may be few, but they are burning with a flame which, however small a spark it starts from, never ceases till it has set the whole ablaze.

Thus it is that the ruling authorities are in such a defenseless position before men who advocate Christianity, that but little is necessary to overthrow this sovereign power which seems so powerful, and has held such an exalted position for so many centuries. And yet social reformers are busy promulgating the idea that it is not necessary and is even pernicious and immoral for every man separately to work out his own freedom. As though, while one set of men have been at work a long while turning a river into a new channel, and had dug out a complete water-course and had only to open the floodgates for the water to rush in and do the rest, another set of men should come along and begin to advise them that it would be much better, instead of letting the water out, to construct a machine which would ladle the water up from one side and pour it over the other side.

But the thing has gone too far. Already ruling governments feel their weak and defenseless position, and men of Christian principles are awakening from their apathy, and already begin to feel their power.

"I am come to send a fire on the earth," said Christ, "and what will I, if it be already kindled?"

And this fire is beginning to burn.

CHAPTER X.

EVIL CANNOT BE SUPPRESSED BY THE PHYSICAL FORCE OF THE GOVERNMENT--THE MORAL PROGRESS OF HUMANITY IS BROUGHT ABOUT NOT ONLY BY INDIVIDUAL RECOGNITION OF TRUTH, BUT ALSO THROUGH THE ESTABLISHMENT OF A PUBLIC OPINION.

Christianity Destroys the State--But Which is Most Necessary: Christianity or the State?--There are Some who Assert the Necessity of a State Organization, and Others who Deny it, both Arguing from same First Principles--Neither Contention can be Proved by Abstract Argument--The Question must be Decided by the Stage in the Development of Conscience of Each Man, which will either Prevent or Allow him to Support a Government Organization--Recognition of the Futility and Immorality of Supporting a State Organization Contrary to Christian Principles will Decide the Question for Every Man, in Spite of any Action on Part of the State--Argument of those who Defend the Government, that it is a Form of Social Life, Needed to Protect the Good from the Wicked, till all Nations and all Members of each Nation have Become Christians--The Most Wicked are Always those in Power--The whole History of Humanity is the History of the Forcible Appropriation of Power by the Wicked and their Oppression of the Good--The Recognition by Governments of the Necessity of Opposing Evil by Force is Equivalent to Suicide on their Part--The Abolition of State-violence cannot Increase the Sum Total of Acts of Violence--The Suppression of the Use of Force is not only Possible, but is even Taking Place before Our Eyes--But it will Never be Suppressed by the Violence of Government, but through Men who have Attained Power by

Evidence Recognizing its Emptiness and Becoming Better and Less Capable of Using Force--Individual Men and also Whole Nations Pass Through this Process--By this Means Christianity is Diffused Through Consciousness of Men, not only in Spite of Use of Violence by Government, but even Through its Action, and therefore the Suppression is not to be Dreaded, but is Brought About by the National Progress of Life--Objection of those who Defend State Organization that Universal Adoption of Christianity is hardly Likely to be Realized at any Time--The General Adoption of the Truths of Christianity is being Brought About not only by the Gradual and Inward Means, that is, by Knowledge of the Truth, Prophetic Insight, and Recognition of the Emptiness of Power, and Renunciation of it by Individuals, but also by Another External Means, the Acceptance of a New Truth by Whole Masses of Men on a Lower Level of Development Through Simple Confidence in their Leaders--When a Certain Stage in the Diffusion of a Truth has been Reached, a Public Opinion is Created which Impels a Whole Mass of Men, formerly Antagonistic to the New Truth, to Accept it--And therefore all Men may Quickly be Brought to Renounce the use of Violence when once a Christian Public Opinion is Established--The Conviction of Force being Necessary Hinders the Establishment of a Christian Public Opinion--The Use of Violence Leads Men to Distrust the Spiritual Force which is the Only Force by which they Advance--Neither Nations nor Individuals have been really Subjugated by Force, but only by Public Opinion, which no Force can Resist--Savage Nations and Savage Men can only be Subdued by the Diffusion of a Christian Standard among them, while actually Christian Nations in order to Subdue them do all they can to Destroy a Christian

Standard--These Fruitless Attempts to Civilize Savages Cannot be Adduced as Proofs that Men Cannot be Subdued by Christianity--Violence by Corrupting Public Opinion, only Hinders the Social Organization from being What it Ought to Be--And by the Use of Violence being Suppressed, a Christian Public Opinion would be Established--Whatever might be the Result of the Suppression of Use of Force, this Unknown Future could not be Worse than the Present Condition, and so there is no Need to Dread it--To Attain Knowledge of the Unknown, and to Move Toward it, is the Essence of Life.

Christianity in its true sense puts an end to government. So it was understood at its very commencement; it was for that cause that Christ was crucified. So it has always been understood by people who were not under the necessity of justifying a Christian government. Only from the time that the heads of government assumed an external and nominal Christianity, men began to invent all the impossible, cunningly devised theories by means of which Christianity can be reconciled with government. But no honest and serious-minded man of our day can help seeing the incompatibility of true Christianity--the doctrine of meekness, forgiveness of injuries, and love--with government, with its pomp, acts of violence, executions, and wars. The profession of true Christianity not only excludes the possibility of recognizing government, but even destroys its very foundations.

But if it is so, and we are right in saying that Christianity is incompatible with government, then the question naturally presents itself: which is more necessary to the good of humanity, in which way is men's happiness best to be secured, by maintaining the organization of government or by destroying it and replacing it by Christianity?

Some people maintain that government is more necessary for humanity, that the destruction of the state organization would involve the destruction of all that humanity has gained, that the state has been and still is the only form in which humanity can develop. The evil which we see among peoples living under a government organization they attribute not to that type of society, but to its abuses, which, they say, can be corrected without destroying it, and thus humanity, without discarding the state organization, can develop and attain a high degree of happiness. And men of this way of thinking bring forward in support of their views arguments which they think irrefutable drawn from history, philosophy, and even religion. But there are men who hold on the contrary that, as there was a time when humanity lived without government, such an organization is temporary, and that a time must come when men need a new organization, and that that time has come now. And men of this way of thinking also bring forward in support of their views arguments which they think irrefutable from philosophy, history, and religion.

Volumes may be written in defense of the former view (and volumes indeed have long ago been written and more will still be written on that side), but much also can be written against it (and much also, and most brilliantly, has been written--though more recently --on this side).

And it cannot be proved, as the champions of the state maintain, that the destruction of government involves a social chaos, mutual spoliation and murder, the destruction of all social institutions, and the return of mankind to barbarism. Nor can it be proved as the opponents of government maintain that men have already become so wise and good that they will not spoil or murder one another, but will prefer peaceful associations to hostilities; that of their own accord, unaided by the state, they will make all the arrangements that they need, and that therefore government, far from being any aid, under show of guarding men exerts a pernicious and brutalizing influence over them. It is impossible to prove either of these contentions by abstract reasoning. Still less possible is it to prove them by experiment, since the whole matter turns on the question, ought we to try the experiment? The question whether or not the time has come to make an end of government would be unanswerable, except that there exists another living means of settling it beyond dispute.

We may dispute upon the question whether the nestlings are ready to do without the mother-hen and to come out of the eggs, or whether they are not yet advanced enough. But the young birds will decide the question without any regard for our arguments when they find themselves cramped for space in the eggs. Then they will begin to try them with their beaks and come out of them of their own accord.

It is the same with the question whether the time has come to do away with the governmental type of society and to replace it by a new type. If a man, through the growth of a higher conscience, can no longer comply with the demands of government, he finds himself cramped by it and at the same time no longer needs its protection. When this comes to pass, the question whether men are ready to discard the governmental type is solved. And the conclusion will be as final for them as for the young birds hatched out of the eggs. Just as no power in the world can put them back into the shells, so can no power in the world bring men again under the governmental type of society when once they have outgrown it.

"It may well be that government was necessary and is still necessary for all the advantages which you attribute to it," says the man who has mastered the Christian theory of life. "I only know that on the one hand, government is no longer necessary for ME, and on the other hand, I can no longer carry out the measures that are necessary to the existence of a government. Settle for yourselves what you need for your life. I cannot prove the need or the harm of governments in general. I know only what I need and do not need, what I can do and what I cannot. I know that I do not need to divide myself off from other nations, and therefore I cannot admit that I belong exclusively to any state or nation, or that I owe allegiance to any government. I know that I do not need all the government institutions organized within the state, and therefore I cannot deprive people who need my labor to give it in the form of taxes to institutions which I do not need, which for all I know may be pernicious. I know that I have no need of the administration or of courts of justice founded upon force, and therefore I can take no part in either. I know that I do not need to attack and slaughter other nations or to defend myself from them with arms, and therefore I can take no part in wars or preparations for wars. It may well be that there are people who cannot help regarding all this as necessary and indispensable. I cannot dispute the question with them, I can only speak for myself; but I can say with absolute certainty that I do not need it, and that I cannot do it. And I do not need this and I cannot do it, not because such is my own, my personal will, but because such is the will of him who sent me into life, and gave me an indubitable law for my conduct through life."

Whatever arguments may be advanced in support of the contention that the suppression of government authority would be injurious and would lead to great calamities, men who have once outgrown the governmental form of society cannot go back to it again. And all the reasoning in the world cannot make the man who has outgrown the governmental form of society take part in actions disallowed by his conscience, any more than the full-grown bird can be made to return into the egg-shell.

"But even it be so," say the champions of the existing order of things, "still the suppression of government violence can only be possible and desirable when all men have become Christians. So long as among people nominally Christians there are unchristian wicked men, who for the gratification of their own lusts are ready to do harm to others, the suppression of government authority, far from being a blessing to others, would only increase their miseries. The suppression of the governmental type of society is not only undesirable so long as there is only a minority of true Christians; it would not even be desirable if the whole of a nation were Christians, but among and around them were still unchristian men of other nations. For these unchristian men would rob, outrage, and kill the Christians with impunity and would make their lives miserable. All that would result, would be that the bad would oppress and outrage the good with impunity. And therefore the authority of government must not be suppressed till all the wicked and rapacious people in the world are extinct. And since this will either never be, or at least cannot be for a long time to come, in spite of the efforts of individual Christians to be independent of government authority, it ought to be maintained in the interests of the majority. The champions of government assert that without it the wicked will oppress and outrage the good, and that the power of the government enables the good to resist the wicked."

But in this assertion the champions of the existing order of things take for granted the proposition they want to prove. When they say that except for the government the bad would oppress the good, they take it for granted that the good are those who at the present time are in possession of power, and the bad are those who are in subjection to it. But this is just what wants proving. It would only be true if the custom of our society were what is, or rather is supposed to be, the custom in China; that is, that the good always rule, and that directly those at the head of government cease to be better than those they rule over, the citizens are bound to remove them. This is supposed to be the custom in China. In reality it is not so and can never be so. For to remove the heads of a government ruling by force, it is not the right alone, but the power to do so that is needed. So that even in China this is only an imaginary custom. And in our Christian world we do not even suppose such a custom, and we have nothing on which to build up the supposition that it is the good or the superior who are in power; in reality it is those who have seized power and who keep it for their own and their retainers' benefit.

The good cannot seize power, nor retain it; to do this men must love power. And love of power is inconsistent with goodness; but quite consistent with the very opposite qualities--pride, cunning, cruelty.

Without the aggrandizement of self and the abasement of others, without hypocrisies and deceptions, without prisons, fortresses, executions, and murders, no power can come into existence or be maintained.

"If the power of government is suppressed the more wicked will oppress the less wicked," say the champions of state authority. But when the Egyptians conquered the Jews, the Romans conquered the Greeks, and the Barbarians conquered the Romans, is it possible that all the conquerors were always better than those they conquered? And the same with the transitions of power within a state from one personage to another: has the power always passed from a worse person to a better one? When Louis XVI. was removed and Robespierre came to power, and afterward Napoleon--who ruled then, a better man or a worse? And when were better men in power, when the Versaillist party or when the Commune was in power? When Charles I. was ruler, or when Cromwell? And when Peter III. was Tzar, or when he was killed and Catherine was Tzaritsa in one-half of Russia and Pougachef ruled the other? Which was bad then, and which was good? All men who happen to be in authority assert that their authority is necessary to keep the bad from oppressing the good, assuming that they themselves are the good PAR EXCELLENCE, who protect other good people from the bad.

But ruling means using force, and using force means doing to him to whom force is used, what he does not like and what he who uses the force would certainly not like done to himself. Consequently ruling means doing to others what we would not they should do unto us, that is, doing wrong.

To submit means to prefer suffering to using force. And to prefer suffering to using force means to be good, or at least less wicked than those who do unto others what they would not like themselves.

And therefore, in all probability, not the better but the worse have always ruled and are ruling now. There may be bad men among those who are ruled, but it cannot be that those who are better have generally ruled those who are worse.

It might be possible to suppose this with the inexact heathen definition of good; but with the clear Christian definition of good and evil, it is impossible to imagine it.

If the more or less good, and the more or less bad cannot be distinguished in the heathen world, the Christian conception of good and evil has so clearly defined the characteristics of the good and the wicked, that it is impossible to confound them. According to Christ's teaching the good are those who are meek and long-suffering, do not resist evil by force, forgive injuries, and love their enemies; those are wicked who exalt themselves, oppress, strive, and use force. Therefore by Christ's teaching there can be no doubt whether the good are to be found among rulers or ruled, and whether the wicked are among the ruled or the rulers. Indeed it is absurd even to speak of Christians ruling.

Non-Christians, that is those who find the aim of their lives in earthly happiness, must always rule Christians, the aim of whose lives is the renunciation of such earthly happiness.

This difference has always existed and has become more and more defined as the Christian religion has been more widely diffused and more correctly understood.

The more widely true Christianity was diffused and the more it penetrated men's conscience, the more impossible it was for Christians to be rulers, and the easier it became for non-Christians to rule them.

"To get rid of governmental violence in a society in which all are not true Christians, will only result in the wicked dominating the good and oppressing them with impunity," say the champions of the existing order of things. But it has never been, and cannot be otherwise. So it has always been from the beginning of the world, and so it is still. THE WICKED WILL ALWAYS DOMINATE THE GOOD, AND WILL ALWAYS OPPRESS THEM. Cain overpowered Abel, the cunning Jacob oppressed the guileless Esau and was in his turn deceived by Laban, Caiaphas and Pilate oppressed Christ, the Roman emperors oppressed Seneca, Epictetus, and the good Romans who lived in their times. John IV. with his favorites, the syphilitic drunken Peter with his buffoons, the vicious Catherine with her paramours, ruled and oppressed the industrious religious Russians of their times.

William is ruling over the Germans, Stambouloff over the Bulgarians, the Russian officials over the Russian people. The Germans have dominated the Italians, now they dominate the Hungarians and Slavonians; the Turks have dominated and still dominate the Slavonians and Greeks; the English dominate the Hindoos, the Mongolians dominate the Chinese.

So that whether governmental violence is suppressed or not, the position of good men, in being oppressed by the wicked, will be unchanged.

To terrify men with the prospect of the wicked dominating the good is impossible, for that is just what has always been, and is now, and cannot but be.

The whole history of pagan times is nothing but a recital of the incidents and means by which the more wicked gained possession of power over the less wicked, and retained it by cruelties and deceptions, ruling over the good under the pretense of guarding the right and protecting the good from the wicked. All the revolutions in history are only examples of the more wicked seizing power and oppressing the good. In declaring that if their authority did not exist the more wicked would oppress the good, the ruling authorities only show their disinclination to let other oppressors come to power who would like to snatch it from them.

But in asserting this they only accuse themselves, say that their power, i. e., violence, is needed to defend men from other possible oppressors in the present or the future [see footnote].

[Footnote: I may quote in this connection the amazingly naive and comic declaration of the Russian authorities, the oppressors of other nationalities--the Poles, the Germans of the Baltic provinces, and the Jews. The Russian Government has oppressed its subjects for centuries, and has never troubled itself about the Little Russians of Poland, or the Letts of the Baltic provinces, or the Russian peasants, exploited by everyone. And now it has all of a sudden become the champion of the oppressed--the very oppressed whom it is itself oppressing.]

The weakness of the use of violence lies in the fact that all the arguments brought forward by oppressors in their own defense can with even better reason be advanced against them. They plead the danger of violence--most often imagined in the future--but they are all the while continuing to practice actual violence themselves. "You say that men used to pillage and murder in the past, and that you are afraid that they will pillage and murder one another if your power were no more. That may happen--or it may not happen. But the fact that you ruin thousands of men in prisons, fortresses, galleys, and exile, break up millions of families and ruin millions of men, physically as well as morally, in the army, that fact is not an imaginary but a real act of violence, which, according to your own argument, one ought to oppose by violence. And so you are yourselves these wicked men against whom, according to your own argument, it is absolutely necessary to use violence," the oppressed are sure to say to their oppressors. And non-Christian men always do say, and think and act on this reasoning. If the oppressed are more wicked than their oppressors, they attack them and try to overthrow them; and in favorable circumstances they succeed in overthrowing them, or what is more common, they rise into the ranks of the oppressors and assist in their acts of violence.

So that the very violence which the champions of government hold up as a terror--pretending that except for its oppressive power the wicked would oppress the good--has really always existed and will exist in human society. And therefore the suppression of state violence cannot in any case be the cause of increased oppression of the good by the wicked.

If state violence ceased, there would be acts of violence perhaps on the part of different people, other than those who had done deeds of violence before. But the total amount of violence could not in any case be increased by the mere fact of power passing from one set of men to another.

"State violence can only cease when there are no more wicked men in society," say the champions of the existing order of things, assuming in this of course that since there will always be wicked men, it can never cease. And that would be right enough if it were the case, as they assume, that the oppressors are always the best of men, and that the sole means of saving men from evil is by violence. Then, indeed, violence could never cease. But since this is not the case, but quite the contrary, that it is not the better oppress the worse, but the worse oppress the better, and since violence will never put an end to evil, and there is, moreover, another means of putting an end to it, the assertion that violence will never cease is incorrect. The use of violence grows less and less and evidently must disappear. But this will not come to pass, as some champions of the existing order imagine, through the oppressed becoming better and better under the influence of government (on the contrary, its influence causes their continual degradation), but through the fact that all men are constantly growing better and better of themselves, so that even the most wicked, who are in power, will become less and less wicked, till at last they are so good as to be incapable of using violence.

The progressive movement of humanity does not proceed from the better elements in society seizing power and making those who are subject to them better, by forcible means, as both conservatives and revolutionists imagine. It proceeds first and principally from the fact that all men in general are advancing steadily and undeviatingly toward a more and more conscious assimilation of the Christian theory of life; and secondly, from the fact that, even apart from conscious spiritual life, men are unconsciously brought into a more Christian attitude to life by the very process of one set of men grasping the power, and again being replaced by others.

The worse elements of society, gaining possession of power, under the sobering influence which always accompanies power, grow less and less cruel, and become incapable of using cruel forms of violence. Consequently others are able to seize their place, and the same process of softening and, so to say, unconscious Christianizing goes on with them. It is something like the process of ebullition. The majority of men, having the non-Christian view of life, always strive for power and struggle to obtain it. In this struggle the most cruel, the coarsest, the least Christian elements of society overpower the most gentle, well-disposed, and Christian, and rise by means of their violence to the upper ranks of society. And in them is Christ's prophecy fulfilled: "Woe to you that are rich! woe unto you that are full! woe unto you when all men shall speak well of you!" For the men who are in possession of power and all that results from it--glory and wealth--and have attained the various aims they set before themselves, recognize the vanity of it all and return to the position from which they came. Charles V., John IV., Alexander I., recognizing the emptiness and the evil of power, renounced it because they were incapable of using violence for their own benefit as they had done.

But they are not the solitary examples of this recognition of the emptiness and evil of power. Everyone who gains a position of power he has striven for, every general, every minister, every millionaire, every petty official who has gained the place he has coveted for ten years, every rich peasant who has laid by some hundred rubles, passes through this unconscious process of softening.

And not only individual men, but societies of men, whole nations, pass through this process.

The seductions of power, and all the wealth, honor, and luxury it gives, seem a sufficient aim for men's efforts only so long as they are unattained. Directly a man reaches them he sees all their vanity, and they gradually lose all their power of attraction. They are like clouds which have form and beauty only from the distance; directly one ascends into them, all their splendor vanishes.

Men who are in possession of power and wealth, sometimes even those who have gained for themselves their power and wealth, but more often their heirs, cease to be so eager for power, and so cruel in their efforts to obtain it.

Having learnt by experience, under the operation of Christian influence, the vanity of all that is gained by violence, men sometimes in one, sometimes in several generations lose the vices which are generated by the passion for power and wealth. They become less cruel and so cannot maintain their position, and are expelled from power by others less Christian and more wicked. Thus they return to a rank of society lower in position, but higher in morality, raising thereby the average level of Christian consciousness in men. But directly after them again the worst, coarsest, least Christian elements of society rise to the top, and are subjected to the same process as their predecessors, and again in a generation or so, seeing the vanity of what is gained by violence, and having imbibed Christianity, they come down again among the oppressed, and their place is again filled by new oppressors, less brutal than former oppressors, though more so than those they oppress. So that, although power remains externally the same as it was, with every change of the men in power there is a constant increase of the number of men who have been brought by experience to the necessity of assimilating the Christian conception of life, and with every change--though it is the coarsest, crudest, and least Christian who come into possession of power, they are less coarse and cruel and more Christian than their predecessors when they gained possession of power.

Power selects and attracts the worst elements of society, transforms them, improves and softens them, and returns them to society.

"Such is the process by means of which Christianity, in spite of the hindrances to human progress resulting from the violence of power, gains more and more hold of men. Christianity penetrates to the consciousness of men, not only in spite of the violence of power, but also by means of it.

And therefore the assertion of the champions of the state, that if the power of government were suppressed the wicked would oppress the good, not only fails to show that that is to be dreaded, since it is just what happens now, but proves, on the contrary, that it is governmental power which enables the wicked to oppress the good, and is the evil most desirable to suppress, and that it is being gradually suppressed in the natural course of things.

"But if it be true that governmental power will disappear when those in power become so Christian that they renounce power of their own accord, and there are no men found willing to take their place, and even if this process is already going on," say the champions of the existing order, "when will that come to pass? If, after eighteen hundred years, there are still so many eager for power, and so few anxious to obey, there seems no likelihood of its happening very soon--or indeed of its ever happening at all.

"Even if there are, as there have always been, some men who prefer renouncing power to enjoying it, the mass of men in reserve, who prefer dominion to subjection, is so great that it is difficult to imagine a time when the number will be exhausted.

"Before this Christianizing process could so affect all men one after another that they would pass from the heathen to the Christian conception of life, and would voluntarily abandon power and wealth, it would be necessary that all the coarse, half-savage men, completely incapable of appreciating Christianity or acting upon it, of whom there are always a great many in every Christian society, should be converted to Christianity. More than this, all the savage and absolutely non-Christian peoples, who are so numerous outside the Christian world, must also be converted. And therefore, even if we admit that this Christianizing process will some day affect everyone, still, judging by the amount of progress it has made in eighteen hundred years, it will be many times eighteen centuries before it will do so. And it is therefore impossible and unprofitable to think at present of anything so impracticable as the suppression of authority. We ought only to try to put authority into the best hands."

And this criticism would be perfectly just, if the transition from one conception of life to another were only accomplished by the single process of all men, separately and successively, realizing, each for himself, the emptiness of power, and reaching Christian truth by the inner spiritual path. That process goes on unceasingly, and men are passing over to Christianity one after another by this inner way.

But there is also another external means by which men reach Christianity and by which the transition is less gradual.

This transition from one organization of life to another is not accomplished by degrees like the sand running through the hourglass grain after grain. It is more like the water filling a vessel floating on water. At first the water only runs in slowly on one side, but as the vessel grows heavier it suddenly begins to sink, and almost instantaneously fills with water.

It is just the same with the transitions of mankind from one conception--and so from one organization of life--to another. At first only gradually and slowly, one after another, men attain to the new truth by the inner spiritual way, and follow it out in life. But when a certain point in the diffusion of the truth has been reached, it is suddenly assimilated by everyone, not by the inner way, but, as it were, involuntarily.

That is why the champions of the existing order are wrong in arguing that, since only a small section of mankind has passed over to Christianity in eighteen centuries, it must be many times eighteen centuries before all the remainder do the same. For in that argument they do not take into account any other means, besides the inward spiritual one, by which men assimilate a new truth and pass from one order of life to another.

Men do not only assimilate a truth through recognizing it by prophetic insight, or by experience of life. When the truth has become sufficiently widely diffused, men at a lower stage of development accept it all at once simply through confidence in those who have reached it by the inner spiritual way, and are applying it to life.

Every new truth, by which the order of human life is changed and humanity is advanced, is at first accepted by only a very small number of men who understand it through inner spiritual intuition. The remainder of mankind who accepted on trust the preceding truth on which the existing order is based, are always opposed to the diffusion of the new truth.

But seeing that, to begin with, men do not stand still, but are steadily advancing to a greater recognition of the truth and a closer adaptation of their life to it, and secondly, all men in varying degrees according to their age, their education, and their race are capable of understanding the new truths, at first those who are nearest to the men who have attained the new truth by spiritual intuition, slowly and one by one, but afterward more and more quickly, pass over to the new truth. Thus the number of men who accept the new truth becomes greater and greater, and the truth becomes more and more comprehensible.

And thus more confidence is aroused in the remainder, who are at a less advanced stage of capacity for understanding the truth. And it becomes easier for them to grasp it, and an increasing number accept it.

And so the movement goes on more and more quickly, and on an ever-increasing scale, like a snowball, till at last a public opinion in harmony with the new truth is created, and then the whole mass of men is carried over all at once by its momentum to the new truth and establishes a new social order in accordance with it.

Those men who accept a new truth when it has gained a certain degree of acceptance, always pass over all at once in masses. They are like the ballast with which every ship is always loaded, at once to keep it upright and enable it to sail properly. If there were no ballast, the ship would not be low enough in the water, and would shift its position at the slightest change in its conditions. This ballast, which strikes one at first as superfluous and even as hindering the progress of the vessel, is really indispensable to its good navigation.

It is the same with the mass of mankind, who not individually, but always in a mass, under the influence of a new social idea pass all at once from one organization of life to another. This mass always hinders, by its inertia, frequent and rapid revolutions in the social order which have not been sufficiently proved by human experience. And it delays every truth a long while till it has stood the test of prolonged struggles, and has thoroughly permeated the consciousness of humanity.

And that is why it is a mistake to say that because only a very small minority of men has assimilated Christianity in eighteen centuries, it must take many times as many centuries for all mankind to assimilate it, and that since that time is so far off we who live in the present need not even think about it. It is a mistake, because the men at a lower stage of culture, the, men and the nations who are represented as the obstacle to the realization of the Christian order of life, are the very people who always pass over in masses all at once to any truth that has once been recognized by public opinion.

And therefore the transformation of human life, through which men in power will renounce it, and there will be none anxious to take their place, will not come only by all men consciously and separately assimilating the Christian conception of life. It will come when a Christian public opinion has arisen, so definite and easily comprehensible as to reach the whole of the inert mass, which is not able to attain truth by its own intuition, and therefore is always under the sway of public opinion.

Public opinion arises spontaneously and spreads for hundreds and thousands of years, but it has the power of working on men by infection, and with great rapidity gains a hold on great numbers of men.

"But," say the champions of the existing order, "even if it is true that public opinion, when it has attained a certain degree of definiteness and precision, can convert the inert mass of men outside the Christian world--the non-Christian races--as well as the coarse and depraved who are living in its midst, what proofs have we that this Christian public opinion has arisen and is able to replace force and render it unnecessary.

"We must not give up force, by which the existing order is

maintained, and by relying on the vague and impalpable influence of public opinion expose Christians to the risk of being pillaged, murdered, and outraged in every way by the savages inside and outside of civilized society.

"Since, even supported by the use of force, we can hardly control the non-Christian elements which are always ready to pour down on us and to destroy all that has been gained by civilization, is it likely that public opinion could take the place of force and render us secure? And besides, how are we to find the moment when public opinion has become strong enough to be able to replace the use of force? To reject the use of force and trust to public opinion to defend us would be as insane as to remove all weapons of defense in a menagerie, and then to let loose all the lions and tigers, relying on the fact that the animals seemed peaceable when kept in their cages and held in check by red-hot irons. And therefore people in power, who have been put in positions of authority by fate or by God, have not the right to run the risk, ruining all that has been gained by civilization, just because they want to try an experiment to see whether public opinion is or is not able to replace the protection given by authority."

A French writer, forgotten now, Alphonse Karr, said somewhere, trying to show the impossibility of doing away with the death penalty: "Que messieurs les assassins commencent par nous donner l'exemple." Often have I heard this BON MOT repeated by men who thought that these words were a witty and convincing argument against the abolition of capital punishment. And yet all the erroneousness of the argument of those who consider that governments cannot give up the use of force till all people are capable of doing the same, could not be more clearly expressed than it is in that epigram.

"Let the murderers," say the champions of state violence, "set us the example by giving up murder and then we will give it up." But the murderers say just the same, only with much more right. They say: "Let those who have undertaken to teach us and guide us set us the example of giving up legal murder, and then we will imitate them." And they say this, not as a jest, but seriously, because it is the actual state of the case.

"We cannot give up the use of violence, because we are surrounded by violent ruffians." Nothing in our days hinders the progress of humanity and the establishment of the organization corresponding to its present development more than this false reasoning. Those in authority are convinced that men are only guided and only progress through the use of force, and therefore they confidently make use of it to support the existing organization. The existing order is maintained, not by force, but by public opinion, the action of which is disturbed by the use of force. So that the effect of using force is to disturb and to weaken the very thing it tries to maintain.

Violence, even in the most favorable case, when it is not used simply for some personal aims of those in power, always punishes under the one inelastic formula of the law what has long before been condemned by public opinion. But there is this difference, that while public opinion censures and condemns all the acts opposed to the moral law, including the most varied cases in its reprobation, the law which rests on violence only condemns and punishes a certain very limited range of acts, and by so doing seems to justify all other acts of the same kind which do not come under its scope.

Public opinion ever since the time of Moses has regarded covetousness, profligacy, and cruelty as wrong, and censured them accordingly. And it condemns every kind of manifestation of covetousness, not only the appropriation of the property of others by force or fraud or trickery, but even the cruel abuse of wealth; it condemns every form of profligacy, whether with concubine, slave, divorced woman, or even one's own wife; it condemns every kind of cruelty, whether shown in blows, in ill-treatment, or in murder, not only of men, but even of animals. The law resting on force only punishes certain forms of covetousness, such as robbery and swindling, certain forms of profligacy and cruelty, such as conjugal infidelity, murder, and wounding. And in this way it seems to countenance all the manifestations of covetousness, profligacy, and cruelty which do not come under its narrow definition.

But besides corrupting public opinion, the use of force leads men to the fatal conviction that they progress, not through the spiritual impulse which impels them to the attainment of truth and its realization in life, and which constitutes the only source of every progressive movement of humanity, but by means of violence, the very force which, far from leading men to truth, always carries them further away from it. This is a fatal error, because it leads men to neglect the chief force underlying their life--their spiritual activity--and to turn all their attention and energy to the use of violence, which is superficial, sluggish, and most generally pernicious in its action.

They make the same mistake as men who, trying to set a steam engine in motion, should turn its wheels round with their hands, not suspecting that the underlying cause of its movement was the expansion of the steam, and not the motion of the wheels. By turning the wheels by hand and by levers they could only produce a semblance of movement, and meantime they would be wrenching the wheels and so preventing their being fit for real movement.

That is just what people are doing who think to make men advance by means of external force.

They say that the Christian life cannot be established without the use of violence, because there are savage races outside the pale of Christian societies in Africa and in Asia (there are some who even represent the Chinese as a danger to civilization), and that in the midst of Christian societies there are savage, corrupt, and, according to the new theory of heredity, congenital criminals. And violence, they say, is necessary to keep savages and criminals from annihilating our civilization.

But these savages within and without Christian society, who are such a terror to us, have never been subjugated by violence, and are not subjugated by it now. Nations have never subjugated other nations by violence alone. If a nation which subjugated another was on a lower level of civilization, it has never happened that it succeeded in introducing its organization of life by violence. On the contrary, it was always forced to adopt the organization of life existing in the conquered nation. If ever any of the nations conquered by force have been really subjugated, or even nearly so, it has always been by the action of public opinion, and never by violence, which only tends to drive a people to further rebellion.

When whole nations have been subjugated by a new religion, and have become Christian or Mohammedan, such a conversion has never been brought about because the authorities made it obligatory (on the contrary, violence has much oftener acted in the opposite direction), but because public opinion made such a change inevitable. Nations, on the contrary, who have been driven by force to accept the faith of their conquerors have always remained antagonistic to it.

It is just the same with the savage elements existing in the midst of our civilized societies. Neither the increased nor the diminished severity of punishment, nor the modifications of prisons, nor the increase of police will increase or diminish the number of criminals. Their number will only be diminished by the change of the moral standard of society. No severities could put an end to duels and vendettas in certain districts. In spite of the number of Tcherkesses executed for robbery, they continue to be robbers from their youth up, for no maiden will marry a Tcherkess youth till he has given proof of his bravery by carrying off a horse, or at least a sheep. If men cease to fight duels, and the Tcherkesses cease to be robbers, it will not be from fear of punishment (indeed, that invests the crime with additional charm for youth), but through a change in the moral standard of public opinion. It is the same with all other crimes. Force can never suppress what is sanctioned by public opinion. On the contrary, public opinion need only be in direct opposition to force to neutralize the whole effect of the use of force. It has always been so and always will be in every case of martyrdom.

What would happen if force were not used against hostile nations and the criminal elements of society we do not know. But we do know by prolonged experience that neither enemies nor criminals have been successfully suppressed by force.

And indeed how could nations be subjugated by violence who are led by their whole education, their traditions, and even their religion to see the loftiest virtue in warring with their oppressors and fighting for freedom? And how are we to suppress by force acts committed in the midst of our society which are regarded as crimes by the government and as daring exploits by the people?

To exterminate such nations and such criminals by violence is possible, and indeed is done, but to subdue them is impossible.

The sole guide which directs men and nations has always been and is the unseen, intangible, underlying force, the resultant of all the spiritual forces of a certain people, or of all humanity, which finds its outward expression in public opinion.

The use of violence only weakens this force, hinders it and corrupts it, and tries to replace it by another which far from being conducive to the progress of humanity, is detrimental to it.

To bring under the sway of Christianity all the savage nations outside the pale of the Christian world--all the Zulus, Mandchoos, and Chinese, whom many regard as savages--and the savages who live in our midst, there is only ONE MEANS. That means is the propagation among these nations of the Christian ideal of society, which can only be realized by a Christian life, Christian actions, and Christian examples. And meanwhile, though this is the ONE ONLY MEANS of gaining a hold over the people who have remained non-Christian, the men of our day set to work in the directly opposite fashion to attain this result.

To bring under the sway of Christianity savage nations who do not attack us and whom we have therefore no excuse for oppressing, we ought before all things to leave them in peace, and in case we need or wish to enter into closer relations with them, we ought only to influence them by Christian manners and Christian teaching, setting them the example of the Christian virtues of patience, meekness, endurance, purity, brotherhood, and love. Instead of that we begin by establishing among them new markets for our commerce, with the sole aim of our own profit; then we appropriate their lands, i. e., rob them; then we sell them spirits, tobacco, and opium, i. e., corrupt them; then we establish our morals among them, teach them the use of violence and new methods of destruction, i, e., we teach them nothing but the animal law of strife, below which man cannot sink, and we do all we can to conceal from them all that is Christian in us.
After this we send some dozens of missionaries prating to them of the hypocritical absurdities of the Church, and then quote the failure of our efforts to turn the heathen to Christianity as an incontrovertible proof of the impossibility of applying the truths of Christianity in practical life.

It is just the same with the so-called criminals living in our midst. To bring these people under the sway of Christianity there is one only means, that is, the Christian social ideal, which can only be realized among them by true Christian teaching and supported by a true example of the Christian life. And to preach this Christian truth and to support it by Christian example we set up among them prisons, guillotines, gallows, preparations for murder; we diffuse among the common herd idolatrous superstitions to stupefy them; we sell them spirits, tobacco, and opium to brutalize them; we even organize legalized prostitution; we give land to those who do not need it; we make a display of senseless luxury in the midst of suffering poverty; we destroy the possibility of anything like a Christian public opinion, and studiously try to suppress what Christian public opinion is existing. And then, after having ourselves assiduously corrupted men, we shut them up like wild beasts in places from which they cannot escape, and where they become still more brutalized, or else we kill them. And these very men whom we have corrupted and brutalized by every means, we bring forward as a proof that one cannot deal with criminals except by brute force.

We are just like ignorant doctors who put a man, recovering from illness by the force of nature, into the most unfavorable conditions of hygiene, and dose him with the most deleterious drugs, and then assert triumphantly that their hygiene and their drugs saved his life, when the patient would have been well long before if they had left him alone.

Violence, which is held up as the means of supporting the Christian organization of life, not only fails to produce that effect, it even hinders the social organization of life from being what it might and ought to be. The social organization is as good as it is not as a result of force, but in spite of it.

And therefore the champions of the existing order are mistaken in arguing that since, even with the aid of force, the bad and non-Christian elements of humanity can hardly be kept from attacking us, the abolition of the use of force and the substitution of public opinion for it would leave humanity quite unprotected.

They are mistaken, because force does not protect humanity, but, on the contrary, deprives it of the only possible means of really protecting itself, that is, the establishment and diffusion of a Christian public opinion. Only by the suppression of violence will a Christian public opinion cease to be corrupted, and be enabled to be diffused without hindrance, and men will then turn their efforts in the spiritual direction by which alone they can advance.

"But how are we to cast off the visible tangible protection of an armed policeman, and trust to something so intangible as public opinion? Does it yet exist? Moreover, the condition of things in which we are living now, we know, good or bad; we know its shortcomings and are used to it, we know what to do, and how to behave under present conditions. But what will happen when we give it up and trust ourselves to something invisible and intangible, and altogether unknown?"

The unknown world on which they are entering in renouncing their habitual ways of life appears itself as dreadful to them. It is all very well to dread the unknown when our habitual position is sound and secure. But our position is so far from being secure that we know, beyond all doubt, that we are standing on the brink of a precipice. If we must be afraid let us be afraid of what is really alarming, and not what we imagine as alarming.

Fearing to make the effort to detach ourselves from our perilous position because the future is not fully clear to us, we are like passengers in a foundering ship who, through being afraid to trust themselves to the boat which would carry them to the shore, shut themselves up in the cabin and refuse to come out of it; or like sheep, who, terrified by their barn being on fire, huddle in a corner and do not go out of the wide-open door.

We are standing on the threshold of the murderous war of social revolution, terrific in its miseries, beside which, as those who are preparing it tell us, the horrors of 1793 will be child's play. And can we talk of the danger threatening us from the warriors of Dahomey, the Zulus, and such, who live so far away and are not dreaming of attacking us, and from some thousands of swindlers, thieves, and murderers, brutalized and corrupted by ourselves, whose number is in no way lessened by all our sentences, prisons, and executions?

Moreover this dread of the suppression of the visible protection of the policeman is essentially a sentiment of townspeople, that is, of people who are living in abnormal and artificial conditions. People living in natural conditions of life, not in towns, but in the midst of nature, and carrying on the struggle with nature, live without this protection and know how little force can protect us from the real dangers with which we are surrounded. There is something sickly in this dread, which is essentially dependent on the artificial conditions in which many of us live and have been brought up.

A doctor, a specialist in insanity, told a story that one summer day when he was leaving the asylum, the lunatics accompanied him to the street door. "Come for a walk in the town with me?" the doctor suggested to them. The lunatics agreed, and a small band followed the doctor. But the further they proceeded along the street where healthy people were freely moving about, the more timid they became, and they pressed closer and closer to the doctor, hindering him from walking. At last they all began to beg him to take them back to the asylum, to their meaningless but customary way of life, to their keepers, to blows, strait waistcoats, and solitary cells.

This is just how men of to-day huddle in terror and draw back to their irrational manner of life, their factories, law courts, prisons, executions, and wars, when Christianity calls them to liberty, to the free, rational life of the future coming age.

People ask, "How will our security be guaranteed when the existing organization is suppressed? What precisely will the new organization be that is to replace it? So long as we do not know precisely how our life will be organized, we will not stir a step forward."

An explorer going to an unknown country might as well ask for a detailed map of the country before he would start.

If a man, before he passed from one stage to another, could know his future life in full detail, he would have nothing to live for.
It is the same with the life of humanity. If it had a programme of the life which awaited it before entering a new stage, it would be the surest sign that it was not living, nor advancing, but simply rotating in the same place.

The conditions of the new order of life cannot be known by us because we have to create them by our own labors. That is all that life is, to learn the unknown, and to adapt our actions to this new knowledge.

That is the life of each individual man, and that is the life of human societies and of humanity.

CHAPTER XI.

THE CHRISTIAN CONCEPTION OF LIFE HAS ALREADY ARISEN IN OUR SOCIETY, AND WILL INFALLIBLY PUT AN END TO THE PRESENT ORGANIZATION OF OUR LIFE BASED ON FORCE--WHEN THAT WILL BE.

The Condition and Organization of our Society are Terrible, but they Rest only on Public Opinion, and can be Destroyed by it--Already Violence is Regarded from a Different Point of View; the Number of those who are Ready to Serve the Government is Diminishing; and even the Servants of Government are Ashamed of their Position, and so often Do Not Perform their Duties--These Facts are all Signs of the Rise of a Public Opinion, which Continually Growing will Lead to No One being Willing to Enter Government Service--Moreover, it Becomes More and More Evident that those Offices are of No Practical Use--Men already Begin to Understand the Futility of all Institutions Based on Violence, and if a Few already Understand it, All will One Day Understand it--The Day of Deliverance is Unknown, but it Depends on Men Themselves, on how far Each Man Lives According to the Light that is in Him.

The position of Christian humanity with its prisons, galleys, gibbets, its factories and accumulation of capital, its taxes, churches, gin-palaces, licensed brothels, its ever-increasing armament and its millions of brutalized men, ready, like chained dogs, to attack anyone against whom their master incites them, would be terrible indeed if it were the product of violence, but it is pre-eminently the product of public opinion. And what has been established by public opinion can be destroyed by public opinion--and, indeed, is being destroyed by public opinion.

Money lavished by hundreds of millions, tens of millions of disciplined troops, weapons of astounding destructive power, all organizations carried to the highest point of perfection, a whole army of men charged with the task of deluding and hypnotizing the people, and all this, by means of electricity which annihilates distance, under the direct control of men who regard such an organization of society not only as necessary for profit, but even for self-preservation, and therefore exert every effort of their ingenuity to preserve it--what an invincible power it would seem! And yet we need only imagine for a moment what will really inevitably come to pass, that is, the Christian social standard replacing the heathen social standard and established with the same power and universality, and the majority of men as much ashamed of taking any part in violence or in profiting by it, as they are to-day of thieving, swindling, begging, and cowardice; and at once we see the whole of this complex, and seemingly powerful organization of society falls into ruins of itself without a struggle.

And to bring this to pass, nothing new need be brought before men's minds. Only let the mist, which veils from men's eyes the true meaning of certain acts of violence, pass away, and the

Christian public opinion which is springing up would overpower the extinct public opinion which permitted and justified acts of violence. People need only come to be as much ashamed to do deeds of violence, to assist in them or to profit by them, as they now are of being, or being reputed a swindler, a thief, a coward, or a beggar. And already this change is beginning to take place. We do not notice it just as we do not notice the movement of the earth, because we are moved together with everything around us.

It is true that the organization of society remains in its principal features just as much an organization based on violence as it was one thousand years ago, and even in some respects, especially in the preparation for war and in war itself, it appears still more brutal. But the rising Christian ideal, which must at a certain stage of development replace the heathen ideal of life, already makes its influence felt. A dead tree stands apparently as firmly as ever--it may even seem firmer because it is harder--but it is rotten at the core, and soon must fall. It is just so with the present order of society, based on force. The external aspect is unchanged. There is the same division of oppressors and oppressed, but their view of the significance and dignity of their respective positions is no longer what it once was.

The oppressors, that is, those who take part in government, and those who profit by oppression, that is, the rich, no longer imagine, as they once did, that they are the elect of the world, and that they constitute the ideal of human happiness and greatness, to attain which was once the highest aim of the oppressed.

Very often now it is not the oppressed who strive to attain the position of the oppressors, and try to imitate them, but on the contrary the oppressors who voluntarily abandon the advantages of their position, prefer the condition of the oppressed, and try to resemble them in the simplicity of their life.

Not to speak of the duties and occupations now openly despised, such as that of spy, agent of secret police, moneylender, and publican, there are a great number of professions formerly regarded as honorable, such as those of police officials, courtiers, judges, and administrative functionaries, clergymen, military officers, speculators, and bankers, which are no longer considered desirable positions by everyone, and are even despised by a special circle of the most respected people. There are already men who voluntarily abandon these professions which were once reckoned irreproachable, and prefer less lucrative callings which are in no way connected with the use of force.
And there are even rich men who, not through religious sentiment, but simply through special sensitiveness to the social standard that is springing up, relinquish their inherited property, believing that a man can only justly consume what he has gained by

his own labor.

The position of a government official or of a rich man is no longer, as it once was, and still is among non-Christian peoples, regarded as necessarily honorable and deserving of respect, and under the special blessing of God. The most delicate and moral people (they are generally also the most cultivated) avoid such positions and prefer more humble callings that are not dependent on the use of force.

The best of our young people, at the age when they are still uncorrupted by life and are choosing a career, prefer the calling of doctor, engineer, teacher, artist, writer, or even that of simple farmer living on his own labor, to legal, administrative, clerical, and military positions in the pay of government, or to an idle existence living on their incomes.

Monuments and memorials in these days are mostly not erected in honor of government dignitaries, or generals, or still less of rich men, but rather of artists, men of science, and inventors, persons who have nothing in common with the government, and often have even been in conflict with it. They are the men whose praises are celebrated in poetry, who are honored by sculpture and received with triumphant jubilations.

The best men of our day are all striving for such places of honor.

Consequently the class from which the wealthy and the government officials are drawn grows less in number and lower in intelligence and education, and still more in moral qualities. So that nowadays the wealthy class and men at the head of government do not constitute, as they did in former days, the ÉLITE of society; on the contrary, they are inferior to the middle class.

In Russia and Turkey as in America and France, however often the government change its officials, the majority of them are self-seeking and corrupt, of so low a moral standard that they do not even come up the elementary requirements of common honesty expected by the government. One may often nowadays hear from persons in authority the naïve complaint that the best people are always, by some strange--as it seems to them--fatality, to be found in the camp of the opposition. As though men were to complain that those who accepted the office of hangman were--by some strange fatality--all persons of very little refinement or beauty of character.

The most cultivated and refined people of our society are not nowadays to be found among the very rich, as used formerly to be the rule. The rich are mostly coarse money grubbers, absorbed only, in increasing their hoard, generally by dishonest means, or else the degenerate heirs of such money grubbers, who, far from playing any prominent part in society, are mostly treated with general contempt.

And besides the fact that the class from which the servants of government and the wealthy are drawn grows less in number and lower in caliber, they no longer themselves attach the same importance to their positions as they once did; often they are ashamed of the ignominy of their calling and do not perform the duties they are bound to perform in their position. Kings and emperors scarcely govern at all; they scarcely ever decide upon an internal reform or a new departure in foreign politics. They mostly leave the decision of such questions to government institutions or to public opinion. All their duties are reduced to representing the unity and majesty of government. And even this duty they perform less and less successfully. The majority of them do not keep up their old unapproachable majesty, but become more and more democratized and even vulgarized, casting aside the external prestige that remained to them, and thereby destroying the very thing it was their function to maintain.

It is just the same with the army. Military officers of the highest rank, instead of encouraging in their soldiers the brutality and ferocity necessary for their work, diffuse education among the soldiers, inculcate humanity, and often even themselves share the socialistic ideas of the masses and denounce war. In the last plots against the Russian Government many of the conspirators were in the army. And the number of the disaffected in the army is always increasing. And it often happens (there was a case, indeed, within the last few days) that when called upon to quell disturbances they refuse to fire upon the people. Military exploits are openly reprobated by the military themselves, and are often the subject of jests among them.

It is the same with judges and public prosecutors. The judges, whose duty it is to judge and condemn criminals, conduct the proceedings so as to whitewash them as far as possible. So that the Russian Government, to procure the condemnation of those whom they want to punish, never intrust them to the ordinary tribunals, but have them tried before a court martial, which is only a parody of justice. The prosecutors themselves often refuse to proceed, and even when they do proceed, often in spite of the law, really defend those they ought to be accusing. The learned jurists whose business it is to justify the violence of authority, are more and more disposed to deny the right of punishment and to replace it by theories of irresponsibility and even of moral insanity, proposing to deal with those they call criminals by medical treatment only.

Jailers and overseers of galleys generally become the champions of those whom they ought to torture. Police officers and detectives are continually assisting the escape of those they ought to arrest. The clergy preach tolerance, and even sometimes condemn the use of force, and the more educated among them try in their sermons to avoid the very deception which is the basis of their position and which it is their duty to support. Executioners refuse to perform their functions, so that in Russia the death penalty cannot be carried out for want of executioners. And in spite of all the advantages bestowed on these men, who are selected from convicts, there is a constantly diminishing number of volunteers for the post. Governors, police officials, tax collectors often have compassion on the people and try to find pretexts for not collecting the tax from them. The rich are not at ease in spending their wealth only on themselves, and lavish it on works of public utility. Landowners build schools and hospitals on their property, and some even give up the ownership of their land and transfer it to the cultivators, or establish communities upon it. Millowners and manufacturers build hospitals, schools, savings banks, asylums, and dwellings for their workpeople. Some of them form co-operative associations in which they have shares on the same terms as the others. Capitalists expend a part of their capital on educational, artistic, philanthropic, and other public institutions. And many, who are not equal to parting with their wealth in their lifetime, leave it in their wills to public institutions.

All these phenomena might seem to be mere exceptions, except that they can all be referred to one common cause. Just as one might fancy the first leaves on the budding trees in April were exceptional if we did not know that they all have a common cause, the spring, and that if we see the branches on some trees shooting and turning green, it is certain that it will soon be so with all.

So it is with the manifestation of the Christian standard of opinion on force and all that is based on force. If this standard already influences some, the most impressionable, and impels each in his own sphere to abandon advantages based on the use of force, then its influence will extend further and further till it transforms the whole order of men's actions and puts it into accord with the Christian ideal which is already a living force in the vanguard of humanity.

And if there are now rulers, who do not decide on any step on their own authority, who try to be as unlike monarchs, and as like plain mortals as possible, who state their readiness to give up their prerogatives and become simply the first citizens of a republic; if there are already soldiers who realize all the sin and harm of war, and are not willing to fire on men either of their own or a foreign country; judges and prosecutors who do not like to try and to condemn criminals; priests, who abjure deception; tax-gatherers who try to perform as little as they can of their duties, and rich men renouncing their wealth--then the same thing will inevitably happen to other rulers, other soldiers, other judges, priests, tax-gatherers, and rich men. And when there are no longer men willing to fill these offices, these offices themselves will disappear too.

But this is not the only way in which public opinion is leading men to the abolition of the prevailing order and the substitution of a new order. As the positions based on the rule of force become less attractive and fewer men are found willing to fill them, the more will their uselessness be apparent.

Everywhere throughout the Christian world the same rulers, and the same governments, the same armies, the same law courts, the same tax-gatherers, the same priests, the same rich men, landowners, manufacturers, and capitalists, as ever, but the attitude of the world to them, and their attitude to themselves is altogether changed.

The same sovereigns have still the same audiences and interviews, hunts and banquets, and balls and uniforms; there are the same diplomats and the same deliberations on alliances and wars; there are still the same parliaments, with the same debates on the Eastern question and Africa, on treaties and violations of treaties, and Home Rule and the eight-hour day; and one set of ministers replacing another in the same way, and the same speeches and the same incidents. But for men who observe how one newspaper article has more effect on the position of affairs than dozens of royal audiences or parliamentary sessions, it becomes more and more evident that these audiences and interviews and debates in parliaments do not direct the course of affairs, but something independent of all that, which cannot be concentrated in one place.

The same generals and officers and soldiers, and cannons and fortresses, and reviews and maneuvers, but no war breaks out. One year, ten, twenty years pass by. And it becomes less and less possible to rely on the army for the pacification of riots, and more and more evident, consequently, that generals, and officers, and soldiers are only figures in solemn processions--objects of amusement for governments--a sort of immense--and far too expensive--CORPS DE BALLET.

The same lawyers and judges, and the same assizes, but it becomes more and more evident that the civil courts decide cases on the most diverse grounds, but regardless of justice, and that criminal trials are quite senseless, because the punishments do not attain the objects aimed at by the judges themselves. These institutions therefore serve no other purpose than to provide a means of livelihood for men who are not capable of doing anything more useful.

The same priests and archbishops and churches and synods, but it becomes more and more evident that they have long ago ceased to believe in what they preach, and therefore they can convince no one of the necessity of believing what they don't believe themselves.

The same tax collectors, but they are less and less capable of taking men's property from them by force, and it becomes more and more evident that people can collect all that is necessary by voluntary subscription without their aid.

The same rich men, but it becomes more and more evident that they can only be of use by ceasing to administer their property in person and giving up to society the whole or at least a part of their wealth.

And when all this has become absolutely evident to everyone, it will be natural for men to ask themselves: "But why should we keep and maintain all these kings, emperors, presidents, and members of all sorts of senates and ministries, since nothing comes of all their debates and audiences? Wouldn't it be better, as some humorist suggested, to make a queen of india-rubber?"

And what good to us are these armies with their generals and bands and horses and drums? And what need is there of them when there is no war, and no one wants to make war? and if there were a war, other nations would not let us gain any advantage from it; while the soldiers refuse to fire on their fellow-countrymen.

And what is the use of these lawyers and judges who don't decide civil cases with justice and recognize themselves the uselessness of punishments in criminal cases?

And what is the use of tax collectors who collect the taxes unwillingly, when it is easy to raise all that is wanted without them?

What is the use of the clergy, who don't believe in what they preach?

And what is the use of capital in the hands of private persons, when it can only be of use as the property of all?

And when once people have asked themselves these questions they cannot help coming to some decision and ceasing to support all these institutions which are no longer of use.

But even before those who support these institutions decide to abolish them, the men who occupy these positions will be reduced to the necessity of throwing them up.

Public opinion more and more condemns the use of force, and therefore men are less and less willing to fill positions which rest on the use of force, and if they do occupy them, are less and less able to make use of force in them. And hence they must become more and more superfluous.

I once took part in Moscow in a religious meeting which used to take place generally in the week after Easter near the church in the Ohotny Row. A little knot of some twenty men were collected together on the pavement, engaged in serious religious discussion. At the same time there was a kind of concert going on in the buildings of the Court Club in the same street, and a police officer noticing the little group collected near the church sent a mounted policeman to disperse it. It was absolutely unnecessary for the officer to disperse it. A group of twenty men was no obstruction to anyone, but he had been standing there the whole morning, and he wanted to do something. The policeman, a young fellow, with a resolute flourish of his right arm and a clink of his saber, came up to us and commanded us severely: "Move on! what's this meeting about?" Everyone looked at the policeman, and one of the speakers, a quiet man in a peasant's dress, answered with a calm and gracious air, "We are speaking of serious matters, and there is no need for us to move on; you would do better, young man, to get off your horse and listen. It might do you good"; and turning round he continued his discourse. The policeman turned his horse and went off without a word.

That is just what should be done in all cases of violence.

The officer was bored, he had nothing to do. He had been put, poor fellow, in a position in which he had no choice but to give orders. He was shut off from all human existence; he could do nothing but superintend and give orders, and give orders and superintend, though his superintendence and his orders served no useful purpose whatever. And this is the position in which all these unlucky rulers, ministers, members of parliament, governors, generals, officers, archbishops, priests, and even rich men find themselves to some extent already, and will find themselves altogether as time goes on. They can do nothing but give orders, and they give orders and send their messengers, as the officer sent the policeman, to interfere with people. And because the people they hinder turn to them and request them not to interfere, they fancy they are very useful indeed.

But the time will come and is coming when it will be perfectly evident to everyone that they are not of any use at all, and only a hindrance, and those whom they interfere with will say gently and quietly to them, like my friend in the street meeting, "Pray don't interfere with us." And all the messengers and those who send them too will be obliged to follow this good advice, that is to say, will leave off galloping about, with their arms akimbo, interfering with people, and getting off their horses and removing their spurs, will listen to what is being said, and mixing with others, will take their place with them in some real human work.

The time will come and is inevitably coming when all institutions based on force will disappear through their uselessness, stupidity, and even inconvenience becoming obvious to all.

The time must come when the men of our modern world who fill offices based upon violence will find themselves in the position of the emperor in Andersen's tale of "The Emperor's New Clothes," when the child seeing the emperor undressed, cried in all simplicity, "Look, he is naked!" And then all the rest, who had seen him and said nothing, could not help recognizing it too.

The story is that there was once an emperor, very fond of new clothes. And to him came two tailors, who promised to make him some extraordinary clothes. The emperor engages them and they begin to sew at them, but they explain that the clothes have the extraordinary property of remaining invisible to anyone who is unfit for his position. The courtiers come to look at the tailors' work and see nothing, for the men are plying their needles in empty space. But remembering the extraordinary property of the clothes, they all declare they see them and are loud in their admiration. The emperor does the same himself. The day of the procession comes in which the emperor is to go out in his new clothes. The emperor undresses and puts on his new clothes, that is to say, remains naked, and naked he walks through the town. But remembering the magic property of the clothes, no one ventures to say that he has nothing on till a little child cries out: "Look, he is naked!"

This will be exactly the situation of all who continue through inertia to fill offices which have long become useless directly someone who has no interest in concealing their uselessness exclaims in all simplicity: "But these people have been of no use to anyone for a long time past!"

The condition of Christian humanity with its fortresses, cannons, dynamite, guns, torpedoes, prisons, gallows, churches, factories, customs offices, and palaces is really terrible. But still cannons and guns will not fire themselves, prisons will not shut men up of themselves, gallows will not hang them, churches will not delude them, nor customs offices hinder them, and palaces and factories are not built nor kept up of themselves. All those things are the work of men. If men come to understand that they ought not to do these things, then they will cease to be. And already they are beginning to understand it. Though all do not understand it yet, the advanced guard understand and the rest will follow them. And the advanced guard cannot cease to understand what they have once understood; and what they understand the rest not only can but must inevitably understand hereafter.

So that the prophecy that the time will come when men will be taught of God, will learn war no more, will beat their swords into plowshares and their spears into reaping-hooks, which means, translating it into our language, the fortresses, prisons, barracks, palaces, and churches will remain empty, and all the gibbets and guns and cannons will be left unused, is no longer a dream, but the definite new form of life to which mankind is approaching with ever-increasing rapidity.

But when will it be?

Eighteen hundred years ago to this question Christ answered that the end of the world (that is, of the pagan organization of life) shall come when the tribulation of men is greater than it has ever been, and when the Gospel of the kingdom of God, that is, the possibility of a new organization of life, shall be preached in the world unto all nations. (Matt. xxiv. 3-28.) But of that day and hour knoweth no man but the Father only (Matt. xxiv. 3-6), said Christ. For it may come any time, in such an hour as ye think not.

To the question when this hour cometh Christ answers that we cannot know, but just because we cannot know when that hour is coming we ought to be always ready to meet it, just as the master ought to watch who guards his house from thieves, as the virgins ought to watch with lamps alight for the bridegroom; and further, we ought to work with all the powers given us to bring that hour to pass, as the servants ought to work with the talents intrusted to them. (Matt. xxiv. 43, and xxvi. 13, 14-30.) And there could be no answer but this one. Men cannot know when the day and the hour of the kingdom of God will come, because its coming depends on themselves alone.

The answer is like that of the wise man who, when asked whether it was far to the town, answered, "Walk!"

How can we tell whether it is far to the goal which humanity is approaching, when we do not know how men are going toward it, while it depends on them whether they go or do not go, stand still, slacken their pace or hasten it? All we can know is what we who make up mankind ought to do, and not to do, to bring about the coming of the kingdom of God. And that we all know. And we need only each begin to do what we ought to do, we need only each live with all the light that is in us, to bring about at once the promised kingdom of God to which every man's heart is yearning.

CHAPTER XII.

CONCLUSION--REPENT YE, FOR THE KINGDOM OF HEAVEN IS AT HAND.

1. Chance Meeting with a Train Carrying Soldiers to Restore Order Among the Famishing Peasants--Reason of the Expedition--How the Decisions of the Higher Authorities are Enforced in Cases of Insubordination on Part of the Peasants--What Happened at Orel, as an Example of How the Rights of the Propertied Classes are Maintained by Murder and Torture--All the Privileges of the Wealthy are Based on Similar Acts of Violence.

2. The Elements that Made up the Force Sent to Toula, and the Conduct of the Men Composing it--How these Men Could Carry Out such Acts--The Explanation is Not to be Found in Ignorance, Conviction, Cruelty, Heartlessness, or Want of Moral Sense--They do these Things Because they are Necessary to Support the Existing Order, which they Consider it Every Man's Duty to Support--The Basis of this Conviction that the Existing Order is Necessary and Inevitable--In the Upper Classes this Conviction is Based on the Advantages of the Existing Order for Themselves--But what Forces Men of the Lower Classes to Believe in the Immutability of the Existing Order, from which they Derive no Advantage, and which they Aid in Maintaining, Facts Contrary to their Conscience?--This is the Result of the Lower Classes being Deluded by the Upper, Both as to the Inevitability of the Existing Order and the Lawfulness of the Acts of Violence Needed to Maintain it--Deception in

General--Special Form of Deception in Regard to Military Service--Conscription.

3. How can Men Allow that Murder is Permissible while they Preach Principles of Morality, and How can they Allow of the Existence in their Midst of a Military Organization of Physical Force which is a Constant Menace to Public Security?--It is only Allowed by the Upper Classes, who Profit by this Organization, Because their Privileges are Maintained by it--The Upper Classes Allow it, and the Lower Classes Carry it into Effect in Spite of their Consciousness of the Immorality of the Deeds of Violence, the More Readily Because Through the Arrangements of the Government the Moral Responsibility for such Deeds is Divided among a Great Number of Participants in it, and Everyone Throws the Responsibility on Someone Else--Moreover, the Sense of Moral Responsibility is Lost through the Delusion of Inequality, and the Consequent Intoxication of Power on the Part of Superiors, and Servility on the Part of Inferiors--The Condition of these Men, Acting against the Dictates of their Conscience, is Like that of Hypnotized Subjects Acting by Suggestion--The Difference between this Obedience to Government Suggestion, and Obedience to Public Opinion, and to the Guidance of Men of a Higher Moral Sense--The Existing Order of Society, which is the Result of an Extinct Public Opinion and is Inconsistent with the Already Existing Public Opinion of the Future, is only Maintained by the Stupefaction of the Conscience, Produced Spontaneously by Self-interest in the Upper Classes and Through Hypnotizing in the Lower Classes--The Conscience or the Common Sense of such Men may Awaken, and there are

Examples of its Sudden Awakening, so that one can Never be Sure of the Deeds of Violence they are Prepared for--It Depends Entirely on the Point which the Sense of the Unlawfulness of Acts of Violence has Reached, and this Sense may Spontaneously Awaken in Men, or may be Reawakened by the Influence of Men of more Conscience.

4. Everything Depends on the Strength of the Consciousness of Christian Truths in Each Individual Man--The Leading Men of Modern Times, however, do not Think it Necessary to Preach or Practice the Truths of Christianity, but Regard the Modification of the External Conditions of Existence within the Limit Imposed by Governments as Sufficient to Reform the Life of Humanity--On this Scientific Theory of Hypocrisy, which has Replaced the Hypocrisy of Religion, Men of the Wealthy Classes Base their Justification of their Position--Through this Hypocrisy they can Enjoy the Exclusive Privileges of their Position by Force and Fraud, and Still Pretend to be Christians to One Another and be Easy in their Minds--This Hypocrisy Allows Men who Preach Christianity to Take Part in Institutions Based on Violence--No External Reformation of Life will Render it Less Miserable--Its Misery the Result of Disunion Caused by Following Lies, not the Truth--Union only Possible in Truth--Hypocrisy Hinders this Union, since Hypocrites Conceal from themselves and Others the Truth they Know--Hypocrisy Turns all Reforms of Life to Evil--Hypocrisy Distorts the Idea of Good and Evil, and so Stands in the Way of the Progress of Men toward Perfection--Undisguised Criminals and Malefactors do Less

Harm than those who Live by Legalized Violence, Disguised by Hypocrisy--All Men Feel the Iniquity of our Life, and would Long Ago have Transformed it if it had not been Dissimulated by Hypocrisy--But Seem to have Reached the Extreme Limits of Hypocrisy, and we Need only Make an Effort of Conscience to Awaken as from a Nightmare to a Different Reality.

5. Can Man Make this Effort?--According to the Hypocritical Theory of the Day, Man is not Free to Transform his Life--Man is not Free in his Actions, but he is Free to Admit or to Deny the Truth he Knows--When Truth is Once Admitted, it Becomes the Basis of Action--Man's Threefold Relation to Truth--The Reason of the Apparent Insolubility of the Problem of Free Will--Man's Freedom Consists in the Recognition of the Truth Revealed to him. There is no Other Freedom--Recognition of Truth Gives Freedom, and Shows the Path Along which, Willingly or Unwillingly by Mankind, Man Must Advance--The Recognition of Truth and Real Freedom Enables Man to Share in the Work of God, not as the Slave, but as the Creator of Life--Men Need only Make the Effort to Renounce all Thought of Bettering the External Conditions of Life and Bend all their Efforts to Recognizing and Preaching the Truth they Know, to put an End to the Existing Miserable State of Things, and to Enter upon the Kingdom of God so far as it is yet Accessible to Man--All that is Needed is to Make an End of Lying and Hypocrisy--But then what Awaits us in the Future?--What will Happen to Humanity if Men Follow the Dictates of their Conscience, and how can Life go on

with the Conditions of Civilized Life to which we are Accustomed? --All Uneasiness on these Points may be Removed by the Reflection that Nothing True and Good can be Destroyed by the Realization of Truth, but will only be Freed from the Alloy of Falsehood.

6. Our Life has Reached the Extreme Limit of Misery and Cannot be Improved by any Systems of Organization--All our Life and all our Institutions are Quite Meaningless--Are we Doing what God Wills of us by Preserving our Privileges and Duties to Government?--We are put in this Position not Because the World is so Made and it is Inevitable, but Because we Wish it to be so, Because it is to the Advantage of Some of us--Our Conscience is in Opposition to our Position and all our Conduct, and the Way Out of the Contradiction is to be Found in the Recognition of the Christian Truth: Do Not unto Others what you Would Not they should Do unto You--As our Duties to Self Must be Subordinated to our Duties to Others, so Must our Duties to Others be Subordinated to our Duties to God--The Only Way Out of our Position Lies, if not in Renouncing our Position and our Privileges, at Least in Recognizing our Sin and not Justifying it nor Disguising it--The Only Object of Life is to Learn the Truth and to Act on it--Acceptance of the Position and of State Action Deprives Life of all Object--It is God's Will that we should Serve Him in our Life, that is, that we should Bring About the Greatest Unity of all that has Life, a Unity only Possible in Truth.

I was finishing this book, which I had been working at for two years, when I happened on the 9th of September to be traveling by rail through the governments of Toula and Riazan, where the peasants were starving last year and where the famine is even more severe now. At one of the railway stations my train passed an extra train which was taking a troop of soldiers under the conduct of the governor of the province, together with muskets, cartridges, and rods, to flog and murder these same famishing peasants.

The punishment of flogging by way of carrying the decrees of the authorities into effect has been more and more frequently adopted of late in Russia, in spite of the fact that corporal punishment was abolished by law thirty years ago.

I had heard of this, I had even read in the newspapers of the fearful floggings which had been inflicted in Tchernigov, Tambov, Saratov, Astrakhan, and Orel, and of those of which the governor of Nijni-Novgorod, General Baranov, had boasted. But I had never before happened to see men in the process of carrying out these punishments.

And here I saw the spectacle of good Russians full of the Christian spirit traveling with guns and rods to torture and kill their starving brethren. The reason for their expedition was as follows:

On one of the estates of a rich landowner the peasants had common rights on the forest, and having always enjoyed these rights, regarded the forest as their own, or at least as theirs in common with the owner. The landowner wished to keep the forest entirely to himself and began to fell the trees. The peasants lodged a complaint. The judges in the first instance gave an unjust decision (I say unjust on the authority of the lawyer and governor, who ought to understand the matter), and decided the case in favor of the landowner. All the later decisions, even that of the senate, though they could see that the matter had been unjustly decided, confirmed the judgment and adjudged the forest to the landowner. He began to cut down the trees, but the peasants, unable to believe that such obvious injustice could be done them by the higher authorities, did not submit to the decision and drove away the men sent to cut down the trees, declaring that the forest belonged to them and they would go to the Tzar before they would let them cut it down.

The matter was referred to Petersburg, and the order was transmitted to the governor to carry the decision of the court into effect. The governor asked for a troop of soldiers. And here were the soldiers with bayonets and cartridges, and moreover, a supply of rods, expressly prepared for the purpose and heaped up in one of the trucks, going to carry the decision of the higher authorities into effect.

The decisions of the higher authorities are carried into effect by means of murder or torture, or threats of one or the other, according to whether they offer resistance or not.

In the first case if the peasants offer resistance the practice is in Russia, and it is the same everywhere where a state organization and private property exist, as follows. The governor delivers an address in which he demands submission. The excited crowd, generally deluded by their leaders, don't understand a word of what the representative of authority is saying in the pompous official language, and their excitement continues. Then the governor announces that if they do not submit and disperse, he will be obliged to have recourse to force. If the crowd does not disperse even on this, the governor gives the order to fire over the heads of the crowd. If the crowd does not even then disperse, the governor gives the order to fire straight into the crowd; the soldiers fire and the killed and wounded fall about the street. Then the crowd usually runs away in all directions, and the troops at the governor's command take those who are supposed to be the ringleaders and lead them off under escort. Then they pick up the dying, the wounded, and the dead, covered with blood, sometimes women and children among them. The dead they bury and the wounded they carry to the hospital. Those whom they regard as the ringleaders they take to the town hall and have them tried by a special court-martial. And if they have had recourse to violence on their side, they are condemned to be hanged. And then the gallows is erected. And they solemnly strangle a few defenseless creatures.

This is what has often been done in Russia, and is and must always be done where the social order is based on force.

But in the second case, when the peasants do submit, something quite special, peculiar to Russia, takes place. The governor arrives on the scene of action and delivers an harangue to the people, reproaching them for their insubordination, and either stations troops in the houses of the villages, where sometimes for a whole month the soldiers drain the resources of the peasants, or contenting himself with threats, he mercifully takes leave of the people, or what is the most frequent course, he announces that the ringleaders must be punished, and quite arbitrarily without any trial selects a certain number of men, regarded as ringleaders, and commands them to be flogged in his presence.

In order to give an idea of how such things are done I will describe a proceeding of the kind which took place in Orel, and received the full approval of the highest authorities.

This is what took place in Orel. Just as here in the Toula province, a landlord wanted to appropriate the property of the peasants and just in the same way the peasants opposed it. The matter in dispute was a fall of water, which irrigated the peasants' fields, and which the landowner wanted to cut off and divert to turn his mill. The peasants rebelled against this being done. The land owner laid a complaint before the district commander, who illegally (as was recognized later even by a legal decision) decided the matter in favor of the landowner, and allowed him to divert the water course. The landowner sent workmen to dig the conduit by which the water was to be let off to turn the mill. The peasants were indignant at this unjust decision, and sent their women to prevent the landowner's men from digging this conduit. The women went to the dykes, overturned the carts, and drove away the men. The landowner made a complaint against the women for thus taking the law into their own hands. The district commander made out an order that from every house throughout the village one woman was to be taken and put in prison. The order was not easily executed. For in every household there were several women, and it was impossible to know which one was to be arrested. Consequently the police did not carry out the order. The landowner complained to the governor of the neglect on the part of the police, and the latter, without examining into the affair, gave the chief official of the police strict orders to carry out the instructions of the district commander without delay. The police official, in obedience to his superior, went to the village and with the insolence peculiar to Russian officials ordered his policemen to take one woman out of each house. But since there were more than one woman in each house, and there was no knowing which one was sentenced to imprisonment, disputes and opposition arose. In spite of these disputes and opposition, however, the officer of police gave orders that some woman, whichever came first, should be taken from each household and led away to prison. The peasants began to defend their wives and mothers, would not let them go, and beat the police and their officer. This was a fresh and terrible crime: resistance was offered to the authorities. A report of this new offense was sent to the town. And so this governor--precisely as the governor of Toula was doing on that day--with a battalion of soldiers with guns and rods, hastily brought together by means of telegraphs and telephones and railways, proceeded by a special train to the scene of action, with a learned doctor whose duty it was to insure the flogging being of an hygienic character. Herzen's prophecy of the modern Ghenghis Khan with his telegrams is completely realized by this governor.

Before the town hall of the district were the soldiery, a battalion of police with their revolvers slung round them with red cords, the persons of most importance among the peasants, and the culprits. A crowd of one thousand or more people were standing round. The governor, on arriving, stepped out of his carriage, delivered a prepared harangue, and asked for the culprits and a bench. The latter demand was at first not understood. But a police constable whom the governor always took about with him, and who undertook to organize such executions--by no means exceptional in that province--explained that what was meant was a bench for flogging. A bench was brought as well as the rods, and then the executioners were summoned (the latter had been selected beforehand from some horsestealers of the same village, as the soldiers refused the office). When everything was ready, the governor ordered the first of the twelve culprits pointed out by the landowner as the most guilty to come forward. The first to come forward was the head of a family, a man of forty who had always stood up manfully for the rights of his class, and therefore was held in the greatest esteem by all the villagers. He was led to the bench and stripped, and then ordered to lie down.

The peasant attempted to supplicate for mercy, but seeing it was useless, he crossed himself and lay down. Two police constables hastened to hold him down. The learned doctor stood by, in readiness to give his aid and his medical science when they should be needed. The convicts spit into their hands, brandished the rods, and began to flog. It seemed, however, that the bench was too narrow, and it was difficult to keep the victim writhing in torture upon it. Then the governor ordered them to bring another bench and to put a plank across them. Soldiers, with their hands raised to their caps, and respectful murmurs of "Yes, your Excellency," hasten obediently to carry out this order. Meanwhile the tortured man, half naked, pale and scowling, stood waiting, his eyes fixed on the ground and his teeth chattering. When another bench had been brought they again made him lie down, and the convicted thieves again began to flog him.

The victim's back and thighs and legs, and even his sides, became more and more covered with scars and wheals, and at every blow there came the sound of the deep groans which he could no longer restrain. In the crowd standing round were heard the sobs of wives, mothers, children, the families of the tortured man and of all the others picked out for punishment.

The miserable governor, intoxicated with power, was counting the strokes on his fingers, and never left off smoking cigarettes, while several officious persons hastened on every opportunity to offer him a burning match to light them. When more than fifty strokes had been given, the peasant ceased to shriek and writhe, and the doctor, who had been educated in a government institution to serve his sovereign and his country with his scientific attainments, went up to the victim, felt his pulse, listened to his heart, and announced to the representative of authority that the man undergoing punishment had lost consciousness, and that, in accordance with the conclusions of science, to continue the punishment would endanger the victim's life. But the miserable governor, now completely intoxicated by the sight of blood, gave orders that the punishment should go on, and the flogging was continued up to seventy strokes, the number which the governor had for some reason fixed upon as necessary. When the seventieth stroke had been reached, the governor said "Enough! Next one!"

And the mutilated victim, his back covered with blood, was lifted up and carried away unconscious, and another was led up. The sobs and groans of the crowd grew louder. But the representative of the state continued the torture.

Thus they flogged each of them up to the twelfth, and each of them received seventy strokes. They all implored mercy, shrieked and groaned. The sobs and cries of the crowd of women grew louder and more heart-rending, and the men's faces grew darker and darker. But they were surrounded by troops, and the torture did not cease till it had reached the limit which had been fixed by the caprice of the miserable half-drunken and insane creature they called the governor.

The officials, and officers, and soldiers not only assisted in it, but were even partly responsible for the affair, since by their presence they prevented any interference on the part of the crowd.

When I inquired of one of the governors why they made use of this kind of torture when people had already submitted and soldiers were stationed in the village, he replied with the important air of a man who thoroughly understands all the subtleties of statecraft, that if the peasants were not thoroughly subdued by flogging, they would begin offering opposition to the decisions of authorities again. When some of them had been thoroughly tortured, the authority of the state would be secured forever among them.

And so that was why the Governor of Toula was going in his turn with his subordinate officials, officers, and soldiers to carry out a similar measure. By precisely the same means, i. e., by murder and torture, obedience to the decision of the higher authorities was to be secured. And this decision was to enable a young landowner, who had an income of one hundred thousand, to gain three thousand rubles more by stealing a forest from a whole community of cold and famished peasants, to spend it, in two or three weeks in the saloons of Moscow, Petersburg, or Paris. That was what those people whom I met were going to do.

After my thoughts had for two years been turned in the same direction, fate seemed expressly to have brought me face to face for the first time in my life with a fact which showed me absolutely unmistakably in practice what had long been clear to me in theory, that the organization of our society rests, not as people interested in maintaining the present order of things like to imagine, on certain principles of jurisprudence, but on simple brute force, on the murder and torture of men.

People who own great estates or fortunes, or who receive great revenues drawn from the class who are in want even of necessities, the working class, as well as all those who like merchants, doctors, artists, clerks, learned professors, coachmen, cooks, writers, valets, and barristers, make their living about these rich people, like to believe that the privileges they enjoy are not the result of force, but of absolutely free and just interchange of services, and that their advantages, far from being gained by such punishments and murders as took place in Orel and several parts of Russia this year, and are always taking place all over Europe and America, have no kind of connection with these acts of violence. They like to believe that their privileges exist apart and are the result of free contract among people; and that the violent cruelties perpetrated on the people also exist apart and are the result of some general judicial, political, or economical laws. They try not to see that they all enjoy their privileges as a result of the same fact which forces the peasants who have tended the forest, and who are in the direct need of it for fuel, to give it up to a rich landowner who has taken no part in caring for its growth and has no need of it whatever--the fact, that is, that if they don't give it up they will be flogged or killed.

And yet if it is clear that it was only by means of menaces, blows, or murder, that the mill in Orel was enabled to yield a larger income, or that the forest which the peasants had planted became the property of a landowner, it should be equally clear that all the other exclusive rights enjoyed by the rich, by robbing the poor of their necessities, rest on the same basis of violence. If the peasants, who need land to maintain their families, may not cultivate the land about their houses, but one man, a Russian, English, Austrian, or any other great landowner, possesses land enough to maintain a thousand families, though he does not cultivate it himself, and if a merchant profiting by the misery of the cultivators, taking corn from them at a third of its value, can keep this corn in his granaries with perfect security while men are starving all around him, and sell it again for three times its value to the very cultivators he bought it from, it is evident that all this too comes from the same cause. And if one man may not buy of another a commodity from the other side of a certain fixed line, called the frontier, without paying certain duties on it to men who have taken no part whatever in its production--and if men are driven to sell their last cow to pay taxes which the government distributes among its functionaries, and spends on maintaining soldiers to murder these very taxpayers--it would appear self-evident that all this does not come about as the result of any abstract laws, but is based on just what was done in Orel, and which may be done in Toula, and is done periodically in one form or another throughout the whole world wherever there is a government, and where there are rich and poor.

Simply because torture and murder are not employed in every instance of oppression by force, those who enjoy the exclusive privileges of the ruling classes persuade themselves and others that their privileges are not based on torture and murder, but on some mysterious general causes, abstract laws, and so on. Yet one would think it was perfectly clear that if men, who consider it unjust (and all the working classes do consider it so nowadays), still pay the principal part of the produce of their labor away to the capitalist and the landowner, and pay taxes, though they know to what a bad use these taxes are put, they do so not from recognition of abstract laws of which they have never heard, but only because they know they will be beaten and killed if they don't do so.

And if there is no need to imprison, beat, and kill men every time the landlord collects his rents, every time those who are in want of bread have to pay a swindling merchant three times its value, every time the factory hand has to be content with a wage less than half of the profit made by the employer, and every time a poor man pays his last ruble in taxes, it is because so many men have been beaten and killed for trying to resist these demands, that the lesson has now been learnt very thoroughly.

Just as a trained tiger, who does not eat meat put under his nose, and jumps over a stick at the word of command, does not act thus because he likes it, but because he remembers the red-hot irons or the fast with which he was punished every time he did not obey; so men submitting to what is disadvantageous or even ruinous to them, and considered by them as unjust, act thus because they remember what they suffered for resisting it.

As for those who profit by the privileges gained by previous acts of violence, they often forget and like to forget how these privileges were obtained. But one need only recall the facts of history, not the history of the exploits of different dynasties of rulers, but real history, the history of the oppression of the majority by a small number of men, to see that all the advantages the rich have over the poor are based on nothing but flogging, imprisonment, and murder.

One need but reflect on the unceasing, persistent struggle of all to better their material position, which is the guiding motive of men of the present day, to be convinced that the advantages of the rich over the poor could never and can never be maintained by anything but force.

There may be cases of oppression, of violence, and of punishments, though they are rare, the aim of which is not to secure the privileges of the propertied classes. But one may confidently assert that in any society where, for every man living in ease, there are ten exhausted by labor, envious, covetous, and often suffering with their families from direct privation, all the privileges of the rich, all their luxuries and superfluities, are obtained and maintained only by tortures, imprisonment, and murder.

The train I met on the 9th of September going with soldiers, guns, cartridges, and rods, to confirm the rich landowner in the possession of a small forest which he had taken from the starving peasants, which they were in the direst need of, and he was in no need of at all, was a striking proof of how men are capable of doing deeds directly opposed to their principles and their conscience without perceiving it.

The special train consisted of one first-class carriage for the governor, the officials, and officers, and several luggage vans crammed full of soldiers. The latter, smart young fellows in their clean new uniforms, were standing about in groups or sitting swinging their legs in the wide open doorways of the luggage vans. Some were smoking, nudging each other, joking, grinning, and laughing, others were munching sunflower seeds and spitting out the husks with an air of dignity. Some of them ran along the platform to drink some water from a tub there, and when they met the officers they slackened their pace, made their stupid gesture of salutation, raising their hands to their heads with serious faces as though they were doing something of the greatest importance. They kept their eyes on them till they had passed by them, and then set off running still more merrily, stamping their heels on the platform, laughing and chattering after the manner of healthy, good-natured young fellows, traveling in lively company.

They were going to assist at the murder of their fathers or grandfathers just as if they were going on a party of pleasure, or at any rate on some quite ordinary business.

The same impression was produced by the well-dressed functionaries and officers who were scattered about the platform and in the first-class carriage. At a table covered with bottles was sitting the governor, who was responsible for the whole expedition, dressed in his half-military uniform and eating something while he chatted tranquilly about the weather with some acquaintances he had met, as though the business he was upon was of so simple and ordinary a character that it could not disturb his serenity and his interest in the change of weather.

At a little distance from the table sat the general of the police. He was not taking any refreshment, and had an impenetrable bored expression, as though he were weary of the formalities to be gone through. On all sides officers were bustling noisily about in their red uniforms trimmed with gold; one sat at a table finishing his bottle of beer, another stood at the buffet eating a cake, and brushing the crumbs off his uniform, threw down his money with a self-confident air; another was sauntering before the carriages of our train, staring at the faces of the women.

All these men who were going to murder or to torture the famishing and defenseless creatures who provide them their sustenance had the air of men who knew very well that they were doing their duty, and some were even proud, were "glorying" in what they were doing.

What is the meaning of it?

All these people are within half an hour of reaching the place where, in order to provide a wealthy young man with three thousand rubles stolen from a whole community of famishing peasants, they may be forced to commit the most horrible acts one can conceive, to murder or torture, as was done in Orel, innocent beings, their brothers. And they see the place and time approaching with untroubled serenity.

To say that all these government officials, officers, and soldiers do not know what is before them is impossible, for they are prepared for it. The governor must have given directions about the rods, the officials must have sent an order for them, purchased them, and entered the item in their accounts. The military officers have given and received orders about cartridges. They all know that they are going to torture, perhaps to kill, their famishing fellow-creatures, and that they must set to work within an hour.

To say, as is usually said, and as they would themselves repeat, that they are acting from conviction of the necessity for supporting the state organization, would be a mistake. For in the first place, these men have probably never even thought about state organization and the necessity of it; in the second place, they cannot possibly be convinced that the act in which they are taking part will tend to support rather than to ruin the state;

and thirdly, in reality the majority, if not all, of these men, far from ever sacrificing their own pleasure or tranquillity to support the state, never let slip an opportunity of profiting at the expense of the state in every way they can increase their own pleasure and ease. So that they are not acting thus for the sake of the abstract principle of the state.

What is the meaning of it?

Yet I know all these men. If I don't know all of them personally, I know their characters pretty nearly, their past, and their way of thinking. They certainly all have mothers, some of them wives and children. They are certainly for the most part good, kind, even tender-hearted fellows, who hate every sort of cruelty, not to speak of murder; many of them would not kill or hurt an animal. Moreover, they are all professed Christians and regard all violence directed against the defenseless as base and disgraceful.

Certainly not one of them would be capable in everyday life, for his own personal profit, of doing a hundredth part of what the Governor of Orel did. Every one of them would be insulted at the supposition that he was capable of doing anything of the kind in private life.

And yet they are within half an hour of reaching the place where they may be reduced to the inevitable necessity of committing this crime.

What is the meaning of it?

But it is not only these men who are going by train prepared for murder and torture. How could the men who began the whole business, the landowner, the commissioner, the judges, and those who gave the order and are responsible for it, the ministers, the Tzar, who are also good men, professed Christians, how could they elaborate such a plan and assent to it, knowing its consequences? The spectators even, who took no part in the affair, how could they, who are indignant at the sight of any cruelty in private life, even the overtaxing of a horse, allow such a horrible deed to be perpetrated? How was it they did not rise in indignation and bar the roads, shouting, "No; flog and kill starving men because they won't let their last possession be stolen from them without resistance, that we won't allow!" But far from anyone doing this, the majority, even of those who were the cause of the affair, such as the commissioner, the landowner, the judge, and those who took part in it and arranged it, as the governor, the ministers, and the Tzar, are perfectly tranquil and do not even feel a prick of conscience. And apparently all the men who are going to carry out this crime are equally undisturbed.

The spectators, who one would suppose could have no personal interest in the affair, looked rather with sympathy than with disapproval at all these people preparing to carry out this infamous action. In the same compartment with me was a wood merchant, who had risen from a peasant. He openly expressed aloud his sympathy with such punishments. "They can't disobey the authorities," he said; "that's what the authorities are for. Let them have a lesson; send their fleas flying! They'll give over making commotions, I warrant you. That's what they want."

What is the meaning of it?

It is not possible to say that all these people who have provoked or aided or allowed this deed are such worthless creatures that, knowing all the infamy of what they are doing, they do it against their principles, some for pay and for profit, others through fear of punishment. All of them in certain circumstances know how to stand up for their principles. Not one of these officials would steal a purse, read another man's letter, or put up with an affront without demanding satisfaction. Not one of these officers would consent to cheat at cards, would refuse to pay a debt of honor, would betray a comrade, run away on the field of battle, or desert the flag. Not one of these soldiers would spit out the holy sacrament or eat meat on Good Friday. All these men are ready to face any kind of privation, suffering, or danger rather than consent to do what they regard as wrong. They have therefore the strength to resist doing what is against their principles.

It is even less possible to assert that all these men are such brutes that it is natural and not distasteful to them to do such deeds. One need only talk to these people a little to see that all of them, the landowner even, and the judge, and the minister and the Tzar and the government, the officers and the soldiers, not only disapprove of such things in the depth of their soul, but suffer from the consciousness of their participation in them when they recollect what they imply. But they try not to think about it.

One need only talk to any of these who are taking part in the affair from the landowner to the lowest policeman or soldier to see that in the depth of their soul they all know it is a wicked thing, that it would be better to have nothing to do with it, and are suffering from the knowledge.

A lady of liberal views, who was traveling in the same train with us, seeing the governor and the officers in the first-class saloon and learning the object of the expedition, began, intentionally raising her voice so that they should hear, to abuse the existing order of things and to cry shame on men who would take part in such proceedings. Everyone felt awkward, none knew where to look, but no one contradicted her. They tried to look as though such remarks were not worth answering. But one could see by their faces and their averted eyes that they were ashamed. I noticed the same thing in the soldiers. They too knew that what they were sent to do was a shameful thing, but they did not want to think about what was before them.

When the wood merchant, as I suspect insincerely only to show that he was a man of education, began to speak of the necessity of such measures, the soldiers who heard him all turned away from him, scowling and pretending not to hear.

All the men who, like the landowner, the commissioner, the minister, and the Tzar, were responsible for the perpetration of this act, as well as those who were now going to execute it, and even those who were mere spectators of it, knew that it was a wickedness, and were ashamed of taking any share in it, and even of being present at it.

Then why did they do it, or allow it to be done?

Ask them the question. And the landowner who started the affair, and the judge who pronounced a clearly unjust even though formally legal decision, and those who commanded the execution of the decision, and those who, like the policemen, soldiers, and peasants, will execute the deed with their own hands, flogging and killing their brothers, all who have devised, abetted, decreed, executed, or allowed such crimes, will make substantially the same reply.

The authorities, those who have started, devised, and decreed the matter, will say that such acts are necessary for the maintenance of the existing order; the maintenance of the existing order is necessary for the welfare of the country and of humanity, for the possibility of social existence and human progress.

Men of the poorer class, peasants and soldiers, who will have to execute the deed of violence with their own hands, say that they do so because it is the command of their superior authority, and the superior authority knows what he is about. That those are in authority who ought to be in authority, and that they know what they are doing appears to them a truth of which there can be no doubt. If they could admit the possibility of mistake or error, it would only be in functionaries of a lower grade; the highest authority on which all the rest depends seems to them immaculate beyond suspicion.

Though expressing the motives of their conduct differently, both those in command and their subordinates are agreed in saying that they act thus because the existing order is the order which must and ought to exist at the present time, and that therefore to support it is the sacred duty of every man.

On this acceptance of the necessity and therefore immutability of the existing order, all who take part in acts of violence on the part of government base the argument always advanced in their justification. "Since the existing order is immutable," they say, "the refusal of a single individual to perform the duties laid upon him will effect no change in things, and will only mean that some other man will be put in his place who may do the work worse, that is to say, more cruelly, to the still greater injury of the victims of the act of violence."

This conviction that the existing order is the necessary and therefore immutable order, which it is a sacred duty for every man to support, enables good men, of high principles in private life, to take part with conscience more or less untroubled in crimes such as that perpetrated in Orel, and that which the men in the Toula train were going to perpetrate.

But what is this conviction based on? It is easy to understand that the landowner prefers to believe that the existing order is inevitable and immutable, because this existing order secures him an income from his hundreds and thousands of acres, by means of which he can lead his habitual indolent and luxurious life.

It is easy to understand that the judge readily believes in the necessity of an order of things through which he receives a wage fifty times as great as the most industrious laborer can earn, and the same applies to all the higher officials. It is only under the existing RÉGIME that as governor, prosecutor, senator, members of the various councils, they can receive their several thousands of rubles a year, without which they and their families would at once sink into ruin, since if it were not for the position they occupy they would never by their own abilities, industry, or acquirements get a thousandth part of their salaries. The minister, the Tzar, and all the higher authorities are in the same position. The only distinction is that the higher and the more exceptional their position, the more necessary it is for them to believe that the existing order is the only possible order of things. For without it they would not only be unable to gain an equal position, but would be found to fall lower than all other people. A man who has of his own free will entered the police force at a wage of ten rubles, which he could easily earn in any other position, is hardly dependent on the preservation of the existing RÉGIME, and so he may not believe in its immutability. But a king or an emperor, who receives millions for his post, and knows that there are thousands of people round him who would like to dethrone him and take his place, who knows that he will never receive such a revenue or so much honor in any other position, who knows, in most cases through his more or less despotic rule, that if he were dethroned he would have to answer for all his abuse of power--he cannot but believe in the necessity and even sacredness of the existing order. The higher and the more profitable a man's position, the more unstable it becomes, and the more terrible and dangerous a fall from it for him, the more firmly the man believes in the existing order, and therefore with the more ease of conscience can such a man perpetrate cruel and wicked acts, as though they were not in his own interest, but for the maintenance of that order.

This is the case with all men in authority, who occupy positions more profitable than they could occupy except for the present RÉGIME, from the lowest police officer to the Tzar. All of them are more or less convinced that the existing order is immutable, because--the chief consideration--it is to their advantage. But the peasants, the soldiers, who are at the bottom of the social scale, who have no kind of advantage from the existing order, who are in the very lowest position of subjection and humiliation, what forces them to believe that the existing order in which they are in their humble and disadvantageous position is the order which ought to exist, and which they ought to support even at the cost of evil actions contrary to their conscience?

What forces these men to the false reasoning that the existing order is unchanging, and that therefore they ought to support it, when it is so obvious, on the contrary, that it is only unchanging because they themselves support it?

What forces these peasants, taken only yesterday from the plow and dressed in ugly and unseemly costumes with blue collars and gilt buttons, to go with guns and sabers and murder their famishing fathers and brothers? They gain no kind of advantage and can be in no fear of losing the position they occupy, because it is worse than that from which they have been taken.

The persons in authority of the higher orders--landowners, merchants, judges, senators, governors, ministers, tzars, and officers--take part in such doings because the existing order is to their advantage. In other respects they are often good and kind-hearted men, and they are more able to take part in such doings because their share in them is limited to suggestions, decisions, and orders. These persons in authority never do themselves what they suggest, decide, or command to be done. For the most part they do not even see how all the atrocious deeds they have suggested and authorized are carried out. But the unfortunate men of the lower orders, who gain no kind of advantage from the existing RÉGIME, but, on the contrary, are treated with the utmost contempt, support it even by dragging people with their own hands from their families, handcuffing them, throwing them in prison, guarding them, shooting them.

Why do they do it? What forces them to believe that the existing order is unchanging and they must support it?

All violence rests, we know, on those who do the beating, the handcuffing, the imprisoning, and the killing with their own hands. If there were no soldiers or armed policemen, ready to kill or outrage anyone as they are ordered, not one of those people who sign sentences of death, imprisonment, or galley-slavery for life would make up his mind to hang, imprison, or torture a thousandth part of those whom, quietly sitting in his study, he now orders to be tortured in all kinds of ways, simply because he does not see it nor do it himself, but only gets it done at a distance by these servile tools.

All the acts of injustice and cruelty which are committed in the ordinary course of daily life have only become habitual because there are these men always ready to carry out such acts of injustice and cruelty. If it were not for them, far from anyone using violence against the immense masses who are now ill-treated, those who now command their punishment would not venture to sentence them, would not even dare to dream of the sentences they decree with such easy confidence at present. And if it were not for these men, ready to kill or torture anyone at their commander's will, no one would dare to claim, as all the idle landowners claim with such assurance, that a piece of land, surrounded by peasants, who are in wretchedness from want of land, is the property of a man who does not cultivate it, or that stores of corn taken by swindling from the peasants ought to remain untouched in the midst of a population dying of hunger because the merchants must make their profit. If it were not for these servile instruments at the disposal of the authorities, it could never have entered the head of the landowner to rob the peasants of the forest they had tended, nor of the officials to think they are entitled to their salaries, taken from the famishing people, the price of their oppression; least of all could anyone dream of killing or exiling men for exposing falsehood and telling the truth. All this can only be done because the authorities are confidently assured that they have always these servile tools at hand, ready to carry all their demands into effect by means of torture and murder.

All the deeds of violence of tyrants from Napoleon to the lowest commander of a company who fires upon a crowd, can only be explained by the intoxicating effect of their absolute power over these slaves. All force, therefore, rests on these men, who carry out the deeds of violence with their own hands, the men who serve in the police or the army, especially the army, for the police only venture to do their work because the army is at their back.

What, then, has brought these masses of honest men, on whom the whole thing depends, who gain nothing by it, and who have to do these atrocious deeds with their own hands, what has brought them to accept the amazing delusion that the existing order, unprofitable, ruinous, and fatal as it is for them, is the order which ought to exist?

Who has led them into this amazing delusion?

They can never have persuaded themselves that they ought to do what is against their conscience, and also the source of misery and ruin for themselves, and all their class, who make up nine-tenths of the population.

"How can you kill people, when it is written in God's commandment: 'Thou shalt not kill'?" I have often inquired of different soldiers. And I always drove them to embarrassment and confusion by reminding them of what they did not want to think about. They knew they were bound by the law of God, "Thou shalt not kill," and knew too that they were bound by their duty as soldiers, but had never reflected on the contradiction between these duties. The drift of the timid answers I received to this question was always approximately this: that killing in war and executing criminals by command of the government are not included in the general prohibition of murder. But when I said this distinction was not made in the law of God, and reminded them of the Christian duty of fraternity, forgiveness of injuries, and love, which could not be reconciled with murder, the peasants usually agreed, but in their turn began to ask me questions. "How does it happen," they inquired, "that the government [which according to their ideas cannot do wrong] sends the army to war and orders criminals to be executed." When I answered that the government does wrong in giving such orders, the peasants fell into still greater confusion, and either broke off the conversation or else got angry with me.

"They must have found a law for it. The archbishops know as much about it as we do, I should hope," a Russian soldier once observed to me. And in saying this the soldier obviously set his mind at rest, in the full conviction that his spiritual guides had found a law which authorized his ancestors, and the tzars and their descendants, and millions of men, to serve as he was doing himself, and that the question I had put him was a kind of hoax or conundrum on my part.

Everyone in our Christian society knows, either by tradition or by revelation or by the voice of conscience, that murder is one of the most fearful crimes a man can commit, as the Gospel tells us, and that the sin of murder cannot be limited to certain persons, that is, murder cannot be a sin for some and not a sin for others. Everyone knows that if murder is a sin, it is always a sin, whoever are the victims murdered, just like the sin of adultery, theft, or any other. At the same time from their childhood up men see that murder is not only permitted, but even sanctioned by the blessing of those whom they are accustomed to regard as their divinely appointed spiritual guides, and see their secular leaders with calm assurance organizing murder, proud to wear murderous arms, and demanding of others in the name of the laws of the country, and even of God, that they should take part in murder. Men see that there is some inconsistency here, but not being able to analyze it, involuntarily assume that this apparent inconsistency is only the result of their ignorance. The very grossness and obviousness of the inconsistency confirms them in this conviction.

They cannot imagine that the leaders of civilization, the educated classes, could so confidently preach two such opposed principles as the law of Christ and murder. A simple uncorrupted youth cannot imagine that those who stand so high in his opinion, whom he regards as holy or learned men, could for any object whatever mislead him so shamefully. But this is just what has always been and always is done to him. It is done (1) by instilling, by example and direct instruction, from childhood up, into the working people, who have not time to study moral and religious questions for themselves, the idea that torture and murder are compatible with Christianity, and that for certain objects of state, torture and murder are not only admissible, but ought to be employed; and (2) by instilling into certain of the people, who have either voluntarily enlisted or been taken by compulsion into the army, the idea that the perpetration of murder and torture with their own hands is a sacred duty, and even a glorious exploit, worthy of praise and reward.

The general delusion is diffused among all people by means of the catechisms or books, which nowadays replace them, in use for the compulsory education of children. In them it is stated that violence, that is, imprisonment and execution, as well as murder in civil or foreign war in the defense and maintenance of the existing state organization (whatever that may be, absolute or limited monarchy, convention, consulate, empire of this or that

Napoleon or Boulanger, constitutional monarchy, commune or republic) is absolutely lawful and not opposed to morality and Christianity.

This is stated in all catechisms or books used in schools. And men are so thoroughly persuaded of it that they grow up, live and die in that conviction without once entertaining a doubt about it.

This is one form of deception, the general deception instilled into everyone, but there is another special deception practiced upon the soldiers or police who are picked out by one means or another to do the torturing and murdering necessary to defend and maintain the existing RÉGIME.

In all military instructions there appears in one form or another what is expressed in the Russian military code in the following words:

ARTICLE 87. To carry out exactly and without comment the orders of a superior officer means: to carry out an order received from a superior officer exactly without considering whether it is good or not, and whether it is possible to carry it out. The superior officer is responsible for the consequences of the order he gives.

ARTICLE 88. The subordinate ought never to refuse to carry out the orders of a superior officer except when he sees clearly that in carrying out his superior officer's command, he breaks [the law of God, one involuntarily expects; not at all] HIS OATH OF FIDELITY AND ALLEGIANCE TO THE TZAR.

It is here said that the man who is a soldier can and ought to carry out all the orders of his superior without exception. And as these orders for the most part involve murder, it follows that he ought to break all the laws of God and man. The one law he may not break is that of fidelity and allegiance to the man who happens at a given moment to be in power.

Precisely the same thing is said in other words in all codes of military instruction. And it could not be otherwise, since the whole power of the army and the state is based in reality on this delusive emancipation of men from their duty to God and their conscience, and the substitution of duty to their superior officer for all other duties.

This, then, is the foundation of the belief of the lower classes that the existing RÉGIME so fatal for them is the RÉGIME which ought to exist, and which they ought therefore to support even by torture and murder.

This belief is founded on a conscious deception practiced on them by the higher classes.

And it cannot be otherwise. To compel the lower classes, which are more numerous, to oppress and ill treat themselves, even at the cost of actions opposed to their conscience, it was necessary to deceive them. And it has been done accordingly.

Not many days ago I saw once more this shameless deception being openly practiced, and once more I marveled that it could be practiced so easily and impudently.

At the beginning of November, as I was passing through Toula, I saw once again at the gates of the Zemsky Courthouse the crowd of peasants I had so often seen before, and heard the drunken shouts of the men mingled with the pitiful lamentations of their wives and mothers. It was the recruiting session.

I can never pass by the spectacle. It attracts me by a kind of fascination of repulsion. I again went into the crowd, took my stand among the peasants, looked about and asked questions. And once again I was amazed that this hideous crime can be perpetrated so easily in broad daylight and in the midst of a large town.

As the custom is every year, in all the villages and hamlets of the one hundred millions of Russians, on the 1st of November, the village elders had assembled the young men inscribed on the lists, often their own sons among them, and had brought them to the town.

On the road the recruits have been drinking without intermission, unchecked by the elders, who feel that going on such an insane errand, abandoning their wives and mothers and renouncing all they hold sacred in order to become a senseless instrument of destruction, would be too agonizing if they were not stupefied with spirits.

And so they have come, drinking, swearing, singing, fighting and scuffling with one another. They have spent the night in taverns. In the morning they have slept off their drunkenness and have gathered together at the Zemsky Court-house.

Some of them, in new sheepskin pelisses, with knitted scarves round their necks, their eyes swollen from drinking, are shouting wildly to one another to show their courage; others, crowded near the door, are quietly and mournfully waiting their turn, between their weeping wives and mothers (I had chanced upon the day of the actual enrolling, that is, the examination of those whose names are on the list); others meantime were crowding into the hall of the recruiting office.

Inside the office the work was going on rapidly. The door is opened and the guard calls Piotr Sidorov. Piotr Sidorov starts, crosses himself, and goes into a little room with a glass door, where the conscripts undress. A comrade of Piotr Sidorov's, who has just been passed for service, and come naked out of the revision office, is dressing hurriedly, his teeth chattering. Sidorov has already heard the news, and can see from his face too that he has been taken. He wants to ask him questions, but they hurry him and tell him to make haste and undress. He throws off his pelisse, slips his boots off his feet, takes off his waistcoat and draws his shirt over his head, and naked, trembling all over, and exhaling an odor of tobacco, spirits, and sweat, goes into the revision office, not knowing what to do with his brawny bare arms.

Directly facing him in the revision office hangs in a great gold frame a portrait of the Tzar in full uniform with decorations, and in the corner a little portrait of Christ in a shirt and a crown of thorns. In the middle of the room is a table covered with green cloth, on which there are papers lying and a three-cornered ornament surmounted by an eagle--the zertzal. Round the table are sitting the revising officers, looking collected and indifferent. One is smoking a cigarette; another is looking through some papers. Directly Sidorov comes in, a guard goes up to him, places him under the measuring frame, raising him under his chin, and straightening his legs.

The man with the cigarette--he is the doctor--comes up, and without looking at the recruit's face, but somewhere beyond it, feels his body over with an air of disgust, measures him, tests him, tells the guard to open his mouth, tells him to breathe, to speak. Someone notes something down. At last without having once looked him in the face the doctor says, "Right. Next one!" and with a weary air sits down again at the table. The soldiers again hustle and hurry the lad. He somehow gets into his trousers, wraps his feet in rags, puts on his boots, looks for his scarf and cap, and bundles his pelisse under his arm. Then they lead him into the main hall, shutting him off apart from the rest by a bench, behind which all the conscripts who have been passed for service are waiting. Another village lad like himself, but from a distant province, now a soldier armed with a gun with a sharp-pointed bayonet at the end, keeps watch over him, ready to run him through the body if he should think of trying to escape.

Meantime the crowd of fathers, mothers, and wives, hustled by the police, are pressing round the doors to hear whose lad has been taken, whose is let off. One of the rejected comes out and announces that Piotr is taken, and at once a shrill cry is heard from Piotr's young wife, for whom this word "taken" means separation for four or five years, the life of a soldier's wife as a servant, often a prostitute.

But here comes a man along the street with flowing hair and in a peculiar dress, who gets out of his droskhy and goes into the Zemsky Court-house. The police clear a way for him through the crowd. It is the "reverend father" come to administer the oath. And this "father," who has been persuaded that he is specially and exclusively devoted to the service of Christ, and who, for the most part, does not himself see the deception in which he lives, goes into the hall where the conscripts are waiting. He throws round him a kind of curtain of brocade, pulls his long hair out over it, opens the very Gospel in which swearing is forbidden, takes the cross, the very cross on which Christ was crucified because he would not do what this false servant of his is telling men to do, and puts them on the lectern. And all these unhappy, defenseless, and deluded lads repeat after him the lie, which he utters with the assurance of familiarity.

He reads and they repeat after him:

"I promise and swear by Almighty God upon his holy Gospel," etc., "to defend," etc., and that is, to murder anyone I am told to, and to do everything I am told by men I know nothing of, and who care nothing for me except as an instrument for perpetrating the crimes by which they are kept in their position of power, and my brothers in their condition of misery. All the conscripts repeat these ferocious words without thinking. And then the so-called "father" goes away with a sense of having correctly and conscientiously done his duty. And all these poor deluded lads believe that these nonsensical and incomprehensible words which they have just uttered set them free for the whole time of their service from their duties as men, and lay upon them fresh and more binding duties as soldiers.

And this crime is perpetrated publicly and no one cries out to the deceiving and the deceived: "Think what you are doing; this is the basest, falsest lie, by which not bodies only, but souls too, are destroyed."

No one does this. On the contrary, when all have been enrolled, and they are to be let out again, the military officer goes with a confident and majestic air into the hall where the drunken, cheated lads are shut up, and cries in a bold, military voice: "Your health, my lads! I congratulate you on 'serving the Tzar!'" And they, poor fellows (someone has given them a hint beforehand), mutter awkwardly, their voices thick with drink, something to the effect that they are glad.

Meantime the crowd of fathers, mothers, and wives is standing at the doors waiting. The women keep their tearful eyes fixed on the doors. They open at last, and out come the conscripts, unsteady, but trying to put a good face on it. Here are Piotr and Vania and Makar trying not to look their dear ones in the face. Nothing is heard but the wailing of the wives and mothers. Some of the lads embrace them and weep with them, others make a show of courage, and others try to comfort them.

The wives and mothers, knowing that they will be left for three, four, or five years without their breadwinners, weep and rehearse their woes aloud. The fathers say little. They only utter a clucking sound with their tongues and sigh mournfully, knowing that they will see no more of the steady lads they have reared and trained to help them, that they will come back not the same quiet hard-working laborers, but for the most part conceited and demoralized, unfitted for their simple life.

And then all the crowd get into their sledges again and move away down the street to the taverns and pot-houses, and louder than ever sounds the medley of singing and sobbing, drunken shouts, and the wailing of the wives and mothers, the sounds of the accordeon and oaths. They all turn into the taverns, whose revenues go to the government, and the drinking bout begins, which stifles their sense of the wrong which is being done them.

For two or three weeks they go on living at home, and most of that time they are "jaunting," that is, drinking.

On a fixed day they collect them, drive them together like a flock of sheep, and begin to train them in the military exercises and drill. Their teachers are fellows like themselves, only deceived and brutalized two or three years sooner. The means of instruction are: deception, stupefaction, blows, and vodka. And before a year has passed these good, intelligent, healthy-minded lads will be as brutal beings as their instructors.

"Come, now, suppose your father were arrested and tried to make his escape?" I asked a young soldier.

"I should run him through with my bayonet," he answered with the foolish intonation peculiar to soldiers; "and if he made off, I ought to shoot him," he added, obviously proud of knowing what he must do if his father were escaping.

And when a good-hearted lad has been brought to a state lower than that of a brute, he is just what is wanted by those who use him as an instrument of violence. He is ready; the man has been destroyed and a new instrument of violence has been created. And all this is done every year, every autumn, everywhere, through all Russia in broad daylight in the midst of large towns, where all may see it, and the deception is so clever, so skillful, that though all men know the infamy of it in their hearts, and see all its horrible results, they cannot throw it off and be free.

When one's eyes are opened to this awful deception practiced upon us, one marvels that the teachers of the Christian religion and of morals, the instructors of youth, or even the good-hearted and intelligent parents who are to be found in every society, can teach any kind of morality in a society in which it is openly admitted (it is so admitted, under all governments and all churches) that murder and torture form an indispensable element in the life of all, and that there must always be special men trained to kill their fellows, and that any one of us may have to become such a trained assassin.

How can children, youths, and people generally be taught any kind of morality--not to speak of teaching in the spirit of Christianity--side by side with the doctrine that murder is necessary for the public weal, and therefore legitimate, and that there are men, of whom each of us may have to be one, whose duty is to murder and torture and commit all sorts of crimes at the will of those who are in possession of authority. If this is so, and one can and ought to murder and torture, there is not, and cannot be, any kind of moral law, but only the law that might is right. And this is just how it is. In reality that is the doctrine--justified to some by the theory of the struggle for existence--which reigns in our society.

And, indeed, what sort of ethical doctrine could admit the legitimacy of murder for any object whatever? It is as impossible as a theory of mathematics admitting that two is equal to three.

There may be a semblance of mathematics admitting that two is equal to three, but there can be no real science of mathematics. And there can only be a semblance of ethics in which murder in the shape of war and the execution of criminals is allowed, but no true ethics. The recognition of the life of every man as sacred is the first and only basis of all ethics.

The doctrine of an eye for an eye and a tooth for a tooth has been abrogated by Christianity, because it is the justification of immorality, and a mere semblance of equity, and has no real meaning. Life is a value which has no weight nor size, and cannot be compared to any other, and so there is no sense in destroying a life for a life. Besides, every social law aims at the amelioration of man's life. What way, then, can the annihilation of the life of some men ameliorate men's life? Annihilation of life cannot be a means of the amelioration of life; it is a suicidal act.

To destroy another life for the sake of justice is as though a man, to repair the misfortune of losing one arm, should cut off the other arm for the sake of equity.

But putting aside the sin of deluding men into regarding the most awful crime as a duty, putting aside the revolting sin of using the name and authority of Christ to sanction what he most condemned, not to speak of the curse on those who cause these "little ones" to offend--how can people who cherish their own way of life, their progress, even from the point of view of their personal security, allow the formation in their midst of an overwhelming force as senseless, cruel, and destructive as every government is organized on the basis of an army? Even the most cruel band of brigands is not so much to be dreaded as such a government.

The power of every brigand chief is at least so far limited that the men of his band preserve at least some human liberty, and can refuse to commit acts opposed to their conscience. But, owing to the perfection to which the discipline of the army has been brought, there is no limit to check men who form part of a regularly organized government. There are no crimes so revolting that they would not readily be committed by men who form part of a government or army, at the will of anyone (such as Boulanger, Napoleon, or Pougachef) who may chance to be at their head.

Often when one sees conscription levies, military drills and maneuvers, police officers with loaded revolvers, and sentinels at their posts with bayonets on their rifles; when one hears for whole days at a time (as I hear it in Hamovniky where I live) the whistle of balls and the dull thud as they fall in the sand; when one sees in the midst of a town where any effort at violence in self-defense is forbidden, where the sale of powder and of chemicals, where furious driving and practicing as a doctor without a diploma, and so on, are not allowed; thousands of disciplined troops, trained to murder, and subject to one man's will; one asks oneself how can people who prize their security quietly allow it, and put up with it? Apart from the immorality and evil effects of it, nothing can possibly be more unsafe. What are people thinking about? I don't mean now Christians, ministers of religion, philanthropists, and moralists, but simply people who value their life, their security, and their comfort. This organization, we know, will work just as well in one man's hands as another's. To-day, let us assume, power is in the hands of a ruler who can be endured, but to-morrow it may be seized by a Biron, an Elizabeth, a Catherine, a Pougachef, a Napoleon I., or a Napoleon III.

And the man in authority, endurable to-day, may become a brute to-morrow, or may be succeeded by a mad or imbecile heir, like the King of Bavaria or our Paul I.

And not only the highest authorities, but all little satraps scattered over everywhere, like so many General Baranovs, governors, police officers even, and commanders of companies, can perpetrate the most awful crimes before there is time for them to be removed from office. And this is what is constantly happening.

One involuntarily asks how can men let it go on, not from higher considerations only, but from regard to their own safety?

The answer to this question is that it is not all people who do tolerate it (some--the greater proportion--deluded and submissive, have no choice and have to tolerate anything). It is tolerated by those who only under such an organization can occupy a position of profit. They tolerate it, because for them the risks of suffering from a foolish or cruel man being at the head of the government or the army are always less than the disadvantages to which they would be exposed by the destruction of the organization itself.

A judge, a commander of police, a governor, or an officer will keep his position just the same under Boulanger or the republic, under Pougachef or Catherine. He will lose his profitable position for certain, if the existing order of things which secured it to him is destroyed. And so all these people feel no uneasiness as to who is at the head of the organization, they will adapt themselves to anyone; they only dread the downfall of the organization itself, and that is the reason--though often an unconscious one--that they support it.

One often wonders why independent people, who are not forced to do so in any way, the so-called ÉLITE of society, should go into the army in Russia, England, Germany, Austria, and even France, and seek opportunities of becoming murderers. Why do even high-principled parents send their boys to military schools? Why do mothers buy their children toy helmets, guns, and swords as playthings? (The peasant's children never play at soldiers, by the way). Why do good men and even women, who have certainly no interest in war, go into raptures over the various exploits of Skobeloff and others, and vie with one another in glorifying them? Why do men, who are not obliged to do so, and get no fee for it, devote, like the marshals of nobility in Russia, whole months of toil to a business physically disagreeable and morally painful--the enrolling of conscripts? Why do all kings and emperors wear the military uniform? Why do they all hold military reviews, why do they organize maneuvers, distribute rewards to the military, and raise monuments to generals and successful commanders? Why do rich men of independent position consider it an honor to perform a valet's duties in attendance on crowned personages, flattering them and cringing to them and pretending to believe in their peculiar superiority? Why do men who have ceased to believe in the superstitions of the mediaeval Church, and who could not possibly believe in them seriously and consistently, pretend to believe in and give their support to the demoralizing and blasphemous institution of the church? Why is it that not only governments but private persons of the higher classes, try so jealously to maintain the ignorance of the people? Why do they fall with such fury on any effort at breaking down religious superstitions or really enlightening the people? Why do historians, novelists, and poets, who have no hope of gaining anything by their flatteries, make heroes of kings, emperors, and conquerors of past times? Why do men, who call themselves learned, dedicate whole lifetimes to making theories to prove that violence employed by authority against the people is not violence at all, but a special right? One often wonders why a fashionable lady or an artist, who, one would think, would take no interest in political or military questions, should always condemn strikes of working people, and defend war; and should always be found without hesitation opposed to the one, favorable to the other.

But one no longer wonders when one realizes that in the higher classes there is an unerring instinct of what tends to maintain and of what tends to destroy the organization by virtue of which they enjoy their privileges. The fashionable lady had certainly not reasoned out that if there were no capitalists and no army to defend them, her husband would have no fortune, and she could not have her entertainments and her ball-dresses. And the artist certainly does not argue that he needs the capitalists and the troops to defend them, so that they may buy his pictures. But instinct, replacing reason in this instance, guides them unerringly. And it is precisely this instinct which leads all men, with few exceptions, to support all the religious, political, and economic institutions which are to their advantage.

But is it possible that the higher classes support the existing order of things simply because it is to their advantage? Cannot they see that this order of things is essentially irrational, that it is no longer consistent with the stage of moral development attained by people, and with public opinion, and that it is fraught with perils? The governing classes, or at least the good, honest, and intelligent people of them, cannot but suffer from these fundamental inconsistencies, and see the dangers with which they are threatened. And is it possible that all the millions of the lower classes can feel easy in conscience when they commit such obviously evil deeds as torture and murder from fear of punishment? Indeed, it could not be so, neither the former nor the latter could fail to see the irrationality of their conduct, if the complexity of government organization did not obscure the unnatural senselessness of their actions.

So many instigate, assist, or sanction the commission of every one of these actions that no one who has a hand in them feels himself morally responsible for it.

It is the custom among assassins to oblige all the witnesses of a murder to strike the murdered victim, that the responsibility may be divided among as large a number of people as possible. The same principle in different forms is applied under the government organization in the perpetration of the crimes, without which no government organization could exist. Rulers always try to implicate as many citizens as possible in all the crimes committed in their support.

Of late this tendency has been expressed in a very obvious manner by the obligation of all citizens to take part in legal processes as jurors, in the army as soldiers, in the local government, or legislative assembly, as electors or members.

Just as in a wicker basket all the ends are so hidden away that it is hard to find them, in the state organization the responsibility for the crimes committed is so hidden away that men will commit the most atrocious acts without seeing their responsibility for them.

In ancient times tyrants got credit for the crimes they committed, but in our day the most atrocious infamies, inconceivable under the Neros, are perpetrated and no one gets blamed for them.

One set of people have suggested, another set have proposed, a third have reported, a fourth have decided, a fifth have confirmed, a sixth have given the order, and a seventh set of men have carried it out. They hang, they flog to death women, old men, and innocent people, as was done recently among us in Russia at the Yuzovsky factory, and is always being done everywhere in Europe and America in the struggle with the anarchists and all other rebels against the existing order; they shoot and hang men by hundreds and thousands, or massacre millions in war, or break men's hearts in solitary confinement, and ruin their souls in the corruption of a soldier's life, and no one is responsible.

At the bottom of the social scale soldiers, armed with guns, pistols, and sabers, injure and murder people, and compel men through these means to enter the army, and are absolutely convinced that the responsibility for the actions rests solely on the officers who command them.

At the top of the scale--the Tzars, presidents, ministers, and parliaments decree these tortures and murders and military conscription, and are fully convinced that since they are either placed in authority by the grace of God or by the society they govern, which demands such decrees from them, they cannot be held responsible. Between these two extremes are the intermediary personages who superintend the murders and other acts of violence, and are fully convinced that the responsibility is taken off their shoulders partly by their superiors who have given the order, partly by the fact that such orders are expected from them by all who are at the bottom of the scale.

The authority who gives the orders and the authority who executes them at the two extreme ends of the state organization, meet together like the two ends of a ring; they support and rest on one another and inclose all that lies within the ring.

Without the conviction that there is a person or persons who will take the whole responsibility of his acts, not one soldier would ever lift a hand to commit a murder or other deed of violence.

Without the conviction that it is expected by the whole people not a single king, emperor, president, or parliament would order murders or acts of violence.

Without the conviction that there are persons of a higher grade who will take the responsibility, and people of a lower grade who require such acts for their welfare, not one of the intermediate class would superintend such deeds.

The state is so organized that wherever a man is placed in the social scale, his irresponsibility is the same. The higher his grade the more he is under the influence of demands from below, and the less he is controlled by orders from above, and VICE VERSA.

All men, then, bound together by state organization, throw the responsibility of their acts on one another, the peasant soldier on the nobleman or merchant who is his officer, and the officer on the nobleman who has been appointed governor, the governor on the nobleman or son of an official who is minister, the minister on the member of the royal family who occupies the post of Tzar, and the Tzar again on all these officials, noblemen, merchants, and peasants. But that is not all. Besides the fact that men get rid of the sense of responsibility for their actions in this way, they lose their moral sense of responsibility also, by the fact that in forming themselves into a state organization they persuade themselves and each other so continually, and so indefatigably, that they are not all equal, but "as the stars apart," that they come to believe it genuinely themselves. Thus some are persuaded that they are not simple people like everyone else, but special people who are to be specially honored. It is instilled into another set of men by every possible means that they are inferior to others, and therefore must submit without a murmur to every order given them by their superiors.

On this inequality, above all, on the elevation of some and the degradation of others, rests the capacity men have of being blind to the insanity of the existing order of life, and all the cruelty and criminality of the deception practiced by one set of men on another.

Those in whom the idea has been instilled that they are invested with a special supernatural grandeur and consequence, are so intoxicated with a sense of their own imaginary dignity that they cease to feel their responsibility for what they do.

While those, on the other hand, in whom the idea is fostered that they are inferior animals, bound to obey their superiors in everything, fall, through this perpetual humiliation, into a strange condition of stupefied servility, and in this stupefied state do not see the significance of their actions and lose all consciousness of responsibility for what they do.

The intermediate class, who obey the orders of their superiors on the one hand and regard themselves as superior beings on the other, are intoxicated by power and stupefied by servility at the same time and so lose the sense of their responsibility.

One need only glance during a review at the commander-in-chief, intoxicated with self-importance, followed by his retinue, all on magnificent and gayly appareled horses, in splendid uniforms and wearing decorations, and see how they ride to the harmonious and solemn strains of music before the ranks of soldiers, all presenting arms and petrified with servility. One need only glance at this spectacle to understand that at such moments, when they are in a state of the most complete intoxication, commander-in-chief, soldiers, and intermediate officers alike, would be capable of committing crimes of which they would never dream under other conditions.

The intoxication produced by such stimulants as parades, reviews, religious solemnities, and coronations, is, however, an acute and temporary condition; but there are other forms of chronic, permanent intoxication, to which those are liable who have any kind of authority, from that of the Tzar to that of the lowest police officer at the street corner, and also those who are in subjection to authority and in a state of stupefied servility. The latter, like all slaves, always find a justification for their own servility, in ascribing the greatest possible dignity and importance to those they serve.

It is principally through this false idea of inequality, and the intoxication of power and of servility resulting from it, that men associated in a state organization are enabled to commit acts opposed to their conscience without the least scruple or remorse. Under the influence of this intoxication, men imagine themselves no longer simply men as they are, but some special beings--noblemen, merchants, governors, judges, officers, tzars, ministers, or soldiers--no longer bound by ordinary human duties, but by other duties far more weighty--the peculiar duties of a nobleman, merchant, governor, judge, officer, tzar, minister, or soldier.

Thus the landowner, who claimed the forest, acted as he did only because he fancied himself not a simple man, having the same rights to life as the peasants living beside him and everyone else, but a great landowner, a member of the nobility, and under the influence of the intoxication of power he felt his dignity offended by the peasants' claims. It was only through this feeling that, without considering the consequences that might follow, he sent in a claim to be reinstated in his pretended rights.

In the same way the judges, who wrongfully adjudged the forest to the proprietor, did so simply because they fancied themselves not simply men like everyone else, and so bound to be guided in everything only by what they consider right, but, under the intoxicating influence of power, imagined themselves the representatives of the justice which cannot err; while under the intoxicating influence of servility they imagined themselves bound to carry out to the letter the instructions inscribed in a certain book, the so-called law. In the same way all who take part in such an affair, from the highest representative of authority who signs his assent to the report, from the superintendent presiding at the recruiting sessions, and the priest who deludes the recruits, to the lowest soldier who is ready now to fire on his own brothers, imagine, in the intoxication of power or of servility, that they are some conventional characters. They do not face the question that is presented to them, whether or not they ought to take part in what their conscience judges an evil act, but fancy themselves various conventional personages--one as the Tzar, God's anointed, an exceptional being, called to watch over the happiness of one hundred millions of men; another as the representative of nobility; another as a priest, who has received special grace by his ordination; another as a soldier, bound by his military oath to carry out all he is commanded without reflection.

Only under the intoxication of the power or the servility of their imagined positions could all these people act as they do.

Were not they all firmly convinced that their respective vocations of tzar, minister, governor, judge, nobleman, landowner, superintendent, officer, and soldier are something real and important, not one of them would even think without horror and aversion of taking part in what they do now.

The conventional positions, established hundreds of years, recognized for centuries and by everyone, distinguished by special names and dresses, and, moreover, confirmed by every kind of solemnity, have so penetrated into men's minds through their senses, that, forgetting the ordinary conditions of life common to all, they look at themselves and everyone only from this conventional point of view, and are guided in their estimation of their own actions and those of others by this conventional standard.

Thus we see a man of perfect sanity and ripe age, simply because he is decked out with some fringe, or embroidered keys on his coat tails, or a colored ribbon only fit for some gayly dressed girl, and is told that he is a general, a chamberlain, a knight of the order of St. Andrew, or some similar nonsense, suddenly become self-important, proud, and even happy, or, on the contrary, grow melancholy and unhappy to the point of falling ill, because he has failed to obtain the expected decoration or title. Or what is still more striking, a young man, perfectly sane in every other matter, independent and beyond the fear of want, simply because he has been appointed judicial prosecutor or district commander, separates a poor widow from her little children, and shuts her up in prison, leaving her children uncared for, all because the unhappy woman carried on a secret trade in spirits, and so deprived the revenue of twenty-five rubles, and he does not feel the least pang of remorse. Or what is still more amazing; a man, otherwise sensible and good-hearted, simply because he is given a badge or a uniform to wear, and told that he is a guard or customs officer, is ready to fire on people, and neither he nor those around him regard him as to blame for it, but, on the contrary, would regard him as to blame if he did not fire. To say nothing of judges and juries who condemn men to death, and soldiers who kill men by thousands without the slightest scruple merely because it has been instilled into them that they are not simply men, but jurors, judges, generals, and soldiers.

This strange and abnormal condition of men under state organization is usually expressed in the following words: "As a man, I pity him; but as guard, judge, general, governor, tzar, or soldier, it is my duty to kill or torture him." Just as though there were some positions conferred and recognized, which would exonerate us from the obligations laid on each of us by the fact of our common humanity.

So, for example, in the case before us, men are going to murder and torture the famishing, and they admit that in the dispute between the peasants and the landowner the peasants are right (all those in command said as much to me). They know that the peasants are wretched, poor, and hungry, and the landowner is rich and inspires no sympathy. Yet they are all going to kill the peasants to secure three thousand rubles for the landowner, only because at that moment they fancy themselves not men but governor, official, general of police, officer, and soldier, respectively, and consider themselves bound to obey, not the eternal demands of the conscience of man, but the casual, temporary demands of their positions as officers or soldiers.

Strange as it may seem, the sole explanation of this astonishing phenomenon is that they are in the condition of the hypnotized, who, they say, feel and act like the creatures they are commanded by the hypnotizer to represent. When, for instance, it is suggested to the hypnotized subject that he is lame, he begins to walk lame, that he is blind, and he cannot see, that he is a wild beast, and he begins to bite. This is the state, not only of those who were going on this expedition, but of all men who fulfill their state and social duties in preference to and in detriment of their human duties.

The essence of this state is that under the influence of one suggestion they lose the power of criticising their actions, and therefore do, without thinking, everything consistent with the suggestion to which they are led by example, precept, or insinuation.

The difference between those hypnotized by scientific men and those under the influence of the state hypnotism, is that an imaginary position is suggested to the former suddenly by one person in a very brief space of time, and so the hypnotized state appears to us in a striking and surprising form, while the imaginary position suggested by state influence is induced slowly, little by little, imperceptibly from childhood, sometimes during years, or even generations, and not in one person alone but in a whole society.

"But," it will be said, "at all times, in all societies, the majority of persons--all the children, all the women absorbed in the bearing and rearing of the young, all the great mass of the laboring population, who are under the necessity of incessant and fatiguing physical labor, all those of weak character by nature, all those who are abnormally enfeebled intellectually by the effects of nicotine, alcohol, opium, or other intoxicants--are always in a condition of incapacity for independent thought, and are either in subjection to those who are on a higher intellectual level, or else under the influence of family or social traditions, of what is called public opinion, and there is nothing unnatural or incongruous in their subjection."

And truly there is nothing unnatural in it, and the tendency of men of small intellectual power to follow the lead of those on a higher level of intelligence is a constant law, and it is owing to it that men can live in societies and on the same principles at all. The minority consciously adopt certain rational principles through their correspondence with reason, while the majority act on the same principles unconsciously because it is required by public opinion.

Such subjection to public opinion on the part of the unintellectual does not assume an unnatural character till the public opinion is split into two.

But there are times when a higher truth, revealed at first to a few persons, gradually gains ground till it has taken hold of such a number of persons that the old public opinion, founded on a lower order of truths, begins to totter and the new is ready to take its place, but has not yet been firmly established. It is like the spring, this time of transition, when the old order of ideas has not quite broken up and the new has not quite gained a footing. Men begin to criticise their actions in the light of the new truth, but in the meantime in practice, through inertia and tradition, they continue to follow the principles which once represented the highest point of rational consciousness, but are now in flagrant contradiction with it.

Then men are in an abnormal, wavering condition, feeling the necessity of following the new ideal, and yet not bold enough to break with the old-established traditions.

Such is the attitude in regard to the truth of Christianity not only of the men in the Toula train, but of the majority of men of our times, alike of the higher and the lower orders.

Those of the ruling classes, having no longer any reasonable justification for the profitable positions they occupy, are forced, in order to keep them, to stifle their higher rational faculty of loving, and to persuade themselves that their positions are indispensable. And those of the lower classes, exhausted by toil and brutalized of set purpose, are kept in a permanent deception, practiced deliberately and continuously by the higher classes upon them.

Only in this way can one explain the amazing contradictions with which our life is full, and of which a striking example was presented to me by the expedition I met on the 9th of September; good, peaceful men, known to me personally, going with untroubled tranquillity to perpetrate the most beastly, senseless, and vile of crimes. Had not they some means of stifling their conscience, not one of them would be capable of committing a hundredth part of such a villainy.

It is not that they have not a conscience which forbids them from acting thus, just as, even three or four hundred years ago, when people burnt men at the stake and put them to the rack they had a conscience which prohibited it; the conscience is there, but it has been put to sleep--in those in command by what the psychologists call auto-suggestion; in the soldiers, by the direct conscious hypnotizing exerted by the higher classes.

Though asleep, the conscience is there, and in spite of the hypnotism it is already speaking in them, and it may awake.

All these men are in a position like that of a man under

hypnotism, commanded to do something opposed to everything he regards as good and rational, such as to kill his mother or his child. The hypnotized subject feels himself bound to carry out the suggestion--he thinks he cannot stop--but the nearer he gets to the time and the place of the action, the more the benumbed conscience begins to stir, to resist, and to try to awake. And no one can say beforehand whether he will carry out the suggestion or not; which will gain the upper hand, the rational conscience or the irrational suggestion. It all depends on their relative strength.

That is just the case with the men in the Toula train and in general with everyone carrying out acts of state violence in our day.

There was a time when men who set out with the object of murder and violence, to make an example, did not return till they had carried out their object, and then, untroubled by doubts or scruples, having calmly flogged men to death, they returned home and caressed their children, laughed, amused themselves, and enjoyed the peaceful pleasures of family life. In those days it never struck the landowners and wealthy men who profited by these crimes, that the privileges they enjoyed had any direct connection with these atrocities. But now it is no longer so. Men know now, or are not far from knowing, what they are doing and for what object they do it. They can shut their eyes and force their conscience to be still, but so long as their eyes are opened and their conscience undulled, they must all--those who carry out and those who profit by these crimes alike--see the import of them. Sometimes they realize it only after the crime has been perpetrated, sometimes they realize it just before its perpetration. Thus those who commanded the recent acts of violence in Nijni-Novgorod, Saratov, Orel, and the Yuzovsky factory realized their significance only after their perpetration, and now those who commanded and those who carried out these crimes are ashamed before public opinion and their conscience. I have talked to soldiers who had taken part in these crimes, and they always studiously turned the conversation off the subject, and when they spoke of it it was with horror and bewilderment. There are cases, too, when men come to themselves just before the perpetration of the crime. Thus I know the case of a sergeant-major who had been beaten by two peasants during the repression of disorder and had made a complaint. The next day, after seeing the atrocities perpetrated on the other peasants, he entreated the commander of his company to tear up his complaint and let off the two peasants. I know cases when soldiers, commanded to fire, have refused to obey, and I know many cases of officers who have refused to command expeditions for torture and murder. So that men sometimes come to their senses long before perpetrating the suggested crime, sometimes at the very moment before perpetrating it, sometimes only afterward.

The men traveling in the Toula train were going with the object of killing and injuring their fellow-creatures, but none could tell whether they would carry out their object or not. However obscure his responsibility for the affair is to each, and however strong the idea instilled into all of them that they are not men, but governors, officials, officers, and soldiers, and as such beings can violate every human duty, the nearer they approach the place of the execution, the stronger their doubts as to its being right, and this doubt will reach its highest point when the very moment for carrying it out has come.

The governor, in spite of all the stupefying effect of his surroundings, cannot help hesitating when the moment comes to give final decisive command. He knows that the action of the Governor of Orel has called down upon him the disapproval of the best people, and he himself, influenced by the public opinion of the circles in which he moves, has more than once expressed his disapprobation of him. He knows that the prosecutor, who ought to have come, flatly refused to have anything to do with it, because he regarded it as disgraceful. He knows, too, that there may be changes any day in the government, and that what was a ground for advancement yesterday may be the cause of disgrace to-morrow. And he knows that there is a press, if not in Russia, at least abroad, which may report the affair and cover him with ignominy forever. He is already conscious of a change in public opinion which condemns what was formerly a duty. Moreover, he cannot feel fully assured that his soldiers will at the last moment obey him. He is wavering, and none can say beforehand what he will do.

All the officers and functionaries who accompany him experience in greater or less degree the same emotions. In the depths of their hearts they all know that what they are doing is shameful, that to take part in it is a discredit and blemish in the eyes of some people whose opinion they value. They know that after murdering and torturing the defenseless, each of them will be ashamed to face his betrothed or the woman he is courting. And besides, they too, like the governor, are doubtful whether the soldiers' obedience to orders can be reckoned on. What a contrast with the confident air they all put on as they sauntered about the station and platform! Inwardly they were not only in a state of suffering but even of suspense. Indeed they only assumed this bold and composed manner to conceal the wavering within. And this feeling increased as they drew near the scene of action.

And imperceptible as it was, and strange as it seems to say so, all that mass of lads, the soldiers, who seemed so submissive, were in precisely the same condition.

These are not the soldiers of former days, who gave up the natural life of industry and devoted their whole existence to debauchery, plunder, and murder, like the Roman legionaries or the warriors of the Thirty Years' War, or even the soldiers of more recent times who served for twenty-five years in the army. They have mostly been only lately taken from their families, and are full of the recollections of the good, rational, natural life they have left behind them.

All these lads, peasants for the most part, know what is the business they have come about; they know that the landowners always oppress their brothers the peasants, and that therefore it is most likely the same thing here. Moreover, a majority of them can now read, and the books they read are not all such as exalt a military life; there are some which point out its immorality. Among them are often free-thinking comrades--who have enlisted voluntarily--or young officers of liberal ideas, and already the first germ of doubt has been sown in regard to the unconditional legitimacy and glory of their occupation.

It is true that they have all passed through that terrible, skillful education, elaborated through centuries, which kills all initiative in a man, and that they are so trained to mechanical obedience that at the word of command: "Fire!--All the line!--Fire!" and so on, their guns will rise of themselves and the habitual movements will be performed. But "Fire!" now does not mean shooting into the sand for amusement, it means firing on their broken-down, exploited fathers and brothers whom they see there in the crowd, with women and children shouting and waving their arms. Here they are--one with his scanty beard and patched coat and plaited shoes of reed, just like the father left at home in Kazan or Riazan province; one with gray beard and bent back, leaning on a staff like the old grandfather; one, a young fellow in boots and a red shirt, just as he was himself a year ago--he, the soldier who must fire upon him. There, too, a woman in reed shoes and PANYOVA, just like the mother left at home.

Is it possible they must fire on them? And no one knows what each soldier will do at the last minute. The least word, the slightest allusion would be enough to stop them.

At the last moment they will all find themselves in the position of a hypnotized man to whom it has been suggested to chop a log, who coming up to what has been indicated to him as a log, with the ax already lifted to strike, sees that it is not a log but his sleeping brother. He may perform the act that has been suggested to him, and he may come to his senses at the moment of performing it. In the same way all these men may come to themselves in time or they may go on to the end.

If they do not come to themselves, the most fearful crime will be committed, as in Orel, and then the hypnotic suggestion under which they act will be strengthened in all other men. If they do come to themselves, not only this terrible crime will not be perpetrated, but many also who hear of the turn the affair has taken will be emancipated from the hypnotic influence in which they were held, or at least will be nearer being emancipated from it.

Even if a few only come to themselves, and boldly explain to the others all the wickedness of such a crime, the influence of these few may rouse the others to shake off the controlling suggestion, and the atrocity will not be perpetrated.

More than that, if a few men, even of those who are not taking part in the affair but are only present at the preparations for it, or have heard of such things being done in the past, do not remain indifferent but boldly and plainly express their detestation of such crimes to those who have to execute them, and point out to them all the senselessness, cruelty, and wickedness of such acts, that alone will be productive of good.

That was what took place in the instance before us. It was enough for a few men, some personally concerned in the affair and others simply outsiders, to express their disapproval of floggings that had taken place elsewhere, and their contempt and loathing for those who had taken part in inflicting them, for a few persons in the Toula case to express their repugnance to having any share in it; for a lady traveling by the train, and a few other bystanders at the station, to express to those who formed the expedition their disgust at what they were doing; for one of the commanders of a company, who was asked for troops for the restoration of order, to reply that soldiers ought not to be butchers--and thanks to these and a few other seemingly insignificant influences brought to bear on these hypnotized men, the affair took a completely different turn, and the troops, when they reached the place, did not inflict any punishment, but contented themselves with cutting down the forest and giving it to the landowner.

Had not a few persons had a clear consciousness that what they were doing was wrong, and consequently influenced one another in that direction, what was done at Orel would have taken place at Toula. Had this consciousness been still stronger, and had the influence exerted been therefore greater than it was, it might well have been that the governor with his troops would not even have ventured to cut down the forest and give it to the landowner.

Had that consciousness been stronger still, it might well have been that the governor would not have ventured to go to the scene of action at all; even that the minister would not have ventured to form this decision or the Tzar to ratify it.

All depends, therefore, on the strength of the consciousness of Christian truth on the part of each individual man.

And, therefore, one would have thought that the efforts of all men of the present day who profess to wish to work for the welfare of humanity would have been directed to strengthening this consciousness of Christian truth in themselves and others.

But, strange to say, it is precisely those people who profess most anxiety for the amelioration of human life, and are regarded as the leaders of public opinion, who assert that there is no need to do that, and that there are other more effective means for the amelioration of men's condition. They affirm that the amelioration of human life is effected not by the efforts of individual men, to recognize and propagate the truth, but by the gradual modification of the general conditions of life, and that therefore the efforts of individuals should be directed to the gradual modification of external conditions for the better. For every advocacy of a truth inconsistent with the existing order by an individual is, they maintain, not only useless but injurious, since in provokes coercive measures on the part of the authorities, restricting these individuals from continuing any action useful to society. According to this doctrine all modifications in human life are brought about by precisely the same laws as in the life of the animals.

So that, according to this doctrine, all the founders of religions, such as Moses and the prophets, Confucius, Lao-Tse, Buddha, Christ, and others, preached their doctrines and their followers accepted them, not because they loved the truth, but because the political, social, and above all economic conditions of the peoples among whom these religions arose were favorable for their origination and development.

And therefore the chief efforts of the man who wishes to serve society and improve the condition of humanity ought, according to this doctrine, to be directed not to the elucidation and propagation of truth, but to the improvement of the external political, social, and above all economic conditions. And the modification of these conditions is partly effected by serving the government and introducing liberal and progressive principles into it, partly in promoting the development of industry and the propagation of socialistic ideas, and most of all by the diffusion of science. According to this theory it is of no consequence whether you profess the truth revealed to you, and therefore realize it in your life, or at least refrain from committing actions opposed to the truth, such as serving the government and strengthening its authority when you regard it as injurious, profiting by the capitalistic system when you regard it as wrong, showing veneration for various ceremonies which you believe to be degrading superstitions, giving support to the law when you believe it to be founded on error, serving as a soldier, taking oaths, and lying, and lowering yourself generally. It is useless to refrain from all that; what is of use is not altering the existing forms of life, but submitting to them against your own convictions, introducing liberalism into the existing institutions, promoting commerce, the propaganda of socialism, and the triumphs of what is called science, and the diffusion of education. According to this theory one can remain a landowner, merchant, manufacturer, judge, official in government pay, officer or soldier, and still be not only a humane man, but even a socialist and revolutionist.

Hypocrisy, which had formerly only a religious basis in the doctrine of original sin, the redemption, and the Church, has in our day gained a new scientific basis and has consequently caught in its nets all those who had reached too high a stage of development to be able to find support in religious hypocrisy. So that while in former days a man who professed the religion of the Church could take part in all the crimes of the state, and profit by them, and still regard himself as free from any taint of sin, so long as he fulfilled the external observances of his creed, nowadays all who do not believe in the Christianity of the Church, find similar well-founded irrefutable reasons in science for regarding themselves as blameless and even highly moral in spite of their participation in the misdeeds of government and the advantages they gain from them.

A rich landowner--not only in Russia, but in France, England, Germany, or America--lives on the rents exacted; from the people living on his land, and robs these generally poverty-stricken people of all he can get from them. This man's right of property in the land rests on the fact that at every effort on the part of the oppressed people, without his consent, to make use of the land he considers his, troops are called out to subject them to punishment and murder. One would have thought that it was obvious that a man living in this way was an evil, egoistic creature and could not possibly consider himself a Christian or a liberal. One would have supposed it evident that the first thing such a man must do, if he wishes to approximate to Christianity or liberalism, would be to cease to plunder and ruin men by means of acts of state violence in support of his claim to the land. And so it would be if it were not for the logic of hypocrisy, which reasons that from a religious point of view possession or non-possession of land is of no consequence for salvation, and from the scientific point of view, giving up the ownership of land is a useless individual renunciation, and that the welfare of mankind is not promoted in that way, but by a gradual modification of external forms. And so we see this man, without the least trouble of mind or doubt that people will believe in his sincerity, organizing an agricultural exhibition, or a temperance society, or sending some soup and stockings by his wife or children to three old women, and boldly in his family, in drawing rooms, in committees, and in the press, advocating the Gospel or humanitarian doctrine of love for one's neighbor in general and the agricultural laboring population in particular whom he is continually exploiting and oppressing. And other people who are in the same position as he believe him, commend him, and solemnly discuss with him measures for ameliorating the condition of the working-class, on whose exploitation their whole life rests, devising all kinds of possible methods for this, except the one without which all improvement of their condition is impossible, i. e., refraining from taking from them the land necessary for their subsistence. (A striking example of this hypocrisy was the solicitude displayed by the Russian landowners last year, their efforts to combat the famine which they had caused, and by which they profited, selling not only bread at the highest price, but even potato haulm at five rubles the dessiatine (about 2 and four-fifths acres) for fuel to the freezing peasants.)

Or take a merchant whose whole trade--like all trade indeed--is founded on a series of trickery, by means of which, profiting by the ignorance or need of others, he buys goods below their value and sells them again above their value. One would have fancied it obvious that a man whose whole occupation was based on what in his own language is called swindling, if it is done under other conditions, ought to be ashamed of his position, and could not any way, while he continues a merchant, profess himself a Christian or a liberal.

But the sophistry of hypocrisy reasons that the merchant can pass for a virtuous man without giving up his pernicious course of action; a religious man need only have faith and a liberal man need only promote the modification of external conditions--the progress of industry. And so we see the merchant (who often goes further and commits acts of direct dishonesty, selling adulterated goods, using false weights and measures, and trading in products injurious to health, such as alcohol and opium) boldly regarding himself and being regarded by others, so long as he does not directly deceive his colleagues in business, as a pattern of probity and virtue. And if he spends a thousandth part of his stolen wealth on some public institution, a hospital or museum or school, then he is even regarded as the benefactor of the people on the exploitation and corruption of whom his whole prosperity has been founded: if he sacrifices, too, a portion of his ill-gotten gains on a

Church and the poor, then he is an exemplary Christian.

A manufacturer is a man whose whole income consists of value squeezed out of the workmen, and whose whole occupation is based on forced, unnatural labor, exhausting whole generations of men. It would seem obvious that if this man professes any Christian or liberal principles, he must first of all give up ruining human lives for his own profit. But by the existing theory he is promoting industry, and he ought not to abandon his pursuit. It would even be injuring society for him to do so. And so we see this man, the harsh slave-driver of thousands of men, building almshouses with little gardens two yards square for the workmen broken down in toiling for him, and a bank, and a poorhouse, and a hospital--fully persuaded that he has amply expiated in this way for all the human lives morally and physically ruined by him--and calmly going on with his business, taking pride in it.

Any civil, religious, or military official in government employ, who serves the state from vanity, or, as is most often the case, simply for the sake of the pay wrung from the harassed and toilworn working classes (all taxes, however raised, always fall on labor), if he, as is very seldom the case, does not directly rob the government in the usual way, considers himself, and is considered by his fellows, as a most useful and virtuous member of society.

A judge or a public prosecutor knows that through his sentence or his prosecution hundreds or thousands of poor wretches are at once torn from their families and thrown into prison, where they may go out of their minds, kill themselves with pieces of broken glass, or starve themselves; he knows that they have wives and mothers and children, disgraced and made miserable by separation from them, vainly begging for pardon for them or some alleviation of their sentence, and this judge or this prosecutor is so hardened in his hypocrisy that he and his fellows and his wife and his household are all fully convinced that he may be a most exemplary man. According to the metaphysics of hypocrisy it is held that he is doing a work of public utility. And this man who has ruined hundreds, thousands of men, who curse him and are driven to desperation by his action, goes to mass, a smile of shining benevolence on his smooth face, in perfect faith in good and in God, listens to the Gospel, caresses his children, preaches moral principles to them, and is moved by imaginary sufferings.

All these men and those who depend on them, their wives, tutors, children, cooks, actors, jockeys, and so on, are living on the blood which by one means or another, through one set of blood-suckers or another, is drawn out of the working class, and every day their pleasures cost hundreds or thousands of days of labor. They see the sufferings and privations of these laborers and their children, their aged, their wives, and their sick, they know the punishments inflicted on those who resist this organized plunder, and far from decreasing, far from concealing their luxury, they insolently display it before these oppressed laborers who hate them, as though intentionally provoking them with the pomp of their parks and palaces, their theaters, hunts, and races. At the same time they continue to persuade themselves and others that they are all much concerned about the welfare of these working classes, whom they have always trampled under their feet, and on Sundays, richly dressed, they drive in sumptuous carriages to the houses of God built in very mockery of Christianity, and there listen to men, trained to this work of deception, who in white neckties or in brocaded vestments, according to their denomination, preach the love for their neighbor which they all gainsay in their lives. And these people have so entered into their part that they seriously believe that they really are what they pretend to be.

The universal hypocrisy has so entered into the flesh and blood of all classes of our modern society, it has reached such a pitch that nothing in that way can rouse indignation. Hypocrisy in the Greek means "acting," and acting--playing a part--is always possible. The representatives of Christ give their blessing to the ranks of murderers holding their guns loaded against their brothers; "for prayer" priests, ministers of various Christian sects are always present, as indispensably as the hangman, at executions, and sanction by their presence the compatibility of murder with Christianity (a clergyman assisted at the attempt at murder by electricity in America)--but such facts cause no one any surprise.

There was recently held at Petersburg an international exhibition of instruments of torture, handcuffs, models of solitary cells, that is to say instruments of torture worse than knouts or rods, and sensitive ladies and gentlemen went and amused themselves by looking at them.

No one is surprised that together with its recognition of liberty, equality, and fraternity, liberal science should prove the necessity of war, punishment, customs, the censure, the regulation of prostitution, the exclusion of cheap foreign laborers, the hindrance of emigration, the justifiableness of colonization, based on poisoning and destroying whole races of men called savages, and so on.

People talk of the time when all men shall profess what is called Christianity (that is, various professions of faith hostile to one another), when all shall be well-fed and clothed, when all shall be united from one end of the world to the other by telegraphs and telephones, and be able to communicate by balloons, when all the working classes are permeated by socialistic doctrines, when the Trades Unions possess so many millions of members and so many millions of rubles, when everyone is educated and all can read newspapers and learn all the sciences.

But what good or useful thing can come of all these improvements, if men do not speak and act in accordance with what they believe to be the truth?

The condition of men is the result of their disunion. Their disunion results from their not following the truth which is one, but falsehoods which are many. The sole means of uniting men is their union in the truth. And therefore the more sincerely men strive toward the truth, the nearer they get to unity.

But how can men be united in the truth or even approximate to it, if they do not even express the truth they know, but hold that there is no need to do so, and pretend to regard as truth what they believe to be false?

And therefore no improvement is possible so long as men are hypocritical and hide the truth from themselves, so long as they do not recognize that their union and therefore their welfare is only possible in the truth, and do not put the recognition and profession of the truth revealed to them higher than everything else.

All the material improvements that religious and scientific men can dream of may be accomplished; all men may accept Christianity, and all the reforms desired by the Bellamys may be brought about with every possible addition and improvement, but if the hypocrisy which rules nowadays still exists, if men do not profess the truth they know, but continue to feign belief in what they do not believe and veneration for what they do not respect, their condition will remain the same, or even grow worse and worse. The more men are freed from privation; the more telegraphs, telephones, books, papers, and journals there are; the more means there will be of diffusing inconsistent lies and hypocrisies, and the more disunited and consequently miserable will men become, which indeed is what we see actually taking place.

All these material reforms may be realized, but the position of humanity will not be improved. But only let each man, according to his powers, at once realize in his life the truth he knows, or at least cease to support the falsehoods he is supporting in the place of the truth, and at once, in this year 1893, we should see such reforms as we do not dare to hope for within a century--the emancipation of men and the reign of truth upon earth.

Not without good reason was Christ's only harsh and threatening reproof directed against hypocrites and hypocrisy. It is not theft nor robbery nor murder nor fornication, but falsehood, the special falsehood of hypocrisy, which corrupts men, brutalizes them and makes them vindictive, destroys all distinction between right and wrong in their conscience, deprives them of what is the true meaning of all real human life, and debars them from all progress toward perfection.

Those who do evil through ignorance of the truth provoke sympathy with their victims and repugnance for their actions, they do harm only to those they attack; but those who know the truth and do evil masked by hypocrisy, injure themselves and their victims, and thousands of other men as well who are led astray by the falsehood with which the wrongdoing is disguised.

Thieves, robbers, murderers, and cheats, who commit crimes recognized by themselves and everyone else as evil, serve as an example of what ought not to be done, and deter others from similar crimes. But those who commit the same thefts, robberies, murders, and other crimes, disguising them under all kinds of religious or scientific or humanitarian justifications, as all landowners, merchants, manufacturers, and government officials do, provoke others to imitation, and so do harm not only to those who are directly the victims of their crimes, but to thousands and millions of men whom they corrupt by obliterating their sense of the distinction between right and wrong.

A single fortune gained by trading in goods necessary to the people or in goods pernicious in their effects, or by financial speculations, or by acquiring land at a low price the value of which is increased by the needs of the population, or by an industry ruinous to the health and life of those employed in it, or by military or civil service of the state, or by any employment which trades on men's evil instincts--a single fortune acquired in any of these ways, not only with the sanction, but even with the approbation of the leading men in society, and masked with an ostentation of philanthropy, corrupts men incomparably more than millions of thefts and robberies committed against the recognized forms of law and punishable as crimes.

A single execution carried out by prosperous educated men uninfluenced by passion, with the approbation and assistance of Christian ministers, and represented as something necessary and even just, is infinitely more corrupting and brutalizing to men than thousands of murders committed by uneducated working people under the influence of passion. An execution such as was proposed by Joukovsky, which would produce even a sentiment of religious emotion in the spectators, would be one of the most perverting actions imaginable. (SEE vol. iv. of the works of Joukovsky.)

Every war, even the most humanely conducted, with all its ordinary consequences, the destruction of harvests, robberies, the license and debauchery, and the murder with the justifications of its necessity and justice, the exaltation and glorification of military exploits, the worship of the flag, the patriotic sentiments, the feigned solicitude for the wounded, and so on, does more in one year to pervert men's minds than thousands of robberies, murders, and arsons perpetrated during hundreds of years by individual men under the influence of passion.

The luxurious expenditure of a single respectable and so-called honorable family, even within the conventional limits, consuming as it does the produce of as many days of labor as would suffice to provide for thousands living in privation near, does more to pervert men's minds than thousands of the violent orgies of coarse tradespeople, officers, and workmen of drunken and debauched habits, who smash up glasses and crockery for amusement.

One solemn religious procession, one service, one sermon from the altar-steps or the pulpit, in which the preacher does not believe, produces incomparably more evil than thousands of swindling tricks, adulteration of food, and so on.

We talk of the hypocrisy of the Pharisees. But the hypocrisy of our society far surpasses the comparatively innocent hypocrisy of the Pharisees. They had at least an external religious law, the fulfillment of which hindered them from seeing their obligations to their neighbors. Moreover, these obligations were not nearly so clearly defined in their day. Nowadays we have no such religious law to exonerate us from our duties to our neighbors (I am not speaking now of the coarse and ignorant persons who still fancy their sins can be absolved by confession to a priest or by the absolution of the Pope). On the contrary, the law of the Gospel which we all profess in one form or another directly defines these duties. Besides, the duties which had then been only vaguely and mystically expressed by a few prophets have now been so clearly formulated, have become such truisms, that they are repeated even by schoolboys and journalists. And so it would seem that men of to-day cannot pretend that they do not know these duties.

A man of the modern world who profits by the order of things based on violence, and at the same time protests that he loves his neighbor and does not observe what he is doing in his daily life to his neighbor, is like a brigand who has spent his life in robbing men, and who, caught at last, knife in hand, in the very act of striking his shrieking victim, should declare that he had no idea that what he was doing was disagreeable to the man he had robbed and was prepared to murder. Just as this robber and murderer could not deny what was evident to everyone, so it would seem that a man living upon the privations of the oppressed classes cannot persuade himself and others that he desires the welfare of those he plunders, and that he does not know how the advantages he enjoys are obtained.

It is impossible to convince ourselves that we do not know that there are a hundred thousand men in prison in Russia alone to guarantee the security of our property and tranquillity, and that we do not know of the law tribunals in which we take part, and which, at our initiative, condemn those who have attacked our property or our security to prison, exile, or forced labor, whereby men no worse than those who condemn them are ruined and corrupted; or that we do not know that we only possess all that we do possess because it has been acquired and is defended for us by murder and violence.

We cannot pretend that we do not see the armed policeman who marches up and down beneath our windows to guarantee our security while we eat our luxurious dinner, or look at the new piece at the theater, or that we are unaware of the existence of the soldiers who will make their appearance with guns and cartridges directly our property is attacked.

We know very well that we are only allowed to go on eating our dinner, to finish seeing the new play, or to enjoy to the end the ball, the Christmas fete, the promenade, the races or, the hunt, thanks to the policeman's revolver or the soldier's rifle, which will shoot down the famished outcast who has been robbed of his share, and who looks round the corner with covetous eyes at our pleasures, ready to interrupt them instantly, were not the policeman and the soldier there prepared to run up at our first call for help.

And therefore just as a brigand caught in broad daylight in the act cannot persuade us that he did not lift his knife in order to rob his victim of his purse, and had no thought of killing him, we too, it would seem, cannot persuade ourselves or others that the soldiers and policemen around us are not to guard us, but only for defense against foreign foes, and to regulate traffic and fêtes and reviews; we cannot persuade ourselves and others that we do not know that men do not like dying of hunger, bereft of the right to gain their subsistence from the earth on which they live; that they do not like working underground, in the water, or in stifling heat, for ten to fourteen hours a day, at night in factories to manufacture objects for our pleasure. One would imagine it impossible to deny what is so obvious. Yet it is denied.

Still, there are, among the rich, especially among the young, and among women, persons whom I am glad to meet more and more frequently, who, when they are shown in what way and at what cost their pleasures are purchased, do not try to conceal the truth, but hiding their heads in their hands, cry: "Ah! don't speak of that. If it is so, life is impossible." But though there are such sincere people who even though they cannot renounce their fault, at least see it, the vast majority of the men of the modern world have so entered into the parts they play in their hypocrisy that they boldly deny what is staring everyone in the face.

"All that is unjust," they say; "no one forces the people to work for the landowners and manufacturers. That is an affair of free contract. Great properties and fortunes are necessary, because they provide and organize work for the working classes. And labor in the factories and workshops is not at all the terrible thing you make it out to be. Even if there are some abuses in factories, the government and the public are taking steps to obviate them and to make the labor of the factory workers much easier, and even agreeable. The working classes are accustomed to physical labor, and are, so far, fit for nothing else. The poverty of the people is not the result of private property in land, nor of capitalistic oppression, but of other causes: it is the result of the ignorance, brutality, and intemperance of the people. And we men in authority who are striving against this impoverishment of the people by wise legislation, we capitalists who are combating it by the extension of useful inventions, we clergymen by religious instruction, and we liberals by the formation of trades unions, and the diffusion of education, are in this way increasing the prosperity of the people without changing our own positions. We do not want all to be as poor as the poor; we want all to be as rich as the rich. As for the assertion that men are ill treated and murdered to force them to work for the profit of the rich, that is a sophism. The army is only called out against the mob, when the people, in ignorance of their own interests, make disturbances and destroy the tranquillity necessary for the public welfare. In the same way, too, it is necessary to keep in restraint the malefactors for whom the prisons and gallows are established. We ourselves wish to suppress these forms of punishment and are working in that direction."

Hypocrisy in our day is supported on two sides: by false religion and by false science. And it has reached such proportions that if we were not living in its midst, we could not believe that men could attain such a pitch of self-deception. Men of the present day have come into such an extraordinary condition, their hearts are so hardened, that seeing they see not, hearing they do not hear, and understand not.

Men have long been living in antagonism to their conscience. If it were not for hypocrisy they could not go on living such a life. This social organization in opposition to their conscience only continues to exist because it is disguised by hypocrisy.

And the greater the divergence between actual life and men's conscience, the greater the extension of hypocrisy. But even hypocrisy has its limits. And it seems to me that we have reached those limits in the present day.

Every man of the present day with the Christian principles assimilated involuntarily in his conscience, finds himself in precisely the position of a man asleep who dreams that he is obliged to do something which even in his dream he knows he ought not to do. He knows this in the depths of his conscience, and all the same he seems unable to change his position; he cannot stop and cease doing what he ought not to do. And just as in a dream, his position becoming more and more painful, at last reaches such a pitch of intensity that he begins sometimes to doubt the reality of what is passing and makes a moral effort to shake off the nightmare which is oppressing him.

This is just the condition of the average man of our Christian society. He feels that all that he does himself and that is done around him is something absurd, hideous, impossible, and opposed to his conscience; he feels that his position is becoming more and more unendurable and reaching a crisis of intensity.

It is not possible that we modern men, with the Christian sense of human dignity and equality permeating us soul and body, with our need for peaceful association and unity between nations, should really go on living in such a way that every joy, every gratification we have is bought by the sufferings, by the lives of our brother men, and moreover, that we should be every instant within a hair's-breadth of falling on one another, nation against nation, like wild beasts, mercilessly destroying men's lives and labor, only because some benighted diplomatist or ruler says or writes some stupidity to another equally benighted diplomatist or ruler.

It is impossible. Yet every man of our day sees that this is so and awaits the calamity. And the situation becomes more and more insupportable.

And as the man who is dreaming does not believe that what appears to him can be truly the reality and tries to wake up to the actual real world again, so the average man of modern days cannot in the bottom of his heart believe that the awful position in which he is placed and which is growing worse and worse can be the reality, and tries to wake up to a true, real life, as it exists in his conscience.

And just as the dreamer need only make a moral effort and ask himself, "Isn't it a dream?" and the situation which seemed to him so hopeless will instantly disappear, and he will wake up to peaceful and happy reality, so the man of the modern world need only make a moral effort to doubt the reality presented to him by his own hypocrisy and the general hypocrisy around him, and to ask himself, "Isn't it all a delusion?" and he will at once, like the dreamer awakened, feel himself transported from an imaginary and dreadful world to the true, calm, and happy reality.

And to do this a man need accomplish no great feats or exploits. He need only make a moral effort.

But can a man make this effort?

According to the existing theory so essential to support hypocrisy, man is not free and cannot change his life.

"Man cannot change his life, because he is not free. He is not free, because all his actions are conditioned by previously existing causes. And whatever the man may do there are always some causes or other through which he does these or those acts, and therefore man cannot be free and change his life," say the champions of the metaphysics of hypocrisy. And they would be perfectly right if man were a creature without conscience and incapable of moving toward the truth; that is to say, if after recognizing a new truth, man always remained at the same stage of moral development. But man is a creature with a conscience and capable of attaining a higher and higher degree of truth. And therefore even if man is not free as regards performing these or those acts because there exists a previous cause for every act, the very causes of his acts, consisting as they do for the man of conscience of the recognition of this or that truth, are within his own control.

So that though man may not be free as regards the performance of his actions, he is free as regards the foundation on which they are performed. Just as the mechanician who is not free to modify the movement of his locomotive when it is in motion, is free to regulate the machine beforehand so as to determine what the movement is to be.

Whatever the conscious man does, he acts just as he does, and not otherwise, only because he recognizes that to act as he is acting is in accord with the truth, or because he has recognized it at some previous time, and is now only through inertia, through habit, acting in accordance with his previous recognition of truth.

In any case, the cause of his action is not to be found in any given previous fact, but in the consciousness of a given relation to truth, and the consequent recognition of this or that fact as a sufficient basis for action.

Whether a man eats or does not eat, works or rests, runs risks or avoids them, if he has a conscience he acts thus only because he considers it right and rational, because he considers that to act thus is in harmony with truth, or else because he has made this reflection in the past.

The recognition or non-recognition of a certain truth depends not on external causes, but on certain other causes within the man himself. So that at times under external conditions apparently very favorable for the recognition of truth, one man will not recognize it, and another, on the contrary, under the most unfavorable conditions will, without apparent cause, recognize it. As it is said in the Gospel, "No man can come unto me, except the Father which hath sent me draw him." That is to say, the recognition of truth, which is the cause of all the manifestations of human life, does not depend on external phenomena, but on certain inner spiritual characteristics of the man which escape our observation.

And therefore man, though not free in his acts, always feels himself free in what is the motive of his acts--the recognition or non-recognition of truth. And he feels himself independent not only of facts external to his own personality, but even of his own actions.

Thus a man who under the influence of passion has committed an act contrary to the truth he recognizes, remains none the less free to recognize it or not to recognize it; that is, he can by refusing to recognize the truth regard his action as necessary and justifiable, or he may recognize the truth and regard his act as wrong and censure himself for it.

Thus a gambler or a drunkard who does not resist temptation and

yields to his passion is still free to recognize gambling and drunkenness as wrong or to regard them as a harmless pastime. In the first case even if he does not at once get over his passion, he gets the more free from it the more sincerely he recognizes the truth about it; in the second case he will be strengthened in his vice and will deprive himself of every possibility of shaking it off.

In the same way a man who has made his escape alone from a house on fire, not having had the courage to save his friend, remains free, recognizing the truth that a man ought to save the life of another even at the risk of his own, to regard his action as bad and to censure himself for it, or, not recognizing this truth, to regard his action as natural and necessary and to justify it to himself. In the first case, if he recognizes the truth in spite of his departure from it, he prepares for himself in the future a whole series of acts of self-sacrifice necessarily flowing from this recognition of the truth; in the second case, a whole series of egoistic acts.

Not that a man is always free to recognize or to refuse to recognize every truth. There are truths which he has recognized long before or which have been handed down to him by education and tradition and accepted by him on faith, and to follow these truths has become a habit, a second nature with him; and there are truths, only vaguely, as it were distantly, apprehended by him. The man is not free to refuse to recognize the first, nor to recognize the second class of truths. But there are truths of a third kind, which have not yet become an unconscious motive of action, but yet have been revealed so clearly to him that he cannot pass them by, and is inevitably obliged to do one thing or the other, to recognize or not to recognize them. And it is in regard to these truths that the man's freedom manifests itself.

Every man during his life finds himself in regard to truth in the position of a man walking in the darkness with light thrown before him by the lantern he carries. He does not see what is not yet lighted up by the lantern; he does not see what he has passed which is hidden in the darkness; but at every stage of his journey he sees what is lighted up by the lantern, and he can always choose one side or the other of the road.

There are always unseen truths not yet revealed to the man's intellectual vision, and there are other truths outlived, forgotten, and assimilated by him, and there are also certain truths that rise up before the light of his reason and require his recognition. And it is in the recognition or non-recognition of these truths that what we call his freedom is manifested.

All the difficulty and seeming insolubility of the question of the freedom of man results from those who tried to solve the question imagining man as stationary in his relation to the truth.

Man is certainly not free if we imagine him stationary, and if we forget that the life of a man and of humanity is nothing but a continual movement from darkness into light, from a lower stage of truth to a higher, from a truth more alloyed with errors to a truth more purified from them.

Man would not be free if he knew no truth at all, and in the same way he would not be free and would not even have any idea of freedom if the whole truth which was to guide him in life had been revealed once for all to him in all its purity without any admixture of error.

But man is not stationary in regard to truth, but every individual man as he passes through life, and humanity as a whole in the same way, is continually learning to know a greater and greater degree of truth, and growing more and more free from error.

And therefore men are in a threefold relation to truth. Some truths have been so assimilated by them that they have become the unconscious basis of action, others are only just on the point of being revealed to him, and a third class, though not yet assimilated by him, have been revealed to him with sufficient clearness to force him to decide either to recognize them or to refuse to recognize them.

These, then, are the truths which man is free to recognize or to refuse to recognize.

The liberty of man does not consist in the power of acting independently of the progress of life and the influences arising from it, but in the capacity for recognizing and acknowledging the truth revealed to him, and becoming the free and joyful participator in the eternal and infinite work of God, the life of the world; or on the other hand for refusing to recognize the truth, and so being a miserable and reluctant slave dragged whither he has no desire to go.

Truth not only points out the way along which human life ought to move, but reveals also the only way along which it can move. And therefore all men must willingly or unwillingly move along the way of truth, some spontaneously accomplishing the task set them in life, others submitting involuntarily to the law of life. Man's freedom lies in the power of this choice.

This freedom within these narrow limits seems so insignificant to men that they do not notice it. Some--the determinists--consider this amount of freedom so trifling that they do not recognize it at all. Others--the champions of complete free will--keep their eyes fixed on their hypothetical free will and neglect this which seemed to them such a trivial degree of freedom.

This freedom, confined between the limits of complete ignorance of the truth and a recognition of a part of the truth, seems hardly freedom at all, especially since, whether a man is willing or unwilling to recognize the truth revealed to him, he will be inevitably forced to carry it out in life.

A horse harnessed with others to a cart is not free to refrain from moving the cart. If he does not move forward the cart will knock him down and go on dragging him with it, whether he will or not. But the horse is free to drag the cart himself or to be dragged with it. And so it is with man.

Whether this is a great or small degree of freedom in comparison with the fantastic liberty we should like to have, it is the only freedom that really exists, and in it consists the only happiness attainable by man.

And more than that, this freedom is the sole means of accomplishing the divine work of the life of the world.

According to Christ's doctrine, the man who sees the significance of life in the domain in which it is not free, in the domain of effects, that is, of acts, has not the true life. According to the Christian doctrine, that man is living in the truth who has transported his life to the domain in which it is free--the domain of causes, that is, the knowledge and recognition, the profession and realization in life of revealed truth.

Devoting his life to works of the flesh, a man busies himself with actions depending on temporary causes outside himself. He himself does nothing really, he merely seems to be doing something. In reality all the acts which seem to be his are the work of a higher power, and he is not the creator of his own life, but the slave of it. Devoting his life to the recognition and fulfillment of the truth revealed to him, he identifies himself with the source of universal life and accomplishes acts not personal, and dependent on conditions of space and time, but acts unconditioned by previous causes, acts which constitute the causes of everything else, and have an infinite, unlimited significance.

"The kingdom of heaven suffereth violence, and the violent take it by force." (Matt. xi. 12.)

It is this violent effort to rise above external conditions to the recognition and realization of truth by which the kingdom of heaven is taken, and it is this effort of violence which must and can be made in our times.

Men need only understand this, they need only cease to trouble themselves about the general external conditions in which they are not free, and devote one-hundredth part of the energy they waste on those material things to that in which they are free, to the recognition and realization of the truth which is before them, and to the liberation of themselves and others from deception and hypocrisy, and, without effort or conflict, there would be an end at once of the false organization of life which makes men miserable, and threatens them with worse calamities in the future. And then the kingdom of God would be realized, or at least that first stage of it for which men are ready now by the degree of development of their conscience.

Just as a single shock may be sufficient, when a liquid is saturated with some salt, to precipitate it at once in crystals, a slight effort may be perhaps all that is needed now that the truth already revealed to men may gain a mastery over hundreds, thousands, millions of men, that a public opinion consistent with conscience may be established, and through this change of public opinion the whole order of life may be transformed. And it depends upon us to make this effort.

Let each of us only try to understand and accept the Christian truth which in the most varied forms surrounds us on all sides and forces itself upon us; let us only cease from lying and pretending that we do not see this truth or wish to realize it, at least in what it demands from us above all else; only let us accept and boldly profess the truth to which we are called, and we should find at once that hundreds, thousands, millions of men are in the same position as we, that they see the truth as we do, and dread as we do to stand alone in recognizing it, and like us are only waiting for others to recognize it also.

Only let men cease to be hypocrites, and they would at once see that this cruel social organization, which holds them in bondage, and is represented to them as something stable, necessary, and ordained of God, is already tottering and is only propped up by the falsehood of hypocrisy, with which we, and others like us, support it.

But if this is so, if it is true that it depends on us to break down the existing organization of life, have we the right to destroy it, without knowing clearly what we shall set up in its place? What will become of human society when the existing order of things is at an end?

> "What shall we find the other side of the walls of the world we are abandoning?
>
> "Fear will come upon us--a void, a vast emptiness, freedom--how are we to go forward not knowing whither, how face loss, not seeing hope of gain? . . . If Columbus had reasoned thus he would never have weighed anchor. It was madness to set off upon the ocean, not knowing the route, on the ocean on which no one had sailed, to sail toward a land whose existence was doubtful. By this madness he discovered a new world. Doubtless if the peoples of the world could simply transfer themselves from one furnished mansion to another and better one--it would make it much easier; but unluckily there is no one to get humanity's new dwelling ready for it. The future is even worse than the ocean--there is nothing there--it will be what men and circumstances make it.
>
> "If you are content with the old world, try to preserve it, it is very sick and cannot hold out much longer. But if you

cannot bear to live in everlasting dissonance between your beliefs and your life, thinking one thing and doing another, get out of the mediaeval whited sepulchers, and face your fears. I know very well it is not easy.

"It is not a little thing to cut one's self off from all to which a man has been accustomed from his birth, with which he has grown up to maturity. Men are ready for tremendous sacrifices, but not for those which life demands of them. Are they ready to sacrifice modern civilization, their manner of life, their religion, the received conventional morality?

"Are we ready to give up all the results we have attained with such effort, results of which we have been boasting for three centuries; to give up every convenience and charm of our existence, to prefer savage youth to the senile decay of civilization, to pull down the palace raised for us by our ancestors only for the pleasure of having a hand in the founding of a new house, which will doubtless be built long after we are gone?" (Herzen, vol. v. p. 55.)

Thus wrote almost half a century ago the Russian writer, who with prophetic insight saw clearly then, what even the most unreflecting man sees to-day, the impossibility, that is, of life continuing on its old basis, and the necessity of establishing new forms of life.

It is clear now from the very simplest, most commonplace point of view, that it is madness to remain under the roof of a building which cannot support its weight, and that we must leave it. And indeed it is difficult to imagine a position more wretched than that of the Christian world to-day, with its nations armed against one another, with its constantly increasing taxation to maintain its armies, with the hatred of the working class for the rich ever growing more intense, with the Damocles sword of war forever hanging over the heads of all, ready every instant to fall, certain to fall sooner or later.

Hardly could any revolution be more disastrous for the great mass of the population than the present order or rather disorder of our life, with its daily sacrifices to exhausting and unnatural toil, to poverty, drunkenness, and profligacy, with all the horrors of the war that is at hand, which will swallow up in one year more victims than all the revolutions of the century.

What will become of humanity if each of us performs the duty God demands of us through the conscience implanted within us? Will not harm come if, being wholly in the power of a master, I carry out, in the workshop erected and directed by him, the orders he gives me, strange though they may seem to me who do not know the Master's final aims?

But it is not even this question "What will happen?" that agitates men when they hesitate to fulfill the Master's will. They are troubled by the question how to live without those habitual conditions of life which we call civilization, culture, art, and science. We feel ourselves all the burdensomeness of life as it is; we see also that this organization of life must inevitably be our ruin, if it continues. At the same time we want the conditions of our life which arise out of this organization--our civilization, culture, art, and science--to remain intact. It is as though a man, living in an old house and suffering from cold and all sorts of inconvenience in it, knowing, too, that it is on the point of falling to pieces, should consent to its being rebuilt, but only on the condition that he should not be required to leave it: a condition which is equivalent to refusing to have it rebuilt at all.

"But what if I leave the house and give up every convenience for a time, and the new house is not built, or is built on a different plan so that I do not find in it the comforts to which I am accustomed?" But seeing that the materials and the builders are here, there is every likelihood that the new house will on the contrary be better built than the old one. And at the same time, there is not only the likelihood but the certainty that the old house will fall down and crush those who remain within it. Whether the old habitual conditions of life are supported, or whether they are abolished and altogether new and better conditions arise; in any case, there is no doubt we shall be forced to leave the old forms of life which have become impossible and fatal, and must go forward to meet the future.

"Civilization, art, science, culture, will disappear!"

Yes, but all these we know are only various manifestations of truth, and the change that is before us is only to be made for the sake of a closer attainment and realization of truth. How then can the manifestations of truth disappear through our realizing it? These manifestations will be different, higher, better, but they will not cease to be. Only what is false in them will be destroyed; all the truth there was in them will only be stronger and more flourishing.

Take thought, oh, men, and have faith in the Gospel, in whose teaching is your happiness. If you do not take thought, you will perish just as the men perished, slain by Pilate, or crushed by the tower of Siloam; as millions of men have perished, slayers and slain, executing and executed, torturers and tortured alike, and as the man foolishly perished, who filled his granaries full and made ready for a long life and died the very night that he planned to begin his life. Take thought and have faith in the Gospel, Christ said eighteen hundred years ago, and he says it with even greater force now that the calamities foretold by him have come to pass, and the senselessness of our life has reached the furthest point of suffering and madness.

Nowadays, after so many centuries of fruitless efforts to make our life secure by the pagan organization of life, it must be evident to everyone that all efforts in that direction only introduce fresh dangers into personal and social life, and do not render it more secure in any way.

Whatever names we dignify ourselves with, whatever uniforms we wear, whatever priests we anoint ourselves before, however many millions we possess, however many guards are stationed along our road, however many policemen guard our wealth, however many so-called criminals, revolutionists, and anarchists we punish, whatever exploits we have performed, whatever states we may have founded, fortresses and towers we may have erected--from Babel to the Eiffel Tower--there are two inevitable conditions of life, confronting all of us, which destroy its whole meaning; (1) death, which may at any moment pounce upon each of us; and (2) the transitoriness of all our works, which so soon pass away and leave no trace. Whatever we may do--found companies, build palaces and monuments, write songs and poems--it is all not for long time. Soon it passes away, leaving no trace. And therefore, however we may conceal it from ourselves, we cannot help seeing that the significance of our life cannot lie in our personal fleshly existence, the prey of incurable suffering and inevitable death, nor in any social institution or organization. Whoever you may be who are reading these lines, think of your position and of your duties--not of your position as landowner, merchant, judge, emperor, president, minister, priest, soldier, which has been temporarily allotted you by men, and not of the imaginary duties laid on you by those positions, but of your real positions in eternity as a creature who at the will of Someone has been called out of unconsciousness after an eternity of non-existence to which you may return at any moment at his will. Think of your duties--not your supposed duties as a landowner to your estate, as a merchant to your business, as emperor, minister, or official to the state, but of your real duties, the duties that follow from your real position as a being called into life and endowed with reason and love.

Are you doing what he demands of you who has sent you into the world, and to whom you will soon return? Are you doing what he wills? Are you doing his will, when as landowner or manufacturer you rob the poor of the fruits of their toil, basing your life on this plunder of the workers, or when, as judge or governor, you ill treat men, sentence them to execution, or when as soldiers you prepare for war, kill and plunder?

You will say that the world is so made that this is inevitable, and that you do not do this of your own free will, but because you are forced to do so. But can it be that you have such a strong aversion to men's sufferings, ill treatment, and murder, that you have such an intense need of love and co-operation with your fellows that you see clearly that only by the recognition of the equality of all, and by mutual services, can the greatest possible happiness be realized; that your head and your heart, the faith you profess, and even science itself tell you the same thing, and yet that in spite of it all you can be forced by some confused and complicated reasoning to act in direct opposition to all this; that as landowner or capitalist you are bound to base your whole life on the oppression of the people; that as emperor or president you are to command armies, that is, to be the head and commander of murderers; or that as government official you are forced to take from the poor their last pence for rich men to profit and share them among themselves; or that as judge or juryman you could be forced to sentence erring men to ill treatment and death because the truth was not revealed to them, or above all, for that is the basis of all the evil, that you could be forced to become a soldier, and renouncing your free will and your human sentiments, could undertake to kill anyone at the command of other men?

It cannot be.

Even if you are told that all this is necessary for the maintenance of the existing order of things, and that this social order with its pauperism, famines, prisons, gallows, armies, and wars is necessary to society; that still greater disasters would ensue if this organization were destroyed; all that is said only by those who profit by this organization, while those who suffer from it--and they are ten times as numerous--think and say quite the contrary. And at the bottom of your heart you know yourself that it is not true, that the existing organization has outlived its time, and must inevitably be reconstructed on new principles, and that consequently there is no obligation upon you to sacrifice your sentiments of humanity to support it.

Above all, even if you allow that this organization is necessary, why do you believe it to be your duty to maintain it at the cost of your best feelings? Who has made you the nurse in charge of this sick and moribund organization? Not society nor the state nor anyone; no one has asked you to undertake this; you who fill your position of landowner, merchant, tzar, priest, or soldier know very well that you occupy that position by no means with the unselfish aim of maintaining the organization of life necessary to men's happiness, but simply in your own interests, to satisfy your own covetousness or vanity or ambition or indolence or cowardice. If you did not desire that position, you would not be doing your utmost to retain it. Try the experiment of ceasing to commit the cruel, treacherous, and base actions that you are constantly committing in order to retain your position, and you will lose it at once. Try the simple experiment, as a government official, of giving up lying, and refusing to take a part in executions and acts of violence; as a priest, of giving up deception; as a soldier, of giving up murder; as landowner or manufacturer, of giving up defending your property by fraud and force; and you will at once lose the position which you pretend is forced upon you, and which seems burdensome to you.

A man cannot be placed against his will in a situation opposed to his conscience.

If you find yourself in such a position it is not because it is necessary to anyone whatever, but simply because you wish it. And therefore knowing that your position is repugnant to your heart and your head, and to your faith, and even to the science in which you believe, you cannot help reflecting upon the question whether in retaining it, and above all trying to justify it, you are doing what you ought to do.

You might risk making a mistake if you had time to see and retrieve your fault, and if you ran the risk for something of some value. But when you know beyond all doubt that you may disappear any minute, without the least possibility either for yourself or those you draw after you into your error, of retrieving the mistake, when you know that whatever you may do in the external organization of life it will all disappear as quickly and surely as you will yourself, and will leave no trace behind, it is clear that you have no reasonable ground for running the risk of such a fearful mistake.

It would be perfectly simple and clear if you did not by your hypocrisy disguise the truth which has so unmistakably been revealed to us.

Share all that you have with others, do not heap up riches, do not steal, do not cause suffering, do not kill, do not unto others what you would not they should do unto you, all that has been said not eighteen hundred, but five thousand years ago, and there could be no doubt of the truth of this law if it were not for hypocrisy. Except for hypocrisy men could not have failed, if not to put the law in practice, at least to recognize it, and admit that it is wrong not to put it in practice.

But you will say that there is the public good to be considered, and that on that account one must not and ought not to conform to these principles; for the public good one may commit acts of violence and murder. It is better for one man to die than that the whole people perish, you will say like Caiaphas, and you sign the sentence of death of one man, of a second, and a third; you load your gun against this man who is to perish for the public good, you imprison him, you take his possessions. You say that you commit these acts of cruelty because you are a part of the society and of the state; that it is your duty to serve them, and as landowner, judge, emperor, or soldier to conform to their laws. But besides belonging to the state and having duties created by that position, you belong also to eternity and to God, who also lays duties upon you. And just as your duties to your family and to society are subordinate to your superior duties to the state, in the same way the latter must necessarily be subordinated to the duties dictated to you by the eternal life and by God. And just as it would be senseless to pull up the telegraph posts for fuel for a family or society and thus to increase its welfare at the expense of public interests, in the same way it is senseless to do violence, to execute, and to murder to increase the welfare of the nation, because that is at the expense of the interests of humanity.

Your duties as a citizen cannot but be subordinated to the superior obligations of the eternal life of God, and cannot be in opposition to them. As Christ's disciples said eighteen centuries ago: "Whether it be right in the sight of God to hearken unto you more than unto God, judge ye" (Acts iv. 19); and, "We ought to obey God rather than men" (Acts v. 29).

It is asserted that, in order that the unstable order of things, established in one corner of the world for a few men, may not be destroyed, you ought to commit acts of violence which destroy the eternal and immutable order established by God and by reason. Can that possibly be?

And therefore you cannot but reflect on your position as landowner, manufacturer, judge, emperor, president, minister, priest, and soldier, which is bound up with violence, deception, and murder, and recognize its unlawfulness.

I do not say that if you are a landowner you are bound to give up your lands immediately to the poor; if a capitalist or manufacturer, your money to your workpeople; or that if you are Tzar, minister, official, judge, or general, you are bound to renounce immediately the advantages of your position; or if a soldier, on whom all the system of violence is based, to refuse immediately to obey in spite of all the dangers of insubordination.

If you do so, you will be doing the best thing possible. But it may happen, and it is most likely, that you will not have the strength to do so. You have relations, a family, subordinates and superiors; you are under an influence so powerful that you cannot shake it off; but you can always recognize the truth and refuse to tell a lie about it. You need not declare that you are remaining a landowner, manufacturer, merchant, artist, or writer because it is useful to mankind; that you are governor, prosecutor, or tzar, not because it is agreeable to you, because you are used to it, but for the public good; that you continue to be a soldier, not from fear of punishment, but because you consider the army necessary to society. You can always avoid lying in this way to yourself and to others, and you ought to do so; because the one aim of your life ought to be to purify yourself from falsehood and to confess the truth. And you need only do that and your situation will change directly of itself.

There is one thing, and only one thing, in which it is granted to you to be free in life, all else being beyond your power: that is to recognize and profess the truth.

And yet simply from the fact that other men as misguided and as pitiful creatures as yourself have made you soldier, tzar, landowner, capitalist, priest, or general, you undertake to commit acts of violence obviously opposed to your reason and your heart, to base your existence on the misfortunes of others, and above all, instead of filling the one duty of your life, recognizing and professing the truth, you feign not to recognize it and disguise it from yourself and others.

And what are the conditions in which you are doing this? You who may die any instant, you sign sentences of death, you declare war, you take part in it, you judge, you punish, you plunder the working people, you live luxuriously in the midst of the poor, and teach weak men who have confidence in you that this must be so, that the duty of men is to do this, and yet it may happen at the moment when you are acting thus that a bacterium or a bull may attack you and you will fall and die, losing forever the chance of repairing the harm you have done to others, and above all to yourself, in uselessly wasting a life which has been given you only once in eternity, without having accomplished the only thing you ought to have done.

However commonplace and out of date it may seem to us, however confused we may be by hypocrisy and by the hypnotic suggestion which results from it, nothing can destroy the certainty of this simple and clearly defined truth. No external conditions can guarantee our life, which is attended with inevitable sufferings and infallibly terminated by death, and which consequently can have no significance except in the constant accomplishment of what is demanded by the Power which has placed us in life with a sole certain guide--the rational conscience.

That is why that Power cannot require of us what is irrational and impossible: the organization of our temporary external life, the life of society or of the state. That Power demands of us only what is reasonable, certain, and possible: to serve the kingdom of God, that is, to contribute to the establishment of the greatest possible union between all living beings--a union possible only in the truth; and to recognize and to profess the revealed truth, which is always in our power.

"But seek ye first the kingdom of God, and his righteousness, and all these things shall be added unto you." (Matt. vi. 33.)

The sole meaning of life is to serve humanity by contributing to the establishment of the kingdom of God, which can only be done by the recognition and profession of the truth by every man.

"The kingdom of God cometh not with outward show; neither shall they say, Lo here! or, Lo there! for behold, the kingdom of God is within you." (Luke xvii. 20, 21.)

THE END.

Printed in Great Britain
by Amazon

50364374R00295